The Vincent in the Barn

The Vincent in the Barn

*Great Stories of
Motorcycle Archaeology*

TOM COTTER

FOREWORD BY DAVID EDWARDS
Editor-in-chief *Cycle World* magazine

DEDICATION

To my nephew Ian, who is battling Lyme disease. A portion of the proceeds from this book will be donated to the cure of this illness.

First published in 2009 by Motorbooks, an imprint of MBI Publishing Company, 400 First Avenue North, Suite 300, Minneapolis, MN 55401 USA

Motorbooks titles are also available at discounts in bulk quantity for industrial or sales-promotional use. For details write to Special Sales Manager at MBI Publishing Company, 400 First Avenue North, Suite 300, Minneapolis, MN 55401 USA.

To find out more about our books, visit us online at www.motorbooks.com.

ISBN-13: 978-0-7603- 3535-2

Editors: Lee Klancher and Zack Miller. Design Manager: Brenda C. Canales. Layout by: Mike Vineski

On the cover, main image: Rick Schunk's 1948 Series B Vincent Black Shadow emerges from a Minnesota barn in an artful interpretation of every motorcycle collector's dream. *Rick Schunk*

Detail: Motorcycle collectors scour the earth looking for long-forgotten machines. This 1943 Indian 741 military model was hiding in a basement near Moscow. *Dick Fritz*

On the frontispiece:

There is something very beautiful in the patina of an unrestored machine. *Tom Cotter*

On the back cover:

Harry R. Paul's home-built racer. Following the age-old hot rod tradition of wedging large engines into smaller machines, Harry equipped his Indian Scout with an Indian Chief motor to make an effective flat-track and scrambles weapon. Dormant for five decades, the machine appeared in a Craigslist ad and was scooped up by collector Dale Walksler. *Tom Cotter (color); Dale Walksler collection (black and white)*

Printed in China

Contents

Search and Rescue

By David Edwards

Everybody loves a good barn-find story. The best of the tales read like juicy detective novels. There are hidden clues, rumor and intrigue, false hope, shadowy characters, high-stakes negotiations, invariably a trying voyage, sometimes even outright danger. But work through the plot twists, stay on the hunt, mix with a little good luck, and at the conclusion we have a happy, satisfying outcome. In the end, barn-find stories are all about resurrection.

Not to belittle the efforts of the car collectors in Tom Cotter's previous two books, *The Cobra in the Barn* and *The Hemi in the Barn,* but they had it easy compared with unearthing hidden motorcycles. Due to its size, a sequestered car does indeed need to be stored in a barn or garage. Not so a two-wheeler. Not much bigger than a Schwinn, many go subterranean and end up in basements. Others ascend: A couple of healthy guys can hump a non-runner up several flights of stairs for safekeeping. Some get bricked in behind walls for the ultimate in antitheft. Heck, break a bike down to its basic components—motor, frame, tinware, and wheels—and it can be stored in a small closet.

As is often the case, my own favorite barn-find story came about completely by accident and turned out to be quite the quest. I was in the *Cycle World* library one day, researching a story, when I spied an old 1954 *Cycle* magazine with the cover blurb "Indian V-8!" Now, Indian never made a V-8, but Bill Drabek, a lanky Texas car mechanic, certainly did. He had a 1940 Indian Four with a duff motor and, by chance, a Ford V8-60, the smaller 2,200cc version of Henry's famous flathead. Drabek combined the two to create an eight-cylinder Indian that spanned 9 feet fender tip–to–fender tip and weighed in at almost a half ton, some 965 pounds. Resplendent in Kelvinator white, it was said to be good for 95 miles per hour in second gear—and there were two more gears to go!

Great story, I thought, I'll contact the builder and see if he still has the bike; a follow-up should make for interesting reading. What then transpired was six months of sleuthing that included tracking down additional stories about the bike in *Mechanix Illustrated* and the *Ford Times,* calls to old newspaper reporters, and inquiries at local motorcycle shops. Frankly, it became a bit of an obsession. Now I wanted the story *and* the bike.

Turns out Drabek had passed away in 1968. After his death, there were several offers to buy the bike, but his grief-stricken wife, Jennie, wouldn't hear of it. The V-8 was pushed into a shed, where it spent most of the next three decades, falling prey to the occasional flood, juvenile delinquents, and a family of rodents. In the mid-1990s, Jennie was diagnosed with Alzheimer's and put in a home. The Drabeks' property and possessions, including the big white bike, went on the auction block.

Someone gave the new owner my phone number—after Jay Leno declined interest—and soon enough I was winging to Corpus Christi with a U-Haul truck reservation and directions to a quonset hut in Kingsville. I was not leaving the Lone Star State without that bike.

Before its (still ongoing) restoration began, I showed the V-8 once in its as-found state. It caught the attention of one of the world's preeminent Indian collectors, a moneyed man with at least 60 Wigwam products in his stash.

"Why don't you let me save you a lot of time, effort, and money," he said. "Sell me the bike."

Not a chance.

David Edwards is editor-in-chief at Cycle World *magazine and also counts a $100 BSA Gold Star among his barn finds . . . but that's another story.*

PREFACE

On the bus ride home from school as a kid, every time I saw an old car in a backyard, I'd make a mental note of the address. Then I'd ride my bicycle back on the weekend to see if it was for sale.

The habit of searching for old cars continued during college, marriage, and various careers. It became second nature; while driving, my head would constantly be scanning the landscape—back and forth—checking for bright metallic objects hidden behind garages and bushes.

On a lark, I wrote a book about my obsession—*The Cobra in the Barn*—in 2005, hoping a least a few enthusiasts would find the title interesting enough to buy it. It sold well, as did the follow up, *The Hemi in the Barn.*

Wow, I'm not the only one who enjoys looking for motorized treasure!

I asked my editors and publishers at Motorbooks if they would consider a motorcycle barn-find book, and they gave me the thumbs-up. The result is in your hands.

I met the greatest folks as I traveled around the United States while writing this book. Whether I was interviewing a collector who proudly owned one bike or the curator of a museum that owned hundreds, many of these folks I am now proud to call friends.

I found it interesting that motorcycle owners were less likely to talk about their barn find discoveries than their car-collecting brothers. Often I had to coax the stories out of bike owners. Motorcyclists are less boastful and more humble than the car guys. It was a very pleasant change for me.

As authors often do, I fell in love with my subject; in this case, motorcycles. No longer will I be satisfied with the old Honda dirt bike parked in my garage, I am now on the lookout for a vintage cycle of my own. This book has transformed me.

If you have a story and "as-found" photographs of a motorcycle you discovered, please email those to me at: tcotter@cobrainthebarn.com. If there is enough interest in *The Vincent in the Barn,* maybe I'll include your piece in a future bike-in-the-barn book.

Enjoy the ride.

Tom Cotter

—Tom Cotter, February 2009

ACKNOWLEDGMENTS

My name may be on the front of this book, but it is the result of many, many people who helped in its production.

Thanks to all the contributing writers who assisted me with their own stories: Somer Hooker, Larry Edsall, Paul Duchene, Steve Rossi, Ed Bauer, Ken Gross, Phillip Tooth, Zack Miller, Lee Klancher, and Kris Palmer.

Thanks to all those who helped me write their stories of motorcycle discovery: David Hansen, Glenn Bator, Jeff Slobodian, Guy Webster, Dale Walksler, Matt Walksler, Jeff Ray, Brian Slark, Lanny Hyde, Russ Aves, Dick Fritz, Dale Seymour, Al Kelly, Ken Kelly, Dale Axlerod, Jon Ennik, Keith Irwin, Skip Irwin, Tim Fortner, John Parham, Chuck Goldsborough, Doug Herbert, and Chet Herbert.

Thanks to all those who provided photographs, particularly to my friend John Lamm.

Thanks to those who acted as catalysts and helped put me in contact with owners of interesting bikes: John Duss, Jay Leno, Herb Harris, and Bruce Meyer.

Thanks to David Edwards for agreeing to write the foreword.

Thanks to the great folks at Motorbooks: Zack Miller and Leah Noel, and my freelance editor, Lee Klancher. This is book number five, guys!

And thanks to my wife Pat and son Brian, who always helps diagnose my computer and photography issues.

I hope you enjoy the results.

CHAPTER ONE

Crimes of Persistence

The Jurassic Junkyard

A l Kelly is a self-described crapoholic. He likes nothing more than to buy, sell, or barter parts for his vintage motorcycle or car restoration projects. In the 1980s, the tool and die maker spotted some old cars and parts behind the Mount Hope Texaco, which was about a 30-minute drive from his home in Branchville, New Jersey. When he spotted the parts, he pulled over his freshly restored 1948 GMC pickup and stopped in to check it out.

"I asked the owner if anything in the junkyard was for sale," said Kelly. "He cursed me out and told me to mind my own business and never come back."

He didn't go back for almost 20 years.

One day he was at his job when he received a call in the late afternoon. The caller told Kelly that the eccentric junkyard owner had suffered a stroke, and the town was demanding that the family clean up the property immediately.

"Apparently he had grown up in the same town and was a bit of an oddball," said Kelly. "He would save every piece of metal he could find—every scrap, every bottle cap. He believed that if there were another world war, he

Al Kelly and his brother Ken are lifelong crapoholics. Ken stands in front of the hole they smashed in the side of a storage building in Mount Hope, New Jersey. It was the only way they could drag out the motorcycle treasure hidden inside. *Ken Kelly*

would become rich from recycling all his metal. All this metal was mounded up in sloppy piles, and you had to make your way through on these small paths between the garbage.

"The town actually jailed him once because he refused to clean up his property."

Kelly knew the old man had also been a motorcycle enthusiast in his younger days. When the call came in at 11:30 a.m., he got up from his desk and simply walked out of the factory without saying anything to anyone.

"I was so excited," he said.

When Kelly arrived at Mount Hope Texaco, he was greeted by the old man's 20-something nephew, Dave.

"I asked if I could look at some of the motorcycles and parts and he said, 'Yeah, sure, go ahead,'" said Kelly.

Kelly came across piles of junk, which reminded him of a scene from the movie *Jurassic Park*. At least 50 old cars were scattered about. The cars were models from between the 1920s and the 1950s. He also found piles of motorcycle parts mixed in with the automotive hulks and scraps.

"Apparently he had some trouble with guys sneaking in and stealing motorcycles and parts," he said, "so he took the bikes partially apart and hid them around the junkyard."

Then Kelly saw something that shocked him and made him realize that time was of the essence.

"There was a crusher in the middle of the yard and it was about to come down on a 1920s Indian," he said. "I was yelling at the crusher operator to stop, and he was yelling at me to get back."

The Indian was lost, but Kelly realized that if they were crushing Indian motorcycles for the value of scrap, he should be able to buy things real cheap.

Inside the shed that had no doors were a number of bikes, including a 1957 Harley, a 1944 military Indian, and this 1930 Indian Scout. The Kelly brothers bought all three bikes for $450 each. *Ken Kelly*

"There were other scavengers in the yard looking for gold, so I knew I had to work quickly," said Kelly. "I saw an old bike leaning against a shed, and it was surrounded by a bunch of old parts. It was about [a] 24-by-30-foot building, but there was so much crap piled against it that I couldn't find the way in.

"I just crawled through some old auto parts until I found a hole in the wall and I crawled in. The place was ready to fall down. It was so dark in there that I really couldn't see, but I put out my hands and felt motorcycles in that building. So I covered my tracks, sealed up the hole in the wall, and left to get my brother Ken, who was also into old bikes."

Before he left, Kelly had accumulated some smaller parts he was interested in—motorcycle seats and vintage motorcycle license plates—and asked Dave if he would take $25 for the parts, all the money in his wallet.

"Sure," said Dave.

Then Kelly said, "Oh, wait, this is all the money I have. Can I give you just $20 so I have $5 for lunch?" Dave agreed and Kelly sped off to pick up his brother from work.

"Ken, listen, you've got to come with me right now," he said. "Don't tell anyone; just jump in because everything in that junkyard is selling fast.

"You got to see this."

Kelly drove fast and made it back in 40 minutes, record time for the roundtrip.

The brothers sold the Harley and the military Indian but kept the 1930 Scout. After several years of work, the Scout was restored to concours condition. *Ken Kelly*

The two Kellys went right back to the barn and climbed back inside. The brothers couldn't see a thing, but they were able to feel a spring front end on one of the bikes, so they knew it was an Indian. They also felt a couple of other bikes but couldn't identify the brands in the dark.

"We climbed back out and asked Dave how much he wanted for each motorcycle," he said.

"I'll take $300 each."

So the brothers dragged out their three-bike stash through a larger hole they ripped in the side of the shed wall. The bikes included the Indian, actually a 1930 101 Scout, a 1957 Harley-Davidson Hummer, and a 1944 Indian Military Scout.

"Hey, you weren't supposed to go in there," barked Dave, reminding Kelly of the similar angry tone his uncle had barked 20 years earlier.

"I can't sell those beauties for $300," he said, even though he never even knew there were bikes in the shed. "I'll need at least $450 each for those bikes."

"Deal," said the two Kellys.

In addition to the three motorcycles, the Kellys also dragged out a complete 1946 Harley Knucklehead engine in good condition and some skirted Indian fenders.

The Kellys sold off the 1944 Indian Military Scout and the 1957 Harley, but to this day, they retain the 1930 Indian.

"Finding these bikes wasn't the only treasure—restoring and riding them is also a treasure," Al Kelly said.

A crapoholic's dream come true.

The Indian under the Tarp

Motorcycle collector Al Kelly is always on the lookout for old bikes. Once when he was driving to Blairstown, New Jersey, to visit his father, he noticed what appeared to be a motorcycle under a tarp next to a house. He saw a few old trucks parked around the property, so he stopped in.

He knocked on the door of the house and nobody answered.

So he peaked under that tarp. It was an Indian.

Next time he drove by the house, he again knocked on the door. A man by the name of Tom answered.

"I was cruising by and saw the bike under the tarp," said Kelly. "I looked under it and saw it was an Indian. Is it for sale?"

Tom answered, "My father and I used to ride the Indians. I have this one and my father has his at his house. But we don't want to sell them; we want to restore them one day."

Those are words Kelly did not want to hear, because he knew that most of the time those restorations never happen.

"The man was a mechanic and was obviously pretty handy," said Kelly. "So I told him about the old Harley I was restoring. He asked me to bring it by to show him when I was finished." Tom said he would call Kelly if he decided to sell.

The two bikes Tom and his father owned were 1952 Indian Chiefs formerly used as police motorcycles. They were purchased at an auction by a man who worked on Indians, and then Tom and his father purchased the two 1952s for $125 each. They also bought a third bike, a 1948 Chief, as a parts bike. But the two were not natural riders and tended to fall off. The bikes were eventually parked.

Twelve long years lapsed, with Kelly stopping by to see the man and his Indian under the tarp on his way to visit his dad. As he drove by one day, he noticed the bike was gone!

"I thought, 'Oh, shit, I missed it,'" said Kelly. Obviously the man wasn't true to his word.

But actually Tom had decided to sell his bike to Kelly and just moved it into the bed of a Ford F-250 pickup truck in the backyard. It was still covered with the same tarp. He agreed to sell his Indian, but the other two were not for sale.

"His intention was to sell all three to me, but his siblings got involved and put a stop to the sale of the other two," said Kelly.

Tom lost Kelly's phone number but got in touch with him through a friend.

"His bike turned out to have matching numbers and the engine was already rebuilt," said Kelly. "The bike had perfect sheet metal, but after all those years under the tarp, condensation had caused surface rust over the entire bike.

"But it was a 1952, which is desirable because it was the second-to-last year for Indian production."

16

What got Kelly most excited, though, was the fact that the proper sidecar that was originally attached to this very bike was still in the garage.

"I would have rather have had that sidecar than the other Indian," he said.

Eventually Tom's father died, but the family would still not sell the other two Indians or the sidecar. Interestingly, the two bikes were only 100 serial numbers off.

Kelly is nearing the end of his restoration on the Indian, but he hasn't stopped trying to purchase the other 1952 Chief, the '48 parts bike, and especially that sidecar.

Parked Warriors

By Phillip Tooth

This story first appeared in Motorcycle Classics, *Jan./Feb. 2007.*

We've all had the dream: opening the door of a tumbledown shed in the back of beyond and finding a battle-scarred race bike that hasn't turned a wheel in 50 years. That's just what happened to Larry Feece Sr., except it wasn't one old warrior he found covered in dust and cobwebs.

After Feece forced open the door to a tin shack that was almost falling into the creek that burbled beside it, he let his eyes adjust to the darkness and slowly counted. One . . . two . . . three . . . four Indian motorcycles.

But before you start wishing that you had been as lucky as Feece, stop and consider this: Luck doesn't just happen, you have to make it.

Twenty years ago, Feece used to help his local Yamaha dealer in northern Indiana by appraising old bikes that were brought in for parts exchange.

"Most of the bikes I looked at were nothing special, although occasionally something interesting would turn up. But I never expected to be asked to

Collector Larry Feece Sr. discovered four Indian race bikes that hadn't left a ramshackle shed in more than half a century. The four were team bikes owned by Buck Rogers, whose son started racing number 29 in 1949.
Phillip Tooth

appraise old Indian racers."

The seller told Feece that he had bought them in the late 1950s from Buck Rogers and had intended to convert them back to road bikes, but he never got around to it. Now he had cancer, and what he really wanted was a new V-Max.

"There were four modified Sport Scout racers in that rusted tin shack, each with the petrol tank finished in the same maroon paint. Every one was wearing the number plate from its last race, and two even had the tech inspection tags still clipped on the handlebars," Feece said. "The tires were flat and rust was breaking out like an ugly rash on some parts, but otherwise they looked just the same as the day they were parked."

When Feece told the owner what he thought they were worth, his face lit up. "Wow!" he said. "But what fool would pay that much for a bunch of old Indians?"

"This fool," responded Feece.

He delivered a new V-Max and set it up in the basement.

"I don't think he ever rode it," said Feece. "But he liked sitting on it."

When Feece started looking for information on the original owner, the

When Feece discovered the bikes, they still wore their original Champion Maroon paint. The paint came courtesy of Rogers' job at the Studebaker plant. *Phillip Tooth*

Buck Rogers was the development engineer at the Studebaker factory in South Bend, Indiana, where he was responsible for fitting V-8 engines into civilian pickup trucks. *Larry Feece Sr. collection/Phillip Tooth*

last thing he expected was to talk to developmental engineer Buck Rogers.

"I phoned him up and heard this real weak voice at the end of the line. But when I told him that I had found his Indians he perked up and spoke loud and clear."

Rogers had been the development engineer for Studebaker and was responsible for getting the V-8 into civilian trucks. He told Feece why the gas tanks of his Indians all wore the same war paint: "That was Champion Maroon, a Studebaker color. Studebaker sponsored an Indian race team, only they didn't know it!"

Feece really wanted to meet Buck, but he kept being put off.

"He always asked me to call back in a month or so, because he didn't feel well enough to see visitors."

Then Feece got a call from Rogers' wife. He had passed away, but before he died he asked her to give all the Indian spares in the workshop to Feece. Could he come over and collect them?

Mrs. Rogers handed Feece a huge bunch of keys and pointed him in the direction of the workshop. He peered through a dusty window and saw stacks of heads, barrels, and cranks. But he was having trouble getting inside.

"There must have been 100 keys, and only one would open the door!" Feece said. Needless to say, it wasn't the first one he tried!

Once inside he found spare wheels, forks, frames, gas tanks, and wheels. There were also a number of experimental pistons with domed tops. Buck Rogers had used his contacts at the Studebaker engineering department as well as the paint shop.

Rogers had bought the first Indian for his son Gene in 1949. It was a 1937 Sport Scout with engine number ECG8851. "What a motorcycle!" screamed the '35 Indian brochure of the 45-cubic-inch (750cc) V-Twin. "Indian engineers have designed it on racing principles for riders who want the utmost in a light, economical, exceptionally fast twin. Being light, it is built with a racing type trussed front fork, making it ideal for amateur competition of all sorts."

That wasn't light enough for Buck. He stripped off the lights, generator, and brakes. Up front is a cotton reel hub, while the bare brake drum remains at the rear because the QD hub on these models carries the sprocket, which makes changing overall gear ratios at the track a cinch.

That trussed front fork had to go. Like most Scout racers, the Rogers bike wears much lighter forks scalped from a Junior Scout. The big Scout gas tank was also junked and replaced with the smaller one from the 30.5-cubic-inch (500cc) twin.

The chassis was pretty much stock except for the Flanders rubber-mounted

Son Gene Rogers (left) and father Buck show off their team bikes. The bikes have changed little since this photo was taken in the early 1950s. *Larry Feece Sr. collection/Phillip Tooth*

Buck Rogers at speed during a flat-track race in the 1950s. The 750cc bikes were modified Scouts using all Indian parts, such as smaller gas tanks from the 50cc models. *Larry Feece Sr. collection/Phillip Tooth*

cow-horn bars, but the 42-degree twin engine was something special. Rogers took the motor to Dowagiac, Michigan, and gave it to top freelance tuner Art Hafer. Besides being an ace in the workshop, Hafer was something of a star on the track as well. He set an 8-mile record for 1-mile tracks in 1940, a record that was still standing 10 years later; but he is best remembered for his skill in cam design. Hafer sponsored Ernie Beckman and tuned his Scout.

If you need to know how good a tuner Hafer was, look at it this way: Top Harley tuner Tom Sifton said that Hafer's Scouts were faster than his WRs. Beckman, Bobby Hill (on a bike tuned by Dick Gross), and Bill Tuman (tuner Erwin Smith) became the new Indian Wrecking Crew that rattled Harley's cage between 1951 and 1953. In October 1953, Beckman took Indian's last dirt track national championship win at Williams Grove, Pennsylvania, while Hafer went on to teach his skills to another famous Indian and Royal Enfield tuner by the name of Sheldon Thuet.

Hafer clearly lavished time on his engine. The Rogers Scout got the special Y motor parts with "extra-heavy-duty" cylinders and high-compression heads with larger cooling fins designed to draw the windstream inward over the top of the motor (the stock unit was the B motor). Y-type heads and barrels were optional on the Sport Scout in 1935 and standard on 1937 models.

Valves were standard, with 1⅝-inch-diameter heads just like on Beckman's bike, but the flywheels were lightened, the inlet port enlarged, and the cylinder heads modified to improve gas flow. Hafer preferred the stock Sport Scout cam followers to the hotter Bonneville followers to go with his all-important cam profiles.

The vintage-looking external oil pump of the dry sump system was junked in favor of the pump and ignition drive body introduced on the 1938 models. It is a simple mod, only needing a swap of the outer timing case cover. On the '35 Sport Scout a battery ignition system was standard with Edison-Splitdorf or Bosch magnetos available at extra cost. But on the Rogers bike, sparks come

Rogers ran his team for five years, but when he finished racing at the Springfield Mile in August 1955, he simply parked the bikes in the shed, locked the door, and walked away. The bikes wouldn't be revealed for 50 years. *Larry Feece Sr. collection/ Phillip Tooth*

courtesy of a four-cylinder Splitdorf. This is no exotic race technology, just a robust, reliable magneto found on everything from tractors to midget race cars. The vertically mounted mag that sits on top of the oil pump was a Tom Sifton idea. A big air filter was fitted to keep dust out of the Linkhert carburetor that replaced the stock Schebler de Luxe.

With one Indian sorted, Rogers decided what he really needed was his own little race team, so he bought two more secondhand Sport Scouts in 1950. These had consecutive engine numbers, FDA 1498 and FDA 1499, and were 1941 models. Both got the full Hafer treatment, along with the Junior tanks and forks. Buck loaned these bikes to up-and-coming riders, sponsoring them with gas and travel costs.

But then he must have thought: "Why let these guys have all the fun?" and so in 1953 he bought the fourth Scout, engine number FCG 1508. Of course, it soon got the same mods as the others in the team, and all four Mile racers were given new paint courtesy of Studebaker. He pulled on his leather riding breeches,

Fifty years after anyone had ridden the bikes, Feece tries out his new purchase. This is number 29, raced by Rogers' son Gene. *Phillip Tooth*

tucked his Indian jersey in, and buckled up. He was going to hit the dirt.

Buck Rogers ran his little team for five years but then decided he'd had enough. The last time Rogers raced was in the Springfield Mile on August 21, 1955. When he got home he simply parked the bikes, shut up shop, and walked away from motorcycling. Rogers' bike wears a green 38H plate, while his son's Scout carries a yellow 29H. One of the sponsored bikes is 15H. All are Indiana numbers. The fourth bike has a white Illinois plate, number 13P.

Feece wanted to get at least one bike up and running so that he could use it in dirt track displays at antique meets like those at Wauseon, Ohio, and Davenport, Iowa. But which one? "Gene's bike was the only one with tires that held air. So that was it!" laughs Feece. It was a good choice.

Team Rogers/Studebaker Indian number 29H fires up after a couple of purposeful prods on the kick starter and spits out a sharp, crisp bark from the open pipes. Feece pushes down the clutch pedal, snicks the tank shifter into first, and squirts it down the dirt road outside his house. Although he's happy to shift up one, there's no way he's going all the way to top. There's a steep drop at the end of the track, and he hasn't got brakes. That snapped-off piece of hacksaw blade friction taped to the right handlebar earths the ignition. It's all there is between a sunny California retirement and eternity.

But get Feece on a dirt track and he's happy to show anyone what an Art Hafer–tuned Sport Scout can do. At Harmony, New Jersey, he was challenged by the father of a Harley rider who was so sure his son's hand-shifter would leave the Indian eating dust that he wagered $100 on winning a three-lap race. Feece replied that he needed to clean the plugs first and then took it out for a quick blast.

"There was so much power the front wheel was getting airborne out of the turns," laughed Feece. "When I got back to the pits the father made his excuses, packed up, and cleared out. If I'd left the plugs alone I'd have been 100 bucks better off!"

The Hard-Ridden Burnt-Down Over-Chromed and Finally Perfect Panhead

John Parham's hard-fought career in the motorcycle business can be summarized by telling the story of his ownership of a 1955 Harley-Davidson.

The ownership of that bike, as well as his business, was not smooth or easy in the early days. But in both cases, he overcame great odds and triumphed.

Parham is the owner of J&P Cycles, the largest motorcycle parts and accessories outlet in the United States. His love of vintage bikes also inspired him to establish the National Motorcycle Museum in Anamosa, Iowa. Yet things were not always so rosy for the 54-year-old entrepreneur.

When Parham and his wife, Jill, were starting out, the two had ambition but not much money. His love of motorcycles at an early age told him to pursue a career in that industry, but putting food on the table necessitated a steady income of working for someone else. So he worked in a factory and in 1979 opened a small dirt-floor motorcycle shop where he worked nights and weekends.

That was the same year he purchased his first collector bike, a 1955 Harley Panhead.

"My wife and I were at a swap meet in Indiana and saw this Panhead," he said. They fell in love with the classic old bike but didn't have the money to purchase it at the show.

"I thought it was $2,500, so I made a deal with the owner that if he could wait a little bit, we'd buy it from him in the near future."

Parham and his wife began to slowly scrape together the funds to purchase the bike. When that year's income tax refund check arrived, they had enough to complete the purchase.

"We drove our van down to Indiana to pick up the bike," he said. "We didn't have enough money for a hotel room, so we slept in the back.

"We drove to this guy's house, a mobile home, and had to go to his storage building to get the bike."

But the excitement of purchasing their first old bike was quickly extinguished when the owner they had met previously at the swap meet told them the bike was not $2,500, as Parham thought, but was in fact $2,900.

This was the first, but not the last, disappointment Parham would experience with this Harley.

"We didn't have the money," Parham said. "But we worked it out that he let us pay him the $2,500 that we had and take the bike home with us. Then we could send him the other $400 in a month."

True to his word, Parham sent the man the funds, then proceeded to "ride the heck out of the old Harley."

"It was Harley yellow, but we decided to do it over," said Parham. "A guy talked me into painting it a kind-of root beer color. It did look good."

Parham's dual careers were still moving along, working at the factory during the day and repairing motorcycles the rest of the time. Everything was going well until he was laid off from the factory in 1982. Then a fire destroyed his shop and all its contents two years later.

Parham made two major decisions in 1984: to rebuild and grow his business and to restore his beloved Panhead.

With his wife, Jill, Parham decided to jump into the motorcycle business full time, giving it all the attention and energy they could muster.

Parham promised himself he would give the poor old Harley similar attention.

This was the second disappointment involving the Harley.

This 1955 Harley-Davidson Panhead has been part of John Parham's life since 1979. This photo was taken soon after the bike was purchased. Parham had plenty of dark hair at the time and had just painted the bike a dark root beer color to match. *John Parham collection*

"The fire destroyed the building, and my bike was inside," he said. "It was burnt but not totally destroyed. But now it certainly needed a total restoration from the ground up."

He restored both the bike and the business. The bike was beautiful, probably too good, according to Parham. Eager to show his capabilities, it was over-restored and lavished with more chrome than it had when new. But as beautiful as the old bike looked, the same couldn't be said about his business.

"The winter of 1990 was a tough time to own a small motorcycle shop in a small town," he said. "I had to sell the Harley to make payroll for my staff."

Harley disappointment number three.

He reluctantly sold the Panhead for $7,500 to a guy who agreed to give Parham the first right to purchase it back if he considered selling it again.

Two years later the gentleman called Parham and agreed to sell him back the old Harley for $10,000.

After Parham had sold the Harley and then bought the bike back, he restored it to its original yellow paint color. Here is the Parham family—Jill and John and young son Zack—with their favorite motorcycle. *John Parham collection*

"I was lucky because at the time this guy was selling lots of classic American motorcycles to Germans, and they would have loved to buy this one."

But the man kept his word and Parham bought it back, promising never to have it leave his possession again.

When his business was back on its feet financially, he set out on a full restoration of the old '55.

"It just had too much chrome and not enough nickel plating," he said. "I wanted to bring it back to AMCA standards of what it looked like when it rolled out of the factory.

"That bike has sentimental and historical value to me," he said. "It represents the struggles I've had in this business.

"Now I love to get it out and ride the heck out of it."

As life for the old Harley has gotten better, so has Parham's life in the motorcycle business. He and Jill have built J&P Cycles from a dirt-floor repair shop into a 180,000-square-foot building with a staff of 300 people. They also have a large presence in Daytona Beach, Florida, and seasonally at the Sturgis Rally in Sturgis, South Dakota.

For the man who now owns more than 200 classic motorcycles, the one bike that has been with him through good and bad, the 1955 Harley-Davidson Panhead, is still his most special.

"It's not going anywhere anytime soon," he said.

After 30 years of ownership, the Parhams—Jill, Zack, and John (left to right)—still enjoy the Panhead. In those 30 years, their family business has grown from a dirt-floor shop to one of the largest Harley parts dealers in the world. *John Parham collection*

THE VINCENT IN THE BARN

The Patient Cleveland

By Kris Palmer

Eric Vaughn runs a small machine shop near Los Angeles out of the building of his dreams—a former Cadillac dealership built in the 1920s, with red brick walls and 3,500 square feet of floor space beneath clear-span bow trusses. Vaughn loves old craftsmanship, which is what drew him to vintage motorcycles. In 1949, a friend's father started the Holiday Motor Excursion in Pasadena for pre-'1916 (later '32-and-older) vehicles. The father, Doug Eastwood, also had a 1932 Indian four-cylinder. When Vaughn saw those bikes, all that iron-horse artistry and rumble got under his skin.

Between 1970 and 1985, Vaughn amassed a collection of 50 old bikes, most of them nice unrestored examples from manufacturers well-known to all-but-forgotten. Only when the old Caddy showroom beckoned did he loosen his grip and turn some of them back into cash. At the turn of the millennium, he sold two dozen bikes for a healthy six-figure sum.

He wasn't looking to bring any more bikes home, but rare machines don't vet potential buyers. They just appear out of nowhere sometimes and either you take the chance or you don't; the choice you make sits well or in time you come to wish you'd listened to the other voice in your mind before the deal walked away.

A man came into Vaughn's shop a few years ago and said he'd heard there was a guy in town who liked old bikes. Vaughn said he'd found him. The man had lived in the area his whole life. His father had started the Burger Basket restaurant two blocks away from Vaughn's ex-Caddy dealer shop in 1951.

In his youth, the man got into motorcycles, though a lot shallower than Vaughn, and more briefly. He bought an old Simplex Servi-Cycle that was made in New Orleans. As a child he'd ridden with his mother on his parents' 1920 Cleveland one-cylinder. He showed Vaughn a picture of himself, about age five, sitting on the tank of the latter bike in 1956. In addition, the man had an Indian engine—a circa-1920 Powerplus Twin—from an old board-track racer. It had all sat in his mother's garage, untouched, for decades. The Cleveland hadn't moved in 50 years.

The man had a present-day picture of the bikes and asked Vaughn what he thought the stuff would be worth. Vaughn gave a figure for each bike, and one for the old board-track Indian mill. The man smiled. "You're the first guy who's been honest," he said. "How would you like to buy this stuff?"

Vaughn thanked him but declined. He was out of the buying business. Besides, the bikes looked rusty and weren't that valuable—small potatoes

30

compared to the treasures he'd collected and sold. The man lingered, hoping Vaughn might change his mind. He didn't.

Vaughn's thoughts were elsewhere, on his shop and his building, when the man returned a few days later with a pickup truck. The old motorcycle loot was in the back. Vaughn had to go out and at least have a look at it. "Man, here's the deal," the burger-peddler's son said. "I sold my house and I'm going to move to San Diego. I want to get rid of this stuff and I want you to have it." He offered it all for much less than what Vaughn had said it was worth.

The man with motorcycling parents had sought out a vintage bike collector for a reason: a love of the goods he had to sell. Vaughn eyed the horde in the pickup bed: an Indian engine and two vintage bikes. The photos were unreliable narrators, even if they did tell 1,000 words. While the Simplex wasn't much better than he'd thought, the Cleveland was. What looked like rust in the photo was just grime. In fact, the bike was solid. Apart from a tattered seat, which is what you'd expect, and a missing front fender, it was complete. The loose engine was nice, too, and from a manufacturer dear to Vaughn: He has a 1929 Indian Scout that does 135 miles per hour in hopped-up salt-flats guise. Facing a steal of a deal, Vaughn's love of vintage motorcycles stepped up to silence his inner critic. He handed over the money for two more old bikes, with an Indian twin thrown in.

It wasn't a transaction Vaughn was expecting to make. Yet now that he had the bikes, he decided to give his son, Todd, a call. Todd had gotten into vintage motorcycles, too, and he liked to tear into them and get his hands dirty. Vaughn described the well-preserved Cleveland, then got to his point: "Well Todd, want to take a stab at this thing?"

The younger Vaughn arrived at 3:00 p.m., and by that evening, he had the Cleveland 90 percent disassembled, including the one-cylinder engine. Vaughn got some new rings for it from a buddy and ordered a pair of tires from Coker.

When they got it back together, Vaughn discovered what may have caused the bike to get mothballed in the first place. The 1920 Cleveland has a little magneto and it was out of phase, which meant the engine wouldn't run. Vaughn reoriented it and the 220cc two-stroke sputtered to life. Taken apart, cleaned up, and fitted with fresh rubber, it took its first ride since Eisenhower was president.

"I have a brochure for it," Vaughn said. It cost $225 in 1920, what Vaughn calls "real money." Worth it, too, he thinks, for a well-made machine.

"It has massive ball bearings," he notes. "It's a cool little bike."

Motorcyclists haven't always felt that way.

"In the 1950s that stuff was worthless," Vaughn recalls. "You couldn't get more than $20."

Newfound value is what time can impart, if a bike is lucky enough to hide from abuse, the scrap yard, and critical eyes tainted by the styles of the day.

THE VINCENT IN THE BARN

The little bike turns heads now and Vaughn has taken it on the Pasadena vintage run that inspired his passion years ago. Vaughn even called the former owner to tell him that he and his son had gotten the bike running. The man wasn't regretful. In fact, he felt vindicated and happy that a memorable possession from his youth was back in service.

The old Cleveland isn't a gold mine, just a nice piece of craftsmanship that managed to find the right home . . . even if it had to wait for 50 years.

The Vincent in the Barn

Lanny Hyde had ridden old British bikes for years. He lived in Northern California, but he'd travel down to Southern California frequently to ride his BSA or Norton relics in all-British rides.

"I'd leave my bikes at my parents' house where I grew up," said the retired salesman.

One day a neighbor, Warren, who lived across the street from his parents' house, wandered over to talk to Hyde's mother, who was working outside.

"I see your son rides old British bikes," said Warren.

"My mother told him, 'Yes, he lives up north, but he keeps them here in our garage,'" said Hyde. "'Well, tell him I have an old Vincent stored in my garage across the street.' My mother called me right away."

This chance conversation occurred in 1982. The next time Hyde traveled to his parent's house he walked across the street to meet Warren.

"He told me he had a Vincent back in the barn, really a shed, but that it was all covered with plywood and junk, and he wasn't too interested in cleaning it off just to let me see it," said Hyde.

"I don't own it," said Warren. "It belongs to a friend who left it here in 1960."

Apparently Warren's friend rode it into the shed and parked it. For the next couple of years, he kept the license plates renewed, but eventually that ended, and the Vincent was all but forgotten and went into long-term hibernation.

Warren was also reluctant to reveal the owner's name.

"It took me about six months for him to tell me who this guy was," said Hyde. "But ultimately he told me his name was Cliff and where he lived. So I decided to pay Cliff a visit."

Hyde stopped in front of the house and walked up to the front door. There was a screen door and a wood door.

"I knocked and he opened the door," said Hyde. "He only opened the wood door and said, 'What do you want?' I told him through the screen door that my mom and dad lived across the street from Warren, and that I understood there was a Vincent in the shed."

Then Hyde popped the question: "I wondered if you might be interested in selling it?"

"No!" and he closed the door. "And that was the end of it," said Hyde. But as luck would have it, Hyde was transferred to Southern California, not far from where Cliff lived. "Because he lived on my way home from work, I'd stop and see him once in a while," he said. Cliff was a machinist by trade and specialized in machining gun barrels and other critical materials. "If the garage door was open, I'd stop and talk to him and never mention the

The owner had parked the Rapide in the shed in 1960 but kept the license and insurance renewed until 1964. When Hyde purchased the bike, it still wore its California black plate. *Lanny Hyde collection*

Vincent," he said. Hyde is nothing if not patient because these visits continued for several years.

Finally, one day in 1988, Hyde gathered up his courage and asked Cliff the same question he had asked six years earlier. "You know, Cliff, I'm still interested in that Vincent," said Hyde. "What's it going to take for me to buy it?"

"What's it worth?" asked Cliff. Hyde had still never even seen the bike because his parents' neighbor Warren was reluctant to unearth the potentially rare cycle.

"I told him I didn't know what it was worth, but I would be glad to take a friend over to take a look at it and he'll tell you what it is worth," said Hyde. "You just give me the authorization and I'll take care of it."

When Warren finally uncovered the Vincent, they discovered the bike in pretty rough shape. It had been stored in an open shed and it was covered with sheets of plywood and cardboard.

"You couldn't even see it," he said. "When we finally pulled everything off to see what was there, the handlebars were actually green with corrosion."

It was in sad shape. "It was missing a few pieces, but the basic bike was all there," said Hyde.

The first thing Hyde noticed was that it was missing the correct front fender. It was also missing the correct horn, taillight, and toolbox.

The bike turned out to be a Touring Rapide model, which was Vincent's standard road-going model equipped with deeply valenced steel fenders. "The most popular Vincent is, of course, the Black Shadow, which was built for both road and track use," said Hyde. "Then there was the Black Lightning, which was strictly for the track."

He made Cliff an offer and the bike changed hands after a nearly three-decade hibernation.

"The Rapide had a beautiful valanced front fender," said Hyde, who feels that is the reason the original was missing.

"Most of the Touring Rapides were turned into sport bikes, so alloy or stainless fenders were often substituted. Owners would get rid of the heavy-looking valanced fenders, so now, of course, guys restoring these bikes are looking for those original fenders. And they are really hard to find."

The incorrect front fender on Hyde's Vincent was an aftermarket unit, but luckily he was able to find one from an ad in *Hemmings Motor News*. "There was a tiny ad for Vincent parts," said Hyde. "So I called and asked the man if he had a front fender for a 1952 Rapide, and he said, 'I think so, but you'll have to call me back in a few days because I have to go up into the barn to find it.' I called him back in three days, and he had the fender. The paint was pretty poor, but at least it was straight and didn't have any dents."

He secured a toolbox, a horn, and an original taillight through the Vincent Club.

Hyde brought his Vincent to restorer Gabe Malloy of Grass Valley, California, for a complete rebuild, but interestingly the bike hasn't been started since its completion nearly a decade ago.

Lanny Hyde's mother helped him discover this Series C Vincent Touring Rapide. It had been stored in a shed next to the house across the street. Lanny begged the owner to sell for six years, and he finally relented in 1988. *Lanny Hyde collection*

Restored by Vincent expert Dave Malloy of Grass Valley, California, the like-new Rapide now sits in the foyer of Hyde's house. *Lanny Hyde collection*

A wise man once said that the only way to prevent a British motorcycle from leaking is to not put oil in it, so after the rebuild it has never had fuel or lubricants installed other than assembly fluids. Curiously, Hyde has no intention of ever riding his showpiece.

"I've wanted one of these so long, and it has been restored to such a high level, that today it sits in a special foyer off my living room," he said. "I have other bikes to ride."

It has come a long way from having corroded green handlebars in an open shed.

CHAPTER TWO

Intriguing Circumstances

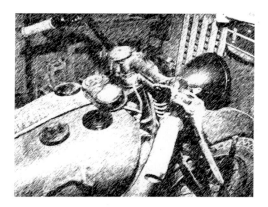

You're Only Crazy Once

"**W**ear your oldest clothes," Dick Fritz said to his colleagues. "And don't forget the Liquid Wrench."

Fritz and his friends Rich and Ben were packing for a trip overseas. Usually, old clothes and Liquid Wrench would never make it onto even the most casual tourist's packing list. But these three were about to embark on the barn-find adventure of a lifetime. In just a few hours, the trio would be on a Delta Airlines flight from New York's Kennedy Airport to the most unlikely destination of Sheremetyevo International Airport in Moscow, Russia.

They were on the hunt for the elusive armor-plated Mercedes 540K Aktion P.

Fritz had been a car guy his whole life. His first car was a 1939 Ford Convertible that he purchased for $125 from a neighbor in 1956. His father warned him, "I wouldn't buy that car if I were you!" But Fritz did what teenaged boys are supposed to do, and he bought it anyway, explaining to his dad, "But you're not me. . . ."

It was in sad condition, with a ripped top and torn upholstery. But the money saved from mowing lawns enabled him to purchase a new top and install seat covers. Eventually he painted the car—using a small compressor he had used to paint model airplanes—and installed a 1953 Mercury V-8 with two carburetors and dual exhaust.

Eventually that car was sold, and a succession of Chevrolets followed, including a 1955 Chevy and a new 1963 fuel-injected Corvette.

It was motorcycles that left the first motor vehicle impression on young Fritz, who at six years old was already witnessing motorcycle circus tricks in his backyard.

"I grew up in a neighborhood near Nyack, New York, and behind us lived a real clown who had traveled with circuses around the world," said Fritz, now 68. "He would have fellow circus performers visit, one of which would arrive pulling a travel trailer and inside was a motorcycle which he used in his act.

"Even though my father would have killed him [if he knew], he would take me for rides when my father was at work."

As he got older, both cars and motorcycles took a backseat to education for Fritz. His intention was to pursue a degree in aeronautical engineering, but when the car bug bit, he changed his major to mechanical engineering and enrolled in the engineering program at Clarkston University in New York.

Enrolled in the same college was the son of a respected auto racing personality, Luigi Chinetti. Chinetti had been a champion race driver in Europe—having won the 24 Hours of Le Mans three times—before emigrating to America in 1940. Chinetti later became Ferrari's first North American importer. Chinetti's son, Luigi Jr., would invite Fritz to work on the racing team's pit crew at tracks such as Watkins Glen, Lime Rock, and Sebring.

"Soon after I graduated from college in 1962 I was called by Mr. Chinetti to come to work at the dealership," said Fritz. "I was 22—what did I know? But Mr. Chinetti said they needed a manager, so I took the job."

He remained there until 1978.

"I handled the importation, sold Ferraris, managed the Ferrari North American Racing Team, designed race car components, handled customer service, designed and installed the first automatic transmission in a Ferrari along with the first Ferrari air pollution control systems, and basically was involved in the whole business," he said.

The Ferrari business wasn't always as robust as the company has been in recent years. There were times, according to Fritz, when the company couldn't make payroll for its small office staff and mechanics.

"With Mr. Chinetti's permission, I opened up a company called Amerispec in 1976," he said. Amerispec was a company that specialized in the legalization of imported cars for use on U.S. roads. "The U.S. Ferrari business wasn't real good in 1975. All they imported to us was the eight-cylinder Dino 308 GT4 model, which not too many people seemed to want so we legalized the 12-cylinder Boxer Berlinettas and 400 Automatics."

"Mr. Chinetti was 75 years old and wanted to sell the business, but I knew I didn't want to work for whoever bought it, so I worked nights and weekends developing my own business in the meantime."

In time, Amerispec thrived as it federalized such cars as the Ferrari Boxer, the Porsche 959, and the McLaren F1 during the boom days of the 1980s. His customers included Jay Leno, Ralph Lauren, and David Letterman.

Then it all went bust as Amerispec tried to tread water during the economic downturn of the early 1990s.

Then one day the phone rang. "Hello," the caller said to Fritz. "Can you help me get my two cars I've imported from Russia out of a container and into this country legally?" Fritz was curious and asked the gentleman, who was obviously also from Russia, "What kind of cars are they?"

"A Mercedes and a Horch, which I hope to sell over here," the gentleman said. He continued, saying there were lots of valuable German cars in Russia to be found.

A light bulb went off in Fritz's head.

"There wasn't much exotic car business going on in 1992 with the recession and all," he said. "So instead of just sitting around the office waiting for the phone to ring, I thought it might be a profitable adventure."

He quickly called his friend Rich Reuter, whose family had owned a restoration business for three generations.

"Because they had restored so many Mercedes-Benzes, I thought of Rich first because he was an expert on the vintage models," said Fritz.

"And it just so happened that Rich had a friend in Moscow who was a writer and a literary guy who could possibly help us out. Then I mentioned it to a customer, Ben, who was instantly interested and said he would be willing to back us financially if we included him."

Suddenly it was a "go" and the three men were packing for a trip to Russia. Because they didn't want to stand out from the Russian population, they decided to wear old clothes and to bring containers of Liquid Wrench in case they needed to remove rusty bolts from any of the cars they were hoping to find.

Reuter knew just one Russian, but word soon began to spread even before they landed that three American car enthusiasts were coming to Russia in search of old cars. In addition, "agents" from Tennessee said they would be glad to show them rare Russian car collections that could be purchased once they landed.

"We brought over $30,000 or $40,000 in American cash, each of us taking a third of the pile of $100 bills," said Fritz. "We carried the cash in our jackets just in case they searched our checked luggage, which they never did. If they had, a less-than-honest customs agent might call his friends on the outside and you'd never be seen again.

"I must admit, though, that carrying around $40,000 cash was frightening, knowing that at the time tourists were being killed in Russia for as little as $200."

When they arrived in Moscow, they checked into a very nice hotel, which was owned by Lufthansa Airlines. It felt somewhat out of place at the very time when the economy of the Soviet Union was collapsing. The plan was to meet their Tennessee connections in the hotel lobby the next morning at 10 a.m.

By 11:30 a.m they had not shown up.

So as Fritz, Reuter, and Ben waited and waited, an interpreter they had hired mentioned that he knew of a motorcycle collector nearby who might be interested in selling some bikes.

"Well, we weren't doing anything there in the hotel, so I said I would go look at them because the other two guys didn't know anything about motorcycles, and at least I knew a little," said Fritz.

Fritz and his interpreter drove across Moscow, into an area crowded with apartment complexes. He was then asked by a young man to crawl through a 4-foot-tall window down under the sidewalk and into a dark basement. He didn't know if he would ever come out again.

He entered the 6-foot-tall basement, and it took a few minutes before his eyes could adjust to the dim light.

"The bikes he had down there were really neat," said Fritz. "There was a military Indian Model 741, which wasn't in very good shape. Then there was a military Harley-Davidson WLA 42, a Matchless, and a BMW R35. He also had several Russian motorcycles, but I wasn't really interested in those because there was really no market for them in the States."

Prior to the trip, Fritz had done some research about American motorcycles in Russia and discovered that the United States had given a couple of thousand Harleys and Indians to the Soviet government during World War II to assist in fighting the Nazi Army. These bikes had been built to U.S. Army specifications but were basically street models that had some different details and were painted Olive Drab.

"I have no idea how he ever got the bikes down here, through that small opening next to the sidewalk," he said. "The owner was a young guy, probably between 25 and 28 years old. He was clean cut, good-looking, and calm. At this point in our trip, I didn't know who I could trust and who I couldn't trust, but dealing with this guy, I got the feeling that I could trust him."

Without consulting his colleagues, he decided to buy the bikes if they could be had for a fair price.

Dick Fritz tired of waiting for his classic car contacts in the Moscow hotel, so he left his two colleagues and pursued the rumor of some classic old motorcycles rusting away in the area. When he arrived at this apartment house, he was told to crawl down into the basement access door under the window. *Dick Fritz*

"I would never come up with a price first," he said. "I would always let the seller come up with a price and then say, 'That's way too much money.'

"Over time we realized that many of the Russians would start by asking $20,000 for a bike or car. When I'd tell them that was too much money, they'd say, 'OK, then how about $2,000?' We'd sometimes be able to negotiate down to $350."

Fritz's negotiation with the young fellow was much easier than most others they would experience, though. He paid about $200 for each bike, so he felt pretty good about his $800 investment when he joined his two colleagues back in the hotel lobby a little while later, who were still waiting for their Tennessee brokers.

"Hey, I think I just bought enough motorcycles to pay for our trip," he said. "I bought four of them."

Reuter was fine with the purchase, but the financier, Ben, was skeptical. "You bought motorcycles?" he asked. "What did you do that for?"

"I told him not to worry, we'd make money with them," said Fritz. "I figured they had to be worth at least $10,000, which would put this trip in the black."

Fritz had arranged with the bikes' owner to store them until shipping arrangements could be secured.

THE VINCENT IN THE BARN

Welcome to Russia! Dick Fritz squats down to fit into the doorway of a basement he was told contained old motorcycles. He didn't know if he would come out dead or alive. In white shirt and light slacks, Fritz was not dressed for a subterranean motorcycle adventure. *Dick Fritz*

Their Tennessee brokers finally showed up the next morning, 24 hours after the appointed time. They led their fellow Yankees to a muddy, dirty field where a number of steel shipping containers were located that people used as garages. The steel doors had three locks on them so that the contents could not be stolen.

"They told us about this very rare four-wheel-drive Mercedes-Benz touring car that had been specially built for a Nazi field marshal," said Fritz. "It was something like a 1937 or '38 230 Mercedes.

"I looked at it and said to Rich, 'This is junk.' He said, 'I know.'" It was the body of a Mercedes mounted onto the chassis, suspension, and drivetrain from some sort of Soviet military truck. And he was trying to tell us that it was all original.

"We didn't want to say anything negative to this guy because who knows if he might turn up something worthwhile in the future."

The Tennessee brokers said they had an option to buy a rare Mercedes 770K and a Horch, but they were 900 miles away, and they needed to sell this Mercedes 4x4 before they could buy those cars. They also showed them photos of a Mercedes 500K and a Horch, which they said they had just sold and were on their way to America, which Fritz studied carefully. He noticed a little red-and-blue sticker under the hood of the Horch and wondered what it might be for.

INTRIGUING CIRCUMSTANCES

In the basement, Fritz was shown this 1935 Matchless, along with an assortment of frames, engines, and other parts. Fritz guesses the owner, Victor Litvak, was in his mid-twenties. *Dick Fritz*

Fritz and his colleagues said they would be in touch and went searching for other cars in the Moscow area.

Their interpreter on this trip, Stash, was a sharp fellow, and he kept asking people throughout Moscow if they knew of any old cars that were for sale.

"We had seen so many cars, but most of them were junk," Fritz said. "Many had some sort of Russian engines adapted into them, were undesirable models, or were in such terrible condition that it didn't make any sense to ship them halfway around the world.

"But the motorcycles kept showing up."

Finally, after they had spent a week in Russia, they were preparing to go home, empty-handed except for the four vintage motorcycles they had secured on the first day they arrived. But clearly, it was rare old cars that would command a small fortune back home that they were after.

Then, at 10 p.m. the night before they had planned to leave, they got a call from Stash. He told them of a friend of his who had a bunch of valuable cars.

"OK, let's go," said Fritz.

So they drove to the outskirts of Moscow and met an interesting, neat older fellow who sported a full beard.

Also in the basement was this 1943 Indian 741, but it had the wrong forks and was missing many parts. Records show that as many as 40,000 motorcycles were shipped by America to the Russian Army to help them battle the Germans during World War II. *Dick Fritz*

"He was apparently a famous artist in Russia. We talked with him for quite a while, then he invited us to see his cars and motorcycles he had in the barn," said Fritz.

"He had quite a few interesting cars and bikes, including a familiar Mercedes 540K and Horch. When he opened the Horch hood to show us the engine, I saw that red-and-blue sticker that I had seen in those photos from the Tennessee guys. I said to Rich, 'Those cars belong to this guy!' Reuter replied, 'I know.'"

The artist said he enjoyed inviting people to tour his collection and take photos, but he wasn't interested in selling any of them. That's when they realized their Tennessee friends were in fact con artists.

So Fritz, Reuter, and Ben returned home without having purchased any ultra-rare classics but secure in their purchase of the four vintage motorcycles.

"We went home without finding any real treasures, but we knew we'd be going back again soon," said Fritz.

A few weeks later, Reuter got word from a friend that a Swede named Peter had contacted her and said he had found an armor-plated Mercedes 540K in Estonia that was for sale. That's all Fritz, Reuter, and Ben needed to hear; they made reservations and flew back to Moscow as soon as they could.

Once in Moscow, they boarded a train for the 11-hour trip to St. Petersburg, then another 11-hour trip to the former Soviet territory of Estonia. They rode in the second-class section so they wouldn't stand out as wealthy Americans. Once in their four-berth sleeping unit, Fritz took a metal clothes hanger he had packed to wire the two door levers shut from the inside so they couldn't be robbed while they slept.

Peter the Swede, a 40-something-year-old adventure-seeker who sported a ponytail and specialized in finding World War II vintage aircraft, met them at the train station. Because he was essentially a scavenger of old things, he said he would occasionally come upon cars and motorcycles as well. Peter, who had once spent prison time in Morocco, was very streetwise, according to Fritz, and had once worked for former race driver Bob Grossman's classic car shop in Southampton, New York.

Peter picked up the Americans at the train station with his 1979 Chevy Nova, making Fritz and his companions a little more comfortable in the foreign land. He informed his passengers that through his friends in the Old Car Club of Estonia, he had arranged for an afternoon visit to a man with an armor-plated Mercedes-Benz called the Aktion P.

Fritz had done research on the Aktion P cars, mostly through an excellent story that had appeared in Volume 28, Issue 1 of *Automobile Quarterly*, and discovered that the heavy-gauge steel plate used inside lightweight aluminum

Fritz decided to buy this Harley WLA42. It was fairly complete and in good condition, and the price of $1,900 seemed reasonable. *Dick Fritz*

Fritz purchased this BMW R35 from a movie studio near St. Petersburg. He believes this is a 1936 model. The price was $1,200. *Dick Fritz*

bodywork and the 1½-inch-thick windshield and side glass made the car virtually bulletproof. The aluminum body, in addition to keeping the overall weight of the car lighter than a steel body, also prevented magnetic bombs from being planted on it, which was apparently a popular assassination technique at the time. The car also was built sans running boards to keep unwanted passengers from hitching a ride and threatening occupants. A total of 20 Aktion Ps were built in 1943 and used by Hitler and his top officials.

Of the 20 Aktion P armored cars produced, only one was known to exist; that lone survivor sat in a museum in Prague. The rest were reputedly destroyed by angry mobs after the war ended because they symbolized Nazi aggression.

At 4 p.m., Peter drove the Americans to a small farm outside of the city of Tallinn, the largest in Estonia. They looked inside the barn, which was beginning to fall in on itself, and saw piles of "stuff."

"There were old car parts, bicycles, all sorts of metal parts, just 7-foot-high unorganized piles of junk," said Fritz. "You couldn't even walk into the barn without climbing on the piles."

"There's no car in there," said Reuter.

There was a rope hanging from the rafters that Peter the Swede used to swing himself to the back of the barn and he began looking around.

"Is there a car back there?" asked Reuter.

"Well, there are pieces of a car," answered Peter.

The aluminum body was here, the chassis was leaning against the wall over there, the fenders over there. Peter used a flashlight to read the chassis numbers to the Americans: "408377." This particular car had been assigned to the motor pool at the Third Reich Chancellery in Berlin, so it had been used by Adolf Hitler, Eva Braun and virtually all the other Nazi high officials and generals.

Fritz and his colleagues had to control their enthusiasm, not wanting the car's owner to see their delight. Reuter later said that it was like winning the lottery. They had just discovered the only other surviving Aktion P.

The owner confirmed that other major components—the engine, rear axle, doors, and so on—were in five other barns in the area. The car was complete when he bought it many years earlier. He explained he had dismantled the car when his teenage daughter was very young because the KGB spy organization, the Estonian Old Car Club, and various other groups knew of the car and wanted it. At one point, the Russian Mafia had threatened to disfigure his young daughter if he didn't present them with the car. By taking it apart, he simply told those interested parties that he had sold it.

"He said he wanted something unique, and that's why he bought it," said Fritz. "He collected lots of things, including a vintage Cleveland motorcycle. He asked if we could stop by our local Cleveland dealership when we returned home and buy a repair manual and some parts for him. I had to explain that the original Cleveland company had been out of business for many years."

After they had dug out many of the parts, the three Americans huddled in the Nova to discuss their next move. "We wanted it," said Fritz. "We were prepared to pay $50,000, $100,000, $200,000, whatever it took to own that car."

They sent their translator to the car's owner to ask how much he wanted for the car. When the translator returned, they couldn't believe their ears; he wasn't interested in selling it!

"We said, 'What?'" said Fritz.

Not wanting to waste any more time, the Americans bid farewell and continued to follow up other cars and motorcycles in the Estonia countryside.

"We looked at some Maybachs, great big sedans, but they were missing too many parts or were too badly deteriorated," said Fritz. "One rare custom-bodied Maybach we saw had been cut up into 2-foot-by-2-foot pieces and stored in an 8-foot-by-8-foot shed. It was a rare car, but you could never restore a car that was destroyed that badly."

They returned to Tallinn and tried for several days to buy the Aktion P. Having no success they flew home with no valuable cars but had purchased four more motorcycles, leaving Peter and his two Estonian friends to try to pry the Aktion P from its owner.

After many phone calls to Peter they learned that maybe if they returned to Estonia they could buy the Mercedes. They first flew to Moscow and pursued several motorcycle leads. One address was on the fifth floor of an Estonia apartment complex. They walked into the young man's small apartment to see his Harley-Davidson WLA 42 in the living room. Another partially assembled motorcycle was leaning against the wall, and wheels, tires, gas tanks, and other parts were neatly stacked on top of cabinets and along the floor.

"We took the elevator up here," said Fritz. "It was about 3 feet square. How did you get these motorcycles up here?"

The young man, Victor, explained that he and a friend had carried them up 5 stories, 10 flights of stairs. He said the threat of theft by parking them on the street was too great.

"He started the motorcycle up right in his apartment just to prove it ran," said Fritz. "Luckily he was a young guy with no family. He actually spoke a few words of English because he watched American television programs."

They bought the Harley for about $800 and arranged to keep the bike stored in the apartment until shipping could be arranged.

From there it was off to another motorcycle collector, this one a father and son who ran a semilegitimate repair and restoration shop in the basement of their building.

"The son would restore bikes to a pretty low quality, but at least he got them back on the road again," said Fritz. "They had a few Indians, but they had a strange method for negotiating the price. It was early evening and they said we should go to the café to have a glass of vodka. At 3 a.m., we left the café, having consumed five bottles of vodka! But we bought a nice Indian 741 for about $1,200.

"We were in pretty bad shape the next day, though."

They also inspected another Indian, a 1919 model, in another fellow's apartment. Fritz said the bike was very nice for its age, at least what he could see of it.

"The guy hadn't paid his electric bill for his apartment, so the lights had been turned off," said Fritz. "I had to inspect the bike using a cigarette lighter as a flashlight.

"Even though we really wanted the bike, we could never come to an agreement on price, so we left his apartment empty-handed."

They also bought another rare BMW R75 complete with a sidecar. An interesting feature of that sidecar was its wheel was driven with a driveshaft from the rear wheel of the motorcycle, making it two-wheel drive and excellent for the duty that model performed with General Rommel's assault on Africa.

After a busy three days, Fritz and Ben returned to Estonia to talk with the Aktion P owner. Another four days of talks failed to have the Mercedes in their hands, so Fritz packed for a flight to America the next morning. Reuter who had stayed in Moscow to hunt for more cars, would meet Fritz at the airport the next day to fly back with him. But the Aktion P, the prize they had sought, still eluded them. Ben had decided to stay in Estonia to try to secure its purchase one more time. Fritz went to bed early and Ben went to the owner's home in the countryside for more negotiations.

"At 5:00 in the morning, Ben comes bounding into the hotel room shouting, 'We got the car. We got the car. Get up! You have to figure out how to get the car to America,'" said Fritz. "I told him that if he was kidding me, I'd kill him."

Ben negotiated a complicated deal that included, "a lot of cash," Fritz's old Mercedes station wagon, and an American boarding school education for the man's daughter.

"What?" Fritz asked, still in a slumber. But once Ben explained the deal, and that the man's daughter's education was his highest priority, it made sense. When Reuter arrived at the airport from Moscow to meet Fritz and he wasn't there, Reuter knew something was up and went to the motel where Fritz and Ben were staying.

The third trip a few weeks later was virtually dedicated to packing up the Aktion P in order to sneak it out of the country under the cover of darkness. The car's exit from Estonia was complicated but included two rented cargo

The real gem in Victor's collection was this 1943 Harley-Davidson WLA 42, which he and a friend had carried up to the fifth floor so it wouldn't be stolen. To show Fritz how well the bike ran, he started it up right in the apartment! *Dick Fritz*

Victor (pictured) had a nice apartment, but part of it was used to store his motorcycle parts. Fritz bought the three motorcycles and some parts, paying about $2,100 for everything. *Dick Fritz*

planes, an 18-wheeler, several delivery vans, payments to the general manager of an airport, hush money, and a foggy night, making their escape that much more hazardous. But after several stressful days trying to stay out of the sight of undesirable Estonians, the car and its new owners escaped and were headed for America. Between the purchase of four motorcycles and the Aktion P, the third trip had been the charm.

The group, now energized from their daring purchase and escape, made a total of seven trips to the former Soviet Union, looking for cars, motorcycles, and even World War II aircraft.

"On one trip, Reuter, Peter the Swede, and I flew across Siberia to the Kuril Islands to see if there [were] any World War II American warplanes to be had," said Fritz. "It was somewhat frightening flying to Petropavlosk on the Komchatka peninsula across the 11 time zones of Russia, over the nothingness of Siberia.

"We took a two-hour helicopter ride to Seviro Kurilsk, a city of 4,500 on the third northernmost island, and drove to some of the old Japanese airbases that had existed there before the Russian occupation," said Fritz. "They did find a number of dismantled King Cobras, Japanese Zeros, and Betty bombers, as well as old tanks and military trucks, but we decided not to pursue them. There was just some bad feeling we had about the area, and we just didn't feel safe being there."

They returned to Moscow and St. Petersburg to search for more motor-cycles. One gentleman they met invited them over to his large basement to see his collection. On the way there, he drove them on a piece of elevated roadway that was about 1,000 feet across and 6 or 7 miles long.

"He explained to us that underneath the road they were driving on was every type of military vehicle you could think of—trucks, tanks, airplanes—and about 1 million people," said Fritz. "This was the Memorial Highway that contained the remains of the city of Leningrad [St. Petersburg] after the Germans had attacked. That was a sobering experience.

"When we made it to his country house, he showed us a very nice Harley-Davidson and a nice Mercedes 170, both of which we purchased. But he was a tough negotiator because he never reduced his price but instead kept adding other items into the deal.

"As we were writing up the deal, he mentioned that it was a shame we weren't there six weeks earlier, because he had just sold two Auto Union Grand Prix race cars.

"We said, 'What?' Then he showed us the photo of the two rear-engined cars in the basement and explained that he had just sold them six weeks earlier to a collector from Europe.

"Can you believe that? These are the priceless cars that Audi restored and displays today."

This military 1943 BMW R75 came complete with Steib sidecar. It was purchased for $3,350 from a man named Igor about 30 miles from Moscow. *Dick Fritz*

The Mercedes, which was purchased for $19,000, never made it to the States. Fritz figures the car was probably stolen before it reached the dock in what was probably an "inside job" among the shipping agents.

On another trip, the trio was invited into a barn that was loaded with old motorcycles and parts.

"This guy had a two-story building stacked with parts, and they were fairly neat and organized," said Fritz. "Upstairs he had gas tanks lined up, wheels, sidecars, fenders, handlebars, and frames. Downstairs he had complete bikes. It was an impressive collection, but his prices were very high, so we didn't buy anything from him."

A number of the bikes they looked at were sitting outside and too far gone to make good investments. One they did purchase was a BMW R75 with a sidecar that had been sitting in a field with grass growing through its frame and wheels.

In all, Fritz believes he inspected at least 100 motorcycles and purchased just 14. Only 3 of the 14 ran, but all of them were nearly 80 to 90 percent complete.

The least amount of money they paid for a motorcycle was $200, and the most they paid was $4,000 for a bright green Indian. They figured that if they

Probably the nicest motorcycle purchased by the Americans was this 1943 BMW R75 built for the Afrika Korps. If you look carefully between the handlebars and the seat, you can see a large dome, which is the cover for the special desert air cleaner used by the Germans in the North African campaign. They paid $4,000 for the bike. *Dick Fritz*

Another BMW R75 military motorcycle equipped for desert operations. This photo better shows the large air cleaner cover that some thought looked like a spare German Army helmet. This bike was found in a field behind a summer house near St. Petersburg. The BMWs built for sidecar use had a power take-off driving the sidecar's rear wheel, giving this bike two-wheel drive. They paid $3,350 for the bike. *Dick Fritz*

could buy a motorcycle and have it transported to the United States for an average of $2,000 each, there would be a healthy profit when they were sold for $7,000 or $8,000 each.

Fritz wishes they had purchased more BMW R75s with sidecars. These turned out to be the most valuable and desirable to buyers in the United States.

"These were made for the Nazis fighting in the Sahara Desert, and they had a few special features to cope with the environment, such as supplemental air filters. The extra-large air cleaner looked like a Nazi helmet that sat on top of the gas tank," said Fritz. "Air would come up inside the helmet and then down through a tube through the center of the gas tank and into the carburetor.

"These bikes were built for the desert, but when Rommel was defeated, they were shipped to Russia for the German offensive against the Russians on the Eastern Front. When Germany was defeated, all those bikes were just left there.

Fritz bought this 1943 Indian 741 military model from a man named Sasha for $2,200. It was discovered in a basement near Moscow. *Dick Fritz*

This military Harley-Davidson was purchased for $2,900 from a second-floor apartment. Fritz said it was one of the nicest bikes they purchased and still had much of the special military equipment installed. *Dick Fritz*

One of the other motorcycles the Americans saw on their many trips to Russia but did not purchase. Fritz believes that Russia still has many interesting vintage motorcycles available to purchase but said he would leave that for younger collectors to pursue. *Dick Fritz*

"After the war, Russia took everything of value they could out of Germany, including the contents of the BMW factory. Soon, Russia was pumping out BMW clones, which they still continue to build versions of today.

"We sold the BMWs for between $8,000 and $10,000, when they were probably worth closer to $20,000."

And even though they didn't buy any of the spare parts they discovered, Fritz said that they did see piles of spare parts as well. "The most interesting was an Ariel Square Four engine and a sidecar with an opening in the front that looked like a jet plane," he said.

"We really didn't make any money on the bikes, but it did pay for our trips."

All 14 bikes were crated and packed into one 20-foot storage container that was put on a ship in Tallinn and arrived in New York a few weeks later. Total shipping cost was about $2,000.

Soon after the bike booty arrived at Fritz's Amerispec shop in Danbury, Connecticut, he brought a couple of his discovered motorcycles to the huge Super Sunday motorcycle rally held nearby. The bikes were a hit.

Instead of marketing the motorcycles in *Hemmings Motor News* or the *New York Times*, all the bikes were sold through word-of-mouth. Fritz said that they were satisfied with the profits their motorcycle sales generated but admits that today, with the extensive use of the Internet, he would utilize sites like eBay to generate a higher return.

Fritz has had many years to reflect since taking the most dynamic barn-finding expedition of a lifetime in 1992. First, he believes there are still places around the world that offer treasure hunters opportunities to search and buy long-forgotten vehicles.

"I think Africa probably still has World War II relics," he said, "especially if you were hunting for motorcycles like the BMW R75 and aircraft. Things certainly wouldn't rust very badly there. And I believe that treasures still exist in Russia."

Fritz believes that searching for cars in Russia would be safer now than it was 16 years ago.

Russians are good negotiators, said Fritz. "They are calculating, rational, and very intelligent," he said. "Remember, some of the best chess players in the world are Russians."

The most unusual negotiation Fritz was involved in was for a motorcycle. Negotiations had ended because Fritz thought the asking price was too high. "Then the seller pulled me aside and informed him that for this price, it included a Russian girl. I said, 'What do you mean a Russian girl?' The seller said, 'We have a lot of Russian girls here. If you want for one night, two nights, she's included in the price.'

"I said, 'No, thank you very much. All we are after is cars and motorcycles; we don't want to bring anything else home.'"

Fritz and his colleagues feel best about the boarding school education they were able to give to the daughter of the Estonian Aktion P owner. She attended two years at an exclusive private school in Massachusetts and, now in her early 30s and again living in Estonia, still stays in touch with him.

Now that Fritz is older and hopefully wiser, has he thought about making another Russian treasure hunt, knowing the risks involved?

"It does occur to me occasionally," he said. "But it's usually after a large meal where I've had too much to drink. In the middle of the night I wake up in a sweat having just dreamed about going back there.

"I've actually heard of a rare Mercedes 500 fastback called the Autobahn Carrier that is sitting in Iran. It was built to celebrate speed record runs on the Autobahn and once belonged to the Shah of Iran. I've seen pictures of it, but am I going there? No way! Maybe someday the conditions will exist to safely go over there and get that car, but I don't see that happening soon.

"With all the dangers we encountered—potential theft, kidnapping, death, Mafia, KGB, and disorganized crime—the modern-day treasure hunt was worthwhile only because of the Aktion P, which was quite valuable. I wouldn't relish being killed over a BMW motorcycle.

"Because you're only crazy once."

The Italian Motorcycle Merchant

Guy Webster loves everything about Italy—the weather, the food, and the wine. He loves the Italian countryside of Tuscany and the hustle-and-bustle of cities like Sicily. But what Webster especially loves are Italian motorcycles.

Webster is a rock-and-roll photographer who has shot portraits of everyone from Keith Richards to Waylon Jennings. He is also well known for his rare motorcycle collection and his knowledge of the subject.

"At one time I had 300 motorcycles, but I'm down to 50 right now," said Webster as he sat on a comfortable leather sofa surrounded by his collection in a generic-looking industrial building in Ojai, California. "I sold about 100 off to collectors around the world about 18 years ago when my wife said she wanted a house on Martha's Vineyard. I did that as an act of love.

"I've sold off my car collection; cars just don't mean anything to me. They don't go fast enough," he said. "I've gone 160 miles per hour [on bikes] on the street for long periods and 180 miles per hour on the track.

"You get out into the country where you can see for 100 miles, with no cops and no place to hide, and you can just go."

To house his large two-wheeled collection, Webster built a huge structure on his property in Ojai. The place looked like an agricultural barn, but inside it was clean and modern with Italian tiled floors. Enthusiasts traveled from all over the world to attend his barn's grand opening.

"Before I sold my ranch, that building was dedicated to restoring old bikes for 30 years," he said.

"These days I collect Italian motorcycles only, ranging from 1950 to 1970, which I consider the hand-made years. These are mostly small-capacity bikes of between 75cc and 500cc and are exquisitely designed. I don't collect 50cc bikes.

"In 1950, Italian bikes still used bicycle seats, but by 1970, they became pretty sophisticated, the manufacturers having used more magnesium and better metals to lighten them up."

Being a well-known collector of vintage motorcycles often means Webster hears about hidden bikes before others. Over the years, he's made some memorable discoveries.

Yoshi's Window Dressing

Webster spent parts of his childhood and adult life living in Italy. In the early 1970s, fresh from a divorce, he took a sabbatical and lived in his adopted country in order to piece his life back together.

"I always had great Italian bikes like MV Agustas and Ducatis, but when I went back to Italy and saw all these great old bikes on the road, I decided it would be fun to buy a few rare old bikes to ride around when I got back home to California."

He went to the vintage motorcycle races at Laguna Seca Raceway in Monterey and saw a bike that spurred his interest, a 1948 Gilera Saturno. "So I walked up to a guy who was with the bike and asked him who owned the bike. He said he had just restored it for a friend.

"So I asked him what something like that costs. He said, 'You don't want to know; it costs too much.'

"In 1972 or '73, it was an outrageous number."

Still, it was such a beautiful bike that Webster kept it in mind.

During the next decade, Webster collected what he calls "minor bikes," which he defines as motorcycles that cost $5,000 to $6,000. Webster walked into a motorcycle shop called the Garage Company in Venice, California. A Gilera motorcycle similar to the one he had seen at Laguna Seca a decade earlier was in the shop window.

"It was a Gilera Saturno Piuma Electron, a very rare motorcycle," he said. "Gilera is the brand. Saturno is the model. Piuma means that it's light-weight, and Electron means it used magnesium in the construction. And it was in shambles but complete except for the tachometer."

Motorcycle collector Guy Webster saw a Gilera Saturno in the early 1970s when he attended a vintage motorcycle race at Laguna Seca Raceway. Many years later he purchased this one, then in very tired condition, having sat in the front window of an LA motorcycle repair shop for many years. *Guy Webster*

The shop was owned by a colorful genius named Yoshi Kosaka.

"I said, 'Hey, Yoshi, what about that bike?' He said it wasn't for sale because it was window dressing.

"But I bugged him for years. It wasn't rusty, just dilapidated and threadbare. All the hoses were gone, the paint was faded, and the decals were crumbling.

"'Come on, Yoshi,' I said. 'It's a mess. I'll restore it.'"

Webster told him that having it in the window didn't bring anyone into the shop, except for oddball collectors like him.

The Gilera was a 1956 500cc single-cylinder factory racing motorcycle or "works" bike that was never sold over the counter. When they were new the Gileras were raced across Europe by professional riders, then shipped to Argentina where the year-old bikes would be campaigned until their useful lives were over.

"So it ended its racing life in Argentina before making its way to California," he said. "Americans were buying Italian racing bikes from Argentina and restoring them."

One day Yoshi called Webster with some news. "I've got a buyer for a couple of your bikes if you'd like to sell them," he said.

This was Webster's chance to own the Gilera. "OK, I'll sell you two or three of my bikes if you sell me the Gilera," said Webster. "You have to understand that I was selling him a couple of beautifully restored Ducatis and he's selling me a piece of junk."

Yoshi didn't like the deal, but he stood to make a nice profit brokering the Ducati sale. After much hemming and hawing, Yoshi finally surrendered.

"OK, bring them on over and let's make the trade," he said.

"I was so excited," said Webster. "I really didn't think he would go for it. I was acting kind of nonchalant, but he had no idea how badly I wanted that bike."

Webster finally had his Gilera, but it now needed to be restored. He remembered the Gilera restorer, Todd Millar, he had met at Laguna Seca many years earlier and convinced him to take on the project.

"Back then, the cost of the restoration was about $10,000, which was a lot of money," said Webster. "But I had done my homework. It was one of four produced and one of two that remain. The other one is apparently in Milan somewhere, but nobody is really sure."

The bike was so complete that it didn't need any parts besides the tachometer, which cost Webster $2,000 by itself.

"I had to find an original, which was tough," he said. "You can find pseudo-original tachs that look pretty good to the average guy, but I had to have a real one. It just happens to be a Smiths gauge made in England.

"Pieces like that tach are like trading commodities," he said. "When the values are high, people let go of their pieces. It's the nature of the game. If you buy the right stuff, the value keeps going up. If inflation happens, prices may flatten out, but they don't go down."

After nearly three decades of Gilera ownership, Webster hasn't lost any enthusiasm for the bike.

"For me, this was the barn find of barn finds," he said. "When Italian collectors come over here they all tell me they'll trade me this or that for the bike, but I've owned it for 26 years and haven't sold it yet."

Even though Webster has raced his vintage bikes extensively, these days his hunger for competition has lessened.

"I'll be 70 years old next year," he said. "I have five kids and grandchildren. I've got to slow down."

Patience for a Parilla

"I was told 25 years ago about a guy who owned a restaurant in Seattle and had a brand new Parilla Grand Sport 250 in his living room," said Webster. "So I contact this guy, who I didn't even know, and ask if it might be for sale."

The man said he had no interest in parting with his bike.

"So I told him flat out, 'When you decide to sell, I want to be the first person on your list once you set a price,'" said Webster.

According to Webster, there are Grand Sports, and there are Grand Sports. "Some have the name Grand Sports, but they are not really racing bikes," he said. "True Grand Sports are racing bikes but look very much like the street versions, which are also called Grand Sports.

"In the day you could actually buy a real racing version over the counter through Cosmopolitan Motors in New Jersey. This guy's was the real thing, even though I never saw it, I just knew it."

The man loved the bike as much as Webster would, which was good. He never abused it and never raced it. They stayed in touch for many years, and each time they spoke, Webster would remind the man that he wanted to buy the bike. And each time the man would say he wasn't selling it.

This relationship of patience on both sides continued until one day the phone rang. The man with the Parilla was calling. "I want to retire and move to Mexico to open a restaurant," he said. "I think I'm ready to sell."

This was music to Webster's ears. "OK, you set the price," he said. "If it's as nice as you say it is, I'll pay it.

"I wanted that bike regardless."

The man agreed and then offered door-to-door service. He delivered the Parilla to Southern California. The delivery included another box. "What's

A Seattle restaurant owner had this Parilla Grand Sport 250 in his living room. Webster had to wait 25 years for him to decide to sell it. This bike is unrestored and has been shown at the Guggenheim Museum in New York in the *Art of the Motorcycle* exhibit. The full faring is made from a single sheet of aluminum.
Guy Webster

this?" asked Webster. "This is the original fairing for the bike, which has never been mounted," said the man.

"I was blown away," said Webster. "I would have paid another $5,000 for it. This was an unrestored racing bike in original condition with an original fairing that no one in the United States has ever seen. It was pristine."

Webster still owns the Parilla and says it's one of the prizes of his collection.

Several years ago, Webster helped curate a motorcycle display at the Guggenheim Museum in New York, and his Parilla was one of the bikes on display there for more than four years.

"I was excited about this rare front racing fairing on the bike and the museum people asked me to take it off," he said. "They said the fairing didn't allow people to see the motor. They were correct, because it has one of the most beautiful motors in motorcycle history."

Basement Box Bike

Webster is known as an Italian bike collector, so he gets calls often from friends giving him tips on potential barn finds.

"People call me from out of the woodwork," he said. "There was this famous guy from the collector car world who once called me and said he wanted to do me a favor. 'I heard of something really unusual about a guy in New Hampshire who has three boxes of motorcycle parts who says it's an MV Agusta. You like MVs, don't you?'"

Webster was all ears. He owned about 10 or 12 MV Agustas at the time, but he was always eager to hear about other discoveries of the special Italian bike.

"Give him a call," his friend said. "I don't know what he's got or what he wants for it, but I thought it might be something you want."

Webster called the man, who actually lived in Connecticut. "Yeah, I have the bike," he said. "It's in my basement.

"I raced it three times back in 1957, then took it apart to restore it. I just don't have the energy to finish it now and would like to sell it."

"He told me it was a 1956 Squalo and that he bought it to race in the Loudon, New Hampshire, races," said Webster.

"I didn't want to screw the guy, but I really wanted that bike."

Webster told him that soon he would be making his annual cross-country trek from his year-round house in Ojai, California, to his summer home on Martha's Vineyard. "I'd like to stop by Connecticut on the way north to see the bike, if that's OK."

Webster liberated this 1956 MV Agusta Squalo from a Connecticut basement where it had been sitting disassembled for nearly 50 years. He was nervous that some parts might be missing, but every piece was there. *Guy Webster*

Webster wanted to clarify how complete the bike was after all these years. "Now, it's all there, right?" he asked.

"Yeah, it's all there, every nut, bolt, and washer," said the man.

"OK, I'll take your word for it," said Webster. "I'm going to trust you, but what is my recourse if I discover it isn't complete after I purchase it?"

The man said he would refund all or a portion of my money to make good on it.

"This was in about 1990, and I was about to gamble a large sum of money," said Webster. "It was $8,000, which was a lot to spend on a motorcycle 18 years ago."

Webster bought it but didn't feel comfortable shipping the boxes of motorcycle components cross-country, but then he had a stroke of luck. Near the man's house in Connecticut was a Ferrari mechanic Webster knew. When he mentioned the bike to the mechanic, the first thing out of his mouth were the words "Man, I'd love to restore an MV Agusta."

Webster was surprised at his comment. "Are you serious? Do you think you could?" Webster asked.

"The guy had never restored a motorcycle before, but he said he could restore anything. It turned out he was a genius. I told him he had a year to assemble the pieces into a complete bike."

One year later it was completed. Webster couldn't pick it up as he had hoped, so he arranged for shipping.

"Mechanically it was perfect, but the bike was unrestored," he said. "But the seller was correct; every single washer was there, right down to the tiny straps that hold the electrical wires to the frame."

When the bike was returned to California, he sent it to his regular restorer for a cosmetic restoration.

"After sitting 50 years in a basement, it looked pretty rough," said Webster. "So I told him not to make it glossy but to make it look like an authentic factory racer. He made it look just right."

The MV Agusta is one of his favorite motorcycles he has ever owned.

"And it was just an act of faith buying three boxes in a basement," said Webster.

Museum Mi-Ta

One of the most renowned motorcycle races in the world is the Motogiro d'Italia, an event where up to 300 participants race through the streets in Italy for between 500 and 1,000 miles. The "Motogiro" is for bikes what the Mille Miglia is for vintage sports cars.

Webster traded a very rare racing engine designed by Ducati's brilliant engineer Fabio Taglioni to a museum in Italy for this 75cc Laverda Mi-Ta. It was unrestored when he received it but has since been brought to as-new condition. *Guy Webster*

"One year in the Motogiro, a group of 14 factory Laverda racing bikes took the first 14 positions in their division," said Webster.

"It's an important race and an important bike, and without exaggeration, it was the only bike I was missing out of my collection. I needed to find a 75cc Laverda Mi-Ta."

Mi-Ta stands for Milano-Taranto, which is a race much like the Giro that races between these two towns.

"I had feelers out, but I could never find a real one," he said. "It was popular for people to make racing replicas out of street models, but they weren't real racers."

In 2005 Webster had an opening at his big bike barn in Ojai and invited hundreds of bike enthusiasts from all over the world to see his collection. A part of his collection was a motorcycle motor with a sign next to it identifying it as being built by the brilliant Ducati designer Fabio Taglioni. The motor was built specifically for a Ceccato. This particular motor was an extra Webster bought for his Ceccato.

An international film crew was documenting the evening's events. The crew shot footage of the crowd but also of the collection of bikes, components, and memorabilia. At the conclusion of the event, that footage was sent to Italy, where it was seen by the staff of the Ceccato Museum in Verase.

"In a slow sweep of the collection, the museum staff sees the Ceccato motor, so they called me," said Webster. "They said, 'Mr. Webster, would you donate that motor to the museum because we have a Ceccato without a motor.'

"I said, 'You must be kidding. I'm not donating it; it must be worth at least $10,000. Besides, where would I get another one?'

"So the museum staff asked if I'd be interested in a trade. 'What if we send you an unrestored bike from our museum in exchange for the motor?'

"I told them, 'the only bike I am looking for is a . . . ,' and before I could get the words out of my mouth they said they had two Laverda Mi-Tas and they would like to send me one.

"They didn't know I was missing the bike or was looking for a Mi-Ta. It's the kind of bike that you can't go out and say you are going to find one because there are just none around.

"So they sent me the bike. It's actually a cheap bike, but to me it was worth trading a $10,000 motor for. It's complete right down to the original racing number plate."

Taglioni's Desmodromic Ceccato

Webster has long been a sucker for Ceccato motorcycles. They are the jewels of the Italian motorcycle world. The bikes were designed by Fabio Taglioni, who made Ducati motorcycles famous by using and perfecting the complex desmodromic valvetrain system.

"It took someone like Taglioni to make it work," said Webster. "He was a genius."

Taglioni built the Ceccato motor while he was still a student in Bologna, and the powerful engine was used to set a world speed record. Webster searched and searched and eventually found a 100cc version for his collection.

"Well, that was a score, I thought," he said. "It took me forever to find one. They were built from 1953 to 1955."

Webster was now friends with the Verase Museum, and he heard they were in need of money. He also knew that they had a 75cc Ceccato dual-overhead-cam version of the bike.

This 75cc Ceccato, also designed by Fabio Taglioni, was purchased from the Ceccato Museum in Italy, but exporting it to the States was forbidden by the Italian government because of its historical significance. Luckily, Webster's daughter, who lived in Italy and owned an export business, was able to ship it within six months. *Guy Webster*

"I said to myself, 'I'd like to have one of those 75cc models,'" he said. "Then I'd have one of each. So I called the museum."

The museum said it would ask a lot of money for the bike, between $40,000 and $50,000, but it was willing to let it go.

So Webster sent them the money only to find out that the Italian government wouldn't allow the bike to leave the country because it was considered a national treasure.

Luckily Webster had a solution. Of his five children, three live in Italy.

"My oldest daughter and her husband are in the international trading business, so they are always importing and exporting," he said. "So they were able to purchase the bike then ship it to me within six months."

The 75cc Ceccato was in fine original condition, so there was no need to restore it.

"It's worth $150,000," he said. "I was just lucky."

Black Shadows of Saigon

By Lee Klancher

The city of Saigon houses many secrets. In the early 1950s, the covert dramas playing out in the majestic city's narrow streets included Corsican drug traffickers stalking American generals, CIA agents covertly supporting the French military who occupied the city, and Viet Minh revolutionaries plotting the downfall of the French.

In a back alley of this giant metropolis now known as Ho Chi Minh City, a crate was abandoned in a warehouse. The crate contained three Vincent motorcycle engines and a pile of other HRD parts that sat forgotten and periodically flooded by murky waters flowing up from the city's underbelly.

While the engines filled with rotting vegetation, Saigon became a sweltering cauldron of unrest as the largely Buddhist population took increasing offense to the Catholic government.

By 1963, the fighting took to the streets as a coup d'état showered bullets on the walls of the city's elegant cathedrals, hotels, and theaters. The president was unceremoniously dragged from the palace to be shot, stabbed, and buried in disgrace. Not long after people danced in the streets to celebrate the nation's new government, those Vincent engines surfaced in a Saigon paper classified ad.

A sharp-eyed Vietnamese man by the name of Nguyen Van Nhon purchased the crate full of Vincent engines and did his best to sell them. He advertised them for sale in the Vincent Owner's Club magazine, *MPH*. He claimed to be courting suitors for the engines from Europe, Australia, and New Zealand.

In letters Van Nhon sent to an American pilot, he described the engines in his possession. He expressed calculated passion for the Vincents, but he also understood the value of his find. In fact, this self-labeled "enthusiast" was doing his best to trade the Vincents for stereo equipment, cars, or motorcycles.

"I have purchased the three bikes last year because first I know it must be a very good and fast bike, a famous name," Van Nhon wrote in a letter dated October 4, 1967. "Secondly it is something like 'vintage' and could not get now, especially new condition like this is almost impossible to find. It is the 'prestige of the past' that any motorcycle enthusiast like me or like any enthusiast would like to have."

Van Nhon wrote that he joined the Vincent HRD Owner's Club in England and was determined to restore at least one of the engines. Perhaps his intentions were authentic, but his actions indicate otherwise.

While corresponding with the pilot, Lieutenant Leon, he expressed his interest in trading the Vincents for Marantz and Fisher stereo components,

Note that the spark plugs are both on the right side of the engine. This indicates that two front cylinders were used, a trick done on race engines, as the fronts flowed a bit better than the rear cylinders. Vincent adopted this setup for all production twins in 1955. *Lee Klancher*

a 1965 Ford Falcon with a three-speed transmission, or parts for a Harley-Davidson motorcycle. Van Nhon was meticulous with his passions, and his lists of desired equipment were very specific.

Van Nhon noted that one of the engines was in pristine condition, was "brand new from shipment in 1953 or 54," and the cylinders both had spark holes on the right-hand side. The spark plug holes are a clue for those in-the-know in Vincent lore. On a stock Black Shadow, the front cylinder has a spark plug on the right side, while the rear has the plug on the left. The front cylinders flow air better than the rear on Shadow engines, and Lightning motors (as well as all 1955 Series D final production Vincents) use two front cylinders, which means they have both spark plug holes on the right-hand side.

He continued to correspond with the lieutenant, urging him to come to Saigon to see the bikes and trade all or just one of them for his desired equipment.

On June 26, 1969, Van Nhon got his wish and sold the "1953 or 54" engine to Bruce Clarke of Florida. The engine was shipped to the United States, but Clarke didn't keep it for long. He sold the engine to another Florida resident, Rudy Nygrin, on September 2, 1970, for $300 in cash.

When Nygrin took the engine apart, he discovered it was not quite as pristine as promised. The engine had been sitting in the warehouse with the drain plug out, and the interior of the cases had marks from periodic flooding. Rotted bits of plants were inside the cases.

Nygrin took the time and expense to install the engine in a Rapide frame and owned it for quite some time.

The bike's history had been publicized in *MPH* in the early 1970s, and readers took a keen interest in how this motorcycle had made its way from Vietnam to the United States. Nygrin saw the articles and letter about his bike and wrote in to describe how he had acquired it. The editor wrote to his readers in one issue, "Many thanks to Rudy for clearing up one of the longest-running Vincent mysteries."

Motorcycle broker Somer Hooker bought the bike years later and eventually sold it to Wayne Brooks of Huntington Beach, California. The bike changed hands again and ended up being owned by Mark Holmes of Oregon.

Holmes was mostly into cars and didn't know quite what to do with the bike, so he put it up for sale on eBay in 2005. Texas collector Herb Harris saw the post and noticed that the ad said the bike had a high-performance specification. Like many serious Vincent enthusiasts, he knew about the engine's Vietnam lineage.

"I bought it because it had history," Harris said. "With the Black Shadow engine, it might be kind of cool. Almost everyone with a Black Shadow engine has been told it has race history. Only in a very few cases is that actually true."

The Montlhéry engine was exported to Vietnam and later brought to America. While the history of how the engine came to the United States is well documented, how it made its way from France to Saigon is a mystery. *Herb Harris collection*

Historic or no, the motorcycle was an assembly of randomly acquired parts.

"The bike was a mess," Harris said. "It was a bitsa—just a piece of this and a piece of that."

Holmes may not have known what to do with the odd assembly of a Vincent, but he was smart enough to research the bike's history. While he was purchasing the machine, he had contacted Vince Farell, the registrar for the Vincent club. When Farrell pulled the paperwork on it, he knew the Vietnam Vincent was something special.

"It's great that this bike has turned up again after all these years; it's one that's a bit special," Farrell wrote. "I have the works records that give all sorts of info on the bikes and where they went in the world. F10AB/1B/9203 was sold as an *engine* only. It left the Vincent factory in 1952 and was sent to Garreau, who was the French agent in Paris. This agrees with the story of it being found in a box unused in Vietnam."

The engine specifications were the race pedigree that Holmes referred to in his eBay ad. The bike left the factory equipped with Lightning cams, 32-millimeter carburetors, and 2-inch straight pipes for the exhaust, along with all kinds of hand-fabricated bits.

This Black Shadow's engine was prepared by the Vincent factory to set a speed record at Montlhéry, France, in 1952. The engine was a spare and never ran, and restorer/collector Herb Harris bought and built this re-creation of the race bike. *Lee Klancher*

The headlamp is a French Marchal unit similar to the "flamethrower" that was put on the original Montlhéry speed record bike. The fuel tank sits just over an inch lower than stock on this bike. *Lee Klancher*

"Clearly it's a spare engine for some kind of works bike," Harris said. He did more research into Vincent history and discovered that the company had sent a large team of riders and bikes to set new world speed records at Montlhéry, France. The engine was built as a works motor and shipped to France just in time for the speed record attempts.

"Bam," Harris said. "There it was."

Montlhéry's 1.5-mile banked concrete oval was a popular place to set speed records, and Vincent was looking to set new records for average speeds over 6, 12, and 24 hours with a Vincent Black Shadow.

They sent a fleet of riders, bikes, and spare engines to France in order to do that. The list of 11 riders included legendary racers John Surtees and Ted Davis.

While they had mechanical troubles that ended the bike's run in the 11th hour, they did set several records. One of them was a six-hour average pace of 100.60 miles per hour, breaking the old record of 96.72 miles per hour.

Vincent's technical manager, Paul Richardson, wrote at length about his experiences at Montlhéry in his book, *Vincent Motor Cycles*. In detail one might expect from a professional gearhead and a melodramatic style worthy of a Formula 1 television announcer, he carefully chronicled the historic event.

Richardson notes that French pit workers told the team to use a brush to lube the chain rather than just pouring oil on it, and urged them to use "some oversize flamethrower of French manufacture" rather than stock HRD lighting.

He also discussed the intensity required of the crew in order to keep a motorcycle running for nearly 12 hours. He noted that the support staff, riders, and crew worked tirelessly. He was also pleased to find that the trackside facilities allowed one to relieve oneself and "keep on enjoying the crispness of the Shadow's exhaust note, lap by lap, even in splendid isolation!"

Despite the fact that the team broke the engine's crank, they set a number of records that clearly meant a lot to Richardson.

"The falling of the first record was a great moment. . . . I had a lump in my throat—tried to congratulate some people—watched the bike on the banking in the brilliant sunshine, sound as a bell."

He went on to describe how the record attempt left him so spent that he and a "Company Director" fell asleep while attending a strip show at a Paris theater the last night of their trip. He added that some fast talking was required after "short riotous celebrating" took place at the "Horse White" hotel.

"A concerted vocal effort convinced Madame the Proprietress and the one and only Head-Waiter that [we] were jolly good fellows," Richardson wrote, "and I don't think we broke anything of value."

Vincent advertised the bike that set the records as a stock Black Shadow. The poorly kept truth was the bike was modified nearly to the Lightning's high-performance specifications and even had hand-fabricated short aluminum manifolds that looked like those used on a Lightning.

"They were selling the project as a standard Black Shadow," Harris said. "It was anything but. . . . It was a racing engine."

So Herb knew he had purchased a piece of lost history. When he and his guys took the Vietnam Shadow's engine apart, they found very little wear and tear.

"I don't think the engine ran at Montlhéry," Harris said. "I think it's all that's left of the works record-setting effort."

One of the other race engines that ran at Montlhéry survived, for a while, but the owner unwittingly stuffed it into a Norton Featherbed frame and eventually parted it out.

Inside the Vietnam Shadow engine's cases, Harris discovered evidence of the water damage that Nygrin described. The flywheel and cases bore watermarks, which Harris and company faithfully left intact. They also found an abundance of unusual marks on the internals of the engine, which they believe were made by the factory in order to indicate it was a very special engine.

"We started seeing these crazy stamps," Harris said. "This bike has the only specially numbered set of cranks I have seen."

This graphic, which mimics a race poster used to advertise the Vincent speed run, is painted on the tank. *Lee Klancher*

Once the surprisingly lightly worn engine was reassembled, Harris had to decide how to restore the bike. He lucked upon an upper frame member that was correct for the bike and started to gather other parts that were as faithful as possible to the original Montlhéry racer.

Harris took the opportunity to create a bike that is an interpretation of the original machine. He used a Black Shadow front end and rear frame, a Lightning saddle, and alloy wheels. Black-painted Lightning fenders were mounted, and the gas tank was lightened and dropped down just over an inch to give the bike a low, racy look. A copy of the original Vincent poster announcing the record event has been added to the top of the fuel tank as well.

A period-correct French Marchal headlamp with a yellow bulb was fitted, and the speedometer was lowered. The result is a rideable Vincent with a unique history.

"It's loud and fast and should do 100 miles per hour in first gear," Harris said.

"History in bikes can be lost in one owner," Harris continued. "My game is to find out what that was. I'm glad I asked the questions. This is one of the most historic bikes I've had."

That's saying a lot, as Harris' Vincent collection includes the well-known race bike *The Beast* and the famous bike Rollie Free set his speed record with in his bathing suit.

The Vietnam Shadow is more than just a 150-mile-per-hour blast from the past. In fact, the best part of this story has not yet been chronicled. How and why did the engine travel from France to that waterlogged warehouse in Saigon?

The most likely scenario is that a French soldier purchased the engine after the race at Montlhéry and transported it to Saigon. The last of the French soldiers left the country in 1956, and it's possible that the engines were abandoned when the owner left. Rumor has it that a Thai prince ordered the machines. But that part of this motorcycle's story is yet to be told.

Another bit of intrigue comes from the letters from Nguyen Van Nhon appealing to Lieutenant Leon to buy the bike. In a long section of one letter, Van Nhon describes each of the three engines and the parts that went along with them in detail. He noted that one of them was a nearly complete motorcycle, which "except for the special tank," looked quite similar to the famous race bike, *Gunga Din*.

Gunga Din was brought to Montlhéry in 1952 to set new top speed records. Ted Davis and John Surtees piloted the bike but failed to break any records due to tire failures caused by the unseasonably warm May temperatures.

Van Nhon's note leads one to believe that another race bike with history—perhaps a back-up to *Gunga Din*?—made its way to that musty warehouse in Saigon.

The speedometer and headlight are dropped an inch or so lower in the front to give the bike a racier appearance. *Lee Klancher*

The crate certainly contained more than just the Montlhéry engine. Somer Hooker said that it also contained a B Rapide that Van Nhon never completed because the government refused to let him import a 20-inch front tire.

He said the crate also contained a new Black Shadow. That Black Shadow was flown out of the country as Saigon was falling by an Air America pilot and ended up in Australia. He believes the bike was modified and then disappeared.

And the *Gunga Din* motor was a Lightning motor, according to Hooker, "at least in spirit."

With Van Nhon peddling history for stereos and cars to buyers in Europe, Australia, and New Zealand, *Gunga Din*'s close cousin could be moldering away in a musty warehouse nearly anywhere in the world.

The key to finding those Vincents may be found in a newspaper article, letter, or bill of sale tucked into a filing cabinet of Ho Chi Minh City. That story is just another secret held close to the bosom of the steamy city of Saigon.

The Indian Chronicles

Granddad's Indian

One day in 1994, Dale Walksler received a call from his friend Ron Christianson, who runs Mid-America Auction Service.

"Ron and I are good buddies, and he regularly calls to bounce ideas off me and to get values on bikes in order to give sellers an accurate idea of what a bike will bring at auction," said Walksler.

"So he calls me and says he heard about a 1903 Indian that some lady has on the East Coast. He heard that the lady's grandfather bought it brand new. He wanted to know my opinion on the value of the bike."

Walksler was on another one of his famous road trips with One-Eye Roy, driving his truck and trailer somewhere in Massachusetts. It was a cold, snowy day, but the owner's house wasn't far out of his way, so he decided to stop in and check out the bike.

"We drove to this lady's house and sat inside and had tea and coffee with her and talked about her family's history," he said. "Afterwards she took us up to the attic where a 1903 Indian sat in incredible condition. Over time, someone had lost the handlebars, muffler, coil, and battery tube, but otherwise it was very complete.

"All Indians in 1903 had blue engines. This one still had its original blue paint on it, but the gas tank looked like it had been repaired and repainted a long time ago."

As the story unfolded, the lady told Walksler that the bike was originally her grandfather's. She told him that her grandfather had purchased the bike new from the Indian factory in Springfield, Massachusetts, in 1903 and rode it 60 miles back to his home. He rode the bike regularly but never raced it. He eventually hung it up in the garage. Neighbors who knew about the motorcycle suggested that the family not keep it in the garage for security reasons, so that's when they put it in the attic.

At some point in the 1960s, her father took the old bike out of the barn and replaced the old wooden rims with newer steel bicycle rims so it would be more usable. Unfortunately, some of the parts Walksler identified as missing were probably lost during that time.

Within a few hours, Walksler was able to negotiate a purchase from the lady, load it on the truck, and drag it back home to Illinois.

"I remember unloading the bike and trying to figure how we were going to get this thing running," said Walksler. "The carburetor looked to be intact, so I got some galvanized tubing for a battery tube and installed a coil.

Dale Walksler retrieved this rare 1903 Indian from the attic of a woman whose grandfather bought it new from the Springfield, Massachusetts, Indian factory and rode it back 60 miles to his home. It had been stored in a barn until it was moved into the attic for security reasons in the 1960s. *Dale Walksler collection*

"I started pedaling and the bike started instantly. Within 30 minutes of unloading the bike, I was able to get it running. I was riding that bike on the same day."

The lady who sold Walksler the bike visited the Wheels Through Time Museum in North Carolina in 2007 (where Walksler is curator) to see her grand-dad's old motorcycle. "This is an amazing story about one-family ownership for 97 years," said Walksler. "When you're buying an antiquity, be it a motorcycle, a car, or a piece of furniture, you're buying a piece of someone's life."

The Tandem Indian

In 2001, Walksler's phone rang at 7 a.m. His friend Rocky Halter was on the line.

"Dale, are you interested in an early 1908 Indian Twin with original paint?" asked Halter.

"Sounds like it's a little bit out of my price range," said Walksler. "By the way, where are you?"

"I'm in your driveway," said Halter.

At the time Walksler lived in an abandoned three-story hospital in a questionable neighborhood outside of Chicago. "I was a bachelor and I lived in the hospital for 13 years," he said.

Walksler ran down the stairs and out into the driveway where Halter's trailer was parked. "I was eager to see if this was a piece of junk or a one-of-a-kind gem because nobody had ever seen anything like it before," he said.

What he discovered that morning was an amazing discovery. The bike was totally unique with tandem seats, tandem handlebars, and tandem gas tanks. Even the tires, as dilapidated as they are, are the original G7J tires with a patent date of 1897 printed on the sidewalls.

Walksler believes this motorcycle was built specifically for Indian designer Roger Hedstrom, which is why it included the tandem components.

"You can look at some of the early Indian catalogues and they offered a tandem unit with dual seats and handlebars," he said, "but this one with the double tanks makes it much more interesting and unique."

The bike also has an unusual twin-cylinder engine design called the Hacksaw Blade Twin because of the unique system it used to operate the valves.

"When people ask 'How do the valves work?' my response is, 'Not very well because they only used the hacksaw blade design for a year and a half before they changed to a pushrod system,'" Walksler said. He explains that the intake and exhaust valves were operated by the same cam lobe through a complicated spring system.

Walksler's friend Halter had just recovered the Indian from a barn in Colorado. Apparently two bachelor brothers who lived together had collected motorcycles for many years. "The brothers got into a heated debate after one of the brothers started dating at 60-plus years of age," said Walksler. "This sidetracked the brothers from their passion of collecting rare motorcycles."

The family feud caused the brothers to break up the collection, and that's how Halter wound up owning the Indian.

"It's one of the motorcycles in our museum that does not run," he said. "I do that for two reasons: I don't want to change those original tires, and you must have round tires to peddle start these bikes. And these tires are pretty warped."

Easy Russ, Junky Joe, One-Eye Roy, and the Snoop

Orvil Parker was an early motorcycle collector. He traveled around the country with his truck and trailer following up leads and snooping in old buildings in search of elusive two-wheeled treasure. The Muskegon, Michigan, resident was tooling through Massachusetts on one of his junkets in the 1960s when he stumbled across a pretty good find: 12 old bikes. As he cleaned out the shed and loaded these bikes into his trailer, he moved an old workbench out of the way and discovered yet another motorcycle behind it. "Great, another old bike," he thought, and loaded it with the other bikes into his trailer.

When his purchase was complete, he drove down the road in search of more hidden treasure troves. He didn't realize that the bike he found tucked behind the workbench was one of the most desirable collector bikes in the world, the Oscar Hedstrom Prototype.

Parker owned the Prototype for 15 to 20 years and eventually sold it to another collector, "Junky" Joe Bisacky, the owner of Joe's Auto Parts in Spring Lake, Michigan. Bisacky was quite a collector, and enthusiasts from around the country made pilgrimages to Spring Lake to see his parts yard, architectural artifacts, and wooden cigar store Indians. But his specialty was old motorcycles and motorcycle parts.

Bisacky was never really interested in selling the rare Hedstrom Prototype, but eventually he did, and the rare bike became part of the collection of another Michigan collector, a gentleman nicknamed Easy Russ from Grand Rapids who had been collecting motorcycles since the early 1970s.

Walksler considers this 1913 Indian the rarest motorcycle in the world. It is believed to have been assembled personally by Indian's brilliant designer and engineer, Oscar Hedstrom. The bike features dual magnetos, dual clutch controls, and dual compression release valves. *Dale Walksler collection*

"He had been through several phases in his motorcycle interest, where, like me, he'd go completely crazy over one model or another," said Wheels Through Time museum curator Dale Walksler. "So at some point in our relationship, Easy Russ tells me about the motorcycle he had purchased from Junky Joe, so I made a point to stop in on my next trip through Michigan."

Walksler toured Russ' barn, which he said contains one of the most amazing collections of antiques in the world. As he was rummaging through the contents of the barn, there between the bumpers of two cars was parked the very unique Indian.

"It was the damnedest looking 1913 Indian I'd seen in my life," he said.

The building was dark, so it was hard to see, but he realized this was no regular Indian.

"It was without tires, but I knew I wanted to own it," he said. "But Easy Russ is an interesting guy, because if he thinks you really want to buy something of his, he becomes Not-So-Easy-Russ."

Walksler didn't necessarily play down the fact that he wanted to own the bike, but he just casually mentioned that it was something he would like to own in the future if he decided to sell it.

"Trying to push Russ into a quick sale is unlikely unless he initiates the sale," he said. "And if he does initiate the sale, you'd better get your money out and buy it right there because if you come back later, it's either not for sale or it's gone or something."

Obviously Walksler was successful in planting a seed in Russ' head, because not too long after that, he called Walksler. "Hey, I'll trade the Indian for an original-paint Harley Knucklehead," he said. Walksler said that Knuckleheads at the time were beginning to become valuable and somewhat hard to find, and certainly one with original paint would be a real prize.

Walksler had an original-paint Knucklehead, a 1947 in original red paint. "It was the most awesome original bike but one that I had become emotionally and personally attached to," said Walksler. "Russ knew I owned the bike, but he never brought it up and neither did I. It was left as a moot point." But Russ' desire for an original-paint Knucklehead got Walksler's mental gears in motion.

Many years earlier, in 1978, when he was a young Harley-Davidson dealer in Mount Vernon, Illinois, he remembered seeing an original-paint Knucklehead.

"Harley had just come out with a new bike called the Brown Classic," said Walksler. "To me it looked like a turd on wheels and I didn't like it, but Harley owners did because it was the latest thing to come out from Harley. So being a young dealer, I decided to try to find one for a potential customer."

Walksler called 15 to 20 dealers and eventually called a fellow Harley dealer in Quincy, Illinois, Gus Trader. Trader was a longtime dealer and a big supporter of motorcycles. When the young Walksler called him up, the conversation went like this:

"Where are you from, son?" asked Trader.

"Mount Vernon, sir," replied Walksler.

"How long you been a dealer, son?" asked Trader.

"I've been a dealer for eight months, sir," said Walksler.

"Well, come on up and I'll sell you this Brown Classic," Trader said.

"I guess he felt sorry for me," Walksler said.

So Walksler went up to see Trader and purchased the Brown Classic for his customer. While he was there, Trader allowed the young Harley dealer to look through his storage barn.

"One of the things he showed me was a 1944 Harley-Davidson Knucklehead in original gray paint," said Walksler. "I logged that image onto the hard drive of my brain for 20 years.

"So when Easy Russ said he wanted an original-paint Knucklehead, I tracked down Gus at his retirement house in Florida. He remembered my dealership, Dale's Harley-Davidson, and the good relationship we had in the past.

"He said, 'I'll sell you that old Knucklehead.'"

As soon as he agreed to buy the bike from Trader, Walksler got on the phone with Easy Russ. "Hey, I found you an original 1944 Knucklehead and it still has its original gray paint. I just bought it from Gus Trader. I haven't seen it in 20 years, but it's awesome."

"We've got a deal," said Russ, and plans were made for the transfer. Easy Russ agreed to deliver the Oscar Hedstrom Prototype Indian to Walksler's home in Mount Vernon, and the exchange was to take place at Walksler's home, which was a former hospital.

"The real problem was that Easy Russ is a real nervous kind of guy, and he showed up at my place even before my truck driver, One-Eye Roy, had returned from Florida with the Knucklehead.

"So we're waiting and waiting, sitting around my old hospital building and it's around midnight. The conversation was getting kind of thin, and they had just driven 10 hours to get to my place."

At about 2 a.m., One-Eye Roy finally arrived, and everyone's spirits picked up again. So Roy rolled the bike out of the truck and into the old hospital. "It's 2 a.m. and everything is real happy until we get down to look at the serial numbers on the frame.

The third digit in the four-digit number had been restamped.

"Russ goes friggin berserk!" said Walksler. "He says, 'I'm not going to buy a re-stamped motorcycle! I'm going home!'

"Russ, it's 2 o'clock in the morning. Why don't you at least spend the night?"

asked Walksler. "He agreed, but he had never spent the night in an abandoned hospital before, so needless to say, nobody got a lot of sleep."

The next morning, Easy Russ is packing to go home and Walksler is trying to stall him to try to make the trade still happen.

"I'm realizing that I had just paid $20,000 for a motorcycle that had been re-stamped," said Walksler, "but I knew Gus Trader had owned it for more than 20 years and the paperwork and title carried back all the way to the original owner. It was just a factory re-stamp, no big deal."

Just before hitting the road back to Grand Rapids, Easy Russ offers a solution. He said he would trade his Indian for Walksler's original red paint 1947 Knucklehead plus $5,000.

"I had a personal attachment to my Knucklehead, but at this moment it became a lot less important," said Walksler. "I wanted that Indian, so I gave up my red Knucklehead and gave Easy Russ $5,000. I got my Indian, and he went down the road."

Later that day, two vintage Harley-Davidson experts happened to stop by Walksler's hospital home. They both agreed that the re-stamped number was simply a factory correction and nothing that would affect the value of the bike.

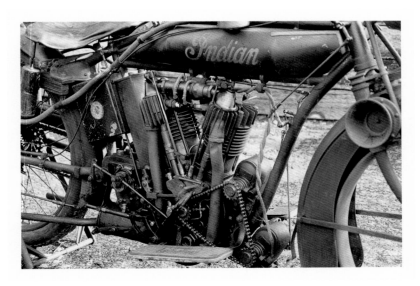

The Hedstrom Prototype finally became Walksler's after a bizarre trade for a 1944 Harley Knucklehead, but only after four type-A personality motorcycle collectors spent the night in an abandoned three-story hospital outside Chicago. *Dale Walksler collection*

INTRIGUING CIRCUMSTANCES

The very next day, cooler heads prevailed. Easy Russ called Walksler and said, "I want to buy the other Knucklehead." Walksler said he could purchase it for the same $20,000 he had paid, forgoing the costs of trucking it up from Florida.

"Great, I'll be there tomorrow," said Russ. He came the next day with $20,000 in cash and purchased the second bike.

A hassle? Yes, but Walksler now owned what he considered the rarest motorcycle in the world, a prototype Indian built by the company's founder.

The Super Supercharged Vincent

Reg Dearden was all set to run for the speed record at Bonneville in 1950. His Vincent Black Lightning was one of the fastest production motorcycles ever constructed and his was even faster. One of only 32 (some historians put the number at 31) Lightnings built, this rare version was retrofitted by the factory with the installation of a supercharger.

Dearden hoped to break the 173.625-mile-per-hour world speed record that had been set in 1937 by a BMW.

Additionally, this particular Black Lightning's frame was stretched by 6 inches—under the direct supervision of company founder Phil Vincent—in order to improve the bike's straight-line stability.

The bike was beautiful, glossy black and purpose-built for speed. Dearden hired famed racer Les Graham to ride the bike. But Graham was killed while racing on a Norton at the Isle of Man and the Vincent never made a single run.

British aviation authorities refused to let Dearden transport the motorcycle from England to the United States in his personal Cessna, so Dearden put the Vincent into storage for 20 years. Around 1970, Deardon decided to part with the bike, and it appeared for sale in a *Cycle World* magazine advertisement.

If the Black Shadow was fast, then the Black Lightning was a rocket ship on wheels. And this factory supercharged model was faster yet. Stretched 6 inches from stock, with a 20 psi boost from a Shorrocks blower, it was built with the intention of breaking the 173.625-mile-per-hour speed record at Bonneville. *Somer Hooker collection*

When Michael Manning from Philadelphia expressed interest in purchasing the rare Vincent, the English government stepped in and put a halt to the sale.

"The Black Lightning was deemed a national treasure of England, and it was not allowed to leave the country," said Somer Hooker, a Vincent expert from the Nashville area. "But the eccentric Manning was determined to own the rare bike."

Manning, with the help of some nonloyal British motorcycle enthusiasts, quietly purchased the bike and disassembled it. He shipped it back in boxes, never attracting the attention of customs agents in England or the United States.

Manning, who owned a couple of Vincents but was not a serious collector, had the bike reassembled and brought to Shadow Lake, a huge Vincent rally in Canada. Manning showed up with the Vincent in the back of his van, among more than 150 other Vincents and scores of enthusiasts from all over the world attending the event. The extremely low-mileage bike—probably less than 100 miles—was on display at the rally when Manning got a wild idea: He promised to fire up the rare motorcycle with the original 20-plus-year-old lubricants in the crankcase.

Owner Reg Dearden (pictured) convinced company head Phil Vincent to personally oversee the construction of the supercharged Lightning. But when the bike's intended rider, Les Graham, was killed at the Isle of Man TT, the record attempt plan was abandoned and Dearden parked the bike. *Somer Hooker collection*

This idea didn't go over well with the Vincent aficionados in attendance, and luckily they talked Manning out of the foolish deed without first changing the fluids. But he did fire it up and he did ride it.

"He took it out to a lonely state highway and it just took off," said Hooker. "I tried to follow him on my Black Shadow, but it didn't kickstart right away and he just took off. That's how fast he was.

"Another day he took it to a nearby town and ran it around the road course."

When Manning left Canada, both he and the bike disappeared for nearly 26 years.

Actually the bike was stored in his carport in Philadelphia, uncovered and unprotected.

Folks had heard about the bike and attempted to purchase it, but Manning was adamant about not selling it, until one day when a nurse he knew convinced him that he should begin selling things of value, such as the motorcycle. The

Vincent owner Michael Manning from Philadelphia saw the supercharged bike advertised in *Cycle World* and bought it from Dearden. He brought the rare machine to the North American Vincent Rally at Canada's Shadow Lake in August 1977. At the show he fired the bike up after decades of hibernation, ran it around a road course, and took high-speed runs on a seldom-used highway. *Tony Cording*

The virtually new 50-plus-year-old Vincent was in surprisingly good condition. Fuel was fed through one large S.U. carburetor that had been sourced from a British bus. *Tony Cording*

strategy she developed was that he offer it to Jay Leno, since he is a well-known motorcycle collector.

"Leno is not interested in vehicles that he can't drive on the streets, so he passed on it," said Hooker. "But he passed along the information to his friend Herb Harris, a lawyer from Texas."

Harris bought it about 12 years ago and has treated it with the respect a motorcycle with this history and condition deserves.

Harris had an excellent detailer clean up the Vincent, which still had all the original stove enameling on the frame, tank, and fenders. The original method for applying stove enamel was to dip the part in a vat of enamel paint, then hang it in an oven—or over a stove—to dry rapidly.

Other items—the cables, handle grips, other hardware—were in amazing condition for a motorcycle that is nearly 60 years old.

The bike had one large S.U. carburetor mounted on it, which was actually sourced to a bus. This carburetor was in need of repair, but once the old fuel was cleaned out, it flowed fuel quite well.

Hooker, who admitted to having owned around 120 Vincent motorcycles in his lifetime, is honest to a fault when it comes to the famous brand.

"Let's face it, these were cantankerous when they were sold new 50 years ago and they haven't gotten any better with age," he said. "However, these

The supercharged Vincent as it appeared in Manning's carport, only partially protected from the elements. Manning is behind the bike, sweeping away leaves. *Bill Weissman*

The special supercharged Vincent Black Lightning as it looks today after having been restored by new owner Herb Harris. *Herb Harris collection*

supercharged bikes are really nice to ride and run well because they have low compression at low rpm."

When it was all cleaned up and running well, Harris took the bike to Jay Leno's to show him what he had passed up several years earlier. According to Hooker, they made quite a bit of noise around Leno's shop when they fired that Vincent up.

"It has great patina, low mileage, and a great history," said Hooker. "It's everything every motorcycle collector would want."

CHAPTER THREE

Strange Journeys

The American Dream

From the time he was a little kid, Keith Irwin knew all about his parents' motorcycle. It seemed to have come up in conversation anytime family or friends got together. "I heard about it pretty much my whole life," said Irwin, who is an auto restorer in Concord, North Carolina. "As long as I could remember, Dad carried that picture with him to show everyone and talk about it."

The bike wasn't anything exotic—just a 1964 Honda Benly 150—but it played a major part in the lives of Irwin's parents, Walter, better known as "Skip," and Dianna.

The year was 1954, and Skip, now 67, was a junior in college at the University of Tennessee, Knoxville, where he was enrolled in environmental studies. He and Dianna were recently married and needed a set of wheels but didn't have much money. So they acquired a Vespa scooter.

"My uncle had this little Vespa that was stolen from his house," said Skip. "I found it about 100 yards from his house, so he let me have it for $25. I used it for about a year."

The young couple rode their Vespa around Knoxville one Saturday and happened to stop by the local Honda dealership to look around. "I wasn't even looking for a motorcycle when I bought it," said Skip. "We went to the dealer and I just fell in love with the Honda. I traded it right there."

Skip and Dianna were living the dream, riding home on their red 1964 Honda Benly 150, complete with whitewall tires and a full windshield. The bike wasn't brand new—it was a year old—but Skip said it didn't have too many miles on it.

"We weren't really motorcycle enthusiasts," he said, "it's just it was the cheapest transportation we could afford. It was a cheap way to get around college and to work. That bike was my sole form of transportation during my junior and senior years."

The young couple often rode their Honda on mini-vacations up into the Great Smoky Mountains.

"Once we parked it in the Smokies near the woods, and we were going to take a hike," he said. "We got about 300 or 400 yards away from the bike, and we heard some growling noises. My wife asked me if that was my stomach making those noises, and I told her no. Then she asked, 'Are there bears around here?' I told her no, that we were too close to Gatlinburg, and bears wouldn't come this far down."

So they continued on their hike. Several hours later, when they returned, there was a surprise waiting for them at their Honda.

Skip Irwin (pictured) and his wife, Dianna, used this Honda Benly 150 as their sole means of transportation while commuting to school, work, and vacation for several years during the mid-1960s. *Skip and Dianna Irwin collection*

"Hot Rod Mama" Dianna poses on the family Honda in front of their apartment in the 1960s. Even though she never rode the motorcycle herself, she spent a lot of time on it as a passenger. *Skip and Dianna Irwin collection*

"When we got back, there was a full-grown black bear sniffing the motorcycle," he said. "Dianna said, 'Oh, and there's no bears around here?' So we just stood next to a tree for about 20 minutes until he got tired and just meandered off. Then we got back on the bike and went further up into the Smokies."

When they arrived at their next hiking spot, there was a man throwing slices of bread to three bears, who went chasing after them. One more bear sat off to the side and observed.

"This big old bear was just watching the man pull bread out of the bag and throwing it so the other bears would chase it," he said. "That bear realized where that bread was coming from, and all of a sudden he makes this hissing sound and lunged at the guy. The guy threw the bread up into the air and everyone went diving for their cars. That was funny."

The Irwins also regularly rode their little motorcycle 150 miles to Bristol, Virginia, where Skip's parents lived.

"I never had any trouble with it, not once," he said, "except once when I wrecked it.

"I worked at the Kroger supermarket over on the Kingston Pike. I worked on Sundays. I was on my way to work one Sunday morning, and it was pouring down rain. Now these bikes don't stop real good in the rain, and I was coming toward a stoplight. This woman in a car to my left just started pulling over into my lane. She was right up against me and in my lane. I was trying to stop and trying to miss her, but she came right into me.

"I hit the curb with the front tire, and the motorcycle stopped, but I didn't. I went right over the top of the windshield and hit a stone wall. I cracked my helmet and hit my back up against the wall. I tore my clothes up a bit.

"The lady stopped and said, 'I'm sorry, I didn't see you.' Well of course, people don't see motorcycles a lot of times."

So Skip climbed back on the Honda and it started up. The bike had some damage—the crash bar up front was torn up, and the back of the seat was skinned up, but the worst damage was the broken windshield that he broke as he flew over the top.

"I went on to work, but by the time I had to go to class the next morning, I couldn't move," said Skip. "I was so sore."

One of the Irwins' favorite adventures with their Honda was once when they were riding to Bristol, Virginia.

"It started raining really heavy, and these things don't handle really well in the rain. The rain was pelting us, and it started to hurt, so we saw this barn out in a field. We cut across the field and went into the barn. The doors were wide open. There were big stacks of hay, so we just lay down in the hay and took a nap until the rain ended. Then we hopped back on our bike and kept going on our way."

After graduation Skip was offered a job as an environmentalist for the state of Georgia where he did subdivision analysis for hotels, schools, and restaurants in several counties.

Now with a steady income, Skip and Dianna purchased another economical mode of transport, a used Austin-Healey Sprite, which the couple used in addition to the Honda.

"That little Honda was economical," he said. "I never really checked the fuel mileage back then, but I'd put 75 cents worth of gas into it and go 150 miles. But gas was only 18.9 cents a gallon back then. It only cost between 75 cents and $1 to fill up the tank, and you could go for a long, long time."

Eventually, the Sprite was traded for a big Healey, and the Honda just sat under a tarp. "I never started it and hadn't ridden it for months," he said. "The battery went dead."

It was time to part with his little Honda.

"A kid next door to where we lived really wanted it," he said. "He brought his dad over to look at it, I gave them a price, and they bought it. I don't remember how much I sold it for. I waited four or five months, but eventually I went over to see how my old motorcycle was doing.

"He stripped it! He made a dirt bike out of it. He took it out into the woods behind his house and hit a tree with it. He bent the frame. It was destroyed. I was just sick."

Skip and Dianna never rode a motorcycle after that, partly because they were now a family. Their son, Keith, was born in 1968, the year they sold the Honda.

"But I loved that bike," he said. "It was such a gorgeous little motorcycle."

Skip and Dianna's motorcycle days were over. Or so they thought.

In 2006, they got a little surprise for Christmas.

Keith decided many years earlier to find a Honda Dream and give it to his parents.

"I searched for about five years before I found the right one," said Keith. "I had heard about a guy from Anderson, South Carolina, who had recently passed away, and his granddaughter had inherited his motorcycle collection, which she was selling. In that collection was a Honda 305 Dream with only 9,000 miles on it.

"Even though the engine was larger than the 150cc that they had, everything else about it was identical, the frame, the color, and whitewall tires. Plus I figured that 40 years later, my parents were a little bit heavier, so the extra horsepower would come in handy."

He spent the next few months tinkering and tuning the motorcycle. Because it had sat for so long, much of the time was spent cleaning the fuel tanks and carburetors.

Skip and Dianna's son Keith had heard about his parents' motorcycle for his entire life, so he decided to find a similar model and rebuild it as a Christmas gift in 2006. Here the Honda is being refurbished in Keith's auto restoration shop. *Keith Irwin*

Skip and Dianna discover their surprise present. With tears in their eyes, Skip and Dianna said it was one of the most memorable Christmases ever. *Keith Irwin*

"I put a new battery in it and rode it around my shop," he said. "The bike even had the same windshield as my parents' original Honda. That's the one my father broke in the accident."

Keith even found a supplier for the original type of white helmets and goggles that his parents used in the 1960s.

"We had no idea at all," said Skip. "Keith made a little game out of finding it on Christmas morning. First we had to search for a clue in the refrigerator, then downstairs, then upstairs, then outside in the U-Haul trailer. And that's where it was."

"It brought tears to both our eyes."

Keith feels good about surprising his parents.

"For all they've done for me, I'm glad I could return the favor," he said.

The Wild Goose Chase

By Steve Rossi

Just yesterday, I did it again. Ever in search of some secret treasure buried behind a random garage door, I hit the highway early after a find in the weekly trader sent me off on what was another day-long descent into moto madness. And even though I'm in an area that's loaded with Ducs and Geese (Ducatis and Moto Guzzis), experience has shown that a pot of gold bullion may be easier to unearth than a worthwhile barn find.

Such is the wild goose chase; I should know because I've been on the prowl for more years than I'd care to share. And even with the efficiency of modern computers to expedite the process, the actual ritual of the "hunt" ultimately relies on that most fragile of human foibles: the owner and his perception of reality.

History has proven that one man's treasure is another's junk. Where I live, history repeats itself every Thursday when the next issue of the bargain shopper hits the newsstand.

So in the interest of pure entertainment—which is really all so many of these expeditions ever turned out to be—I thought I'd share a few of the more memorable jaunts. The stories you are about to read are true, but the names and locations have been withheld to protect the guilty.

Changing Plans

My first wild goose chase concerned itself with a Moto Guzzi. The bike in question was a low-mileage, three-year-old Le Mans III that was on the other side of my home state. I usually do my best to make a real "experience" out of these adventures. For example, I take two-lane roads and turn what could be a 150-mile inspection into a 250-mile expedition.

The bike proved to be everything I wanted, and it was even white, the color I preferred as opposed to the more common red. The owner was selling the bike in order to acquire a new Le Mans 1000 (also in white). I believed that in addition to a motorcycle, I had also found a new friend. We obviously had similar tastes and interests, and I was only too happy to help him buy his new ride. We were both enthusiastic, each of us looking forward to a new Le Mans. What could be better than that? I should have known that it was too good to be true.

On the morning I was scheduled to pick up the bike, I got up early and got ready to head off in my pickup. Before I left my house, the owner called to tell me some bad news.

"I know you're supposed to come down today to pick up the bike, but I don't have it anymore," he said.

"Excuse me?"

"But don't worry. It's okay. You see, the weather was so nice yesterday, I just couldn't wait 'til this morning, so I ran down to the dealer after work and traded it in so I could pickup my new Le Mans 1000. So my old bike is down there instead of at my house. Just call the dealer and go buy it from him. I told him you wanted it. The 1000 is a wonderful bike, by the way. I really like it."

"Great, congratulations. . . ."

Since I already jumped through hoops and was high on this specific Le Mans III, I called the dealer who was better known as the area's most notorious horse trader.

"Sure, the Le Mans III is here, ready and waiting for you," he said. "My Le Mans 1000 customer said that you'd be calling. The price is $#x/@&!"

Wait a minute. How did this thing go up $1,000 overnight? Long story short: after a couple of days of haggling, I only took it in the shorts for an additional $500. The dealer got me coming and, no doubt, the previous owner going. So much for my new friend.

Stuffing a BMW

Sometime after my Moto Guzzi adventure, I got the itch for a bevel-drive Ducati. I set my sights on a Hailwood Replica or maybe an even rarer S2 Mille. After some months, I located an immaculate S2—three states away.

"The only reason I'm selling is because I want to do more touring, so I'm looking to buy a new BMW K75S," said the owner. "But it's got to be a black K75, which my dealer is expecting shortly."

So a deposit on the S2 changed hands, and I waited. A few weeks later his local dealer came through, and we were all systems go. I decided to fly down and ride the Ducati home.

Ticket in hand, I was ready to leave for the airport and called the owner to arrange for him to meet me at the airport.

"Don't bother, I had a fight with the dealer over some accessory equipment and told him to stuff it," he said. "I've got a better idea. I'll just ride the Duc up to your place, buy a BMW from a dealer near you, and ride home. You think you can call around and find a black K75S for me?"

Once again, feeling already committed to the cause, I found him the BMW of his dreams and put him in touch with my local dealer. There was, however, the issue of my nonrefundable airline ticket I had bought. . . .

He called back and said, "Your local dealer is a great guy. I really want to buy the BMW from him. We have a little problem, though: The latest shipment of K75s have a 3 percent price increase. If you're willing to cover the increase we've got a deal. My delivery of the Ducati will offset your expense for the airplane ticket."

This time I told *him* to stuff it!

The Italian-Japanese Connection

On the rebound of my Ducati deal-gone-bad, I heard about a cache of two Ducatis and a Moto Guzzi located in an old gristmill close to where the S2 calamity was located. So I hot-footed it over there and stumbled across a wonderful Ducati 900SS instead. This time, taking no chances, I was there with the truck and cash in hand, since the bikes were advertised as "ready to go." Okay, I was in. Sign me up.

"Great, I'm ready to sell you the bike," the owner said. "If my other arrangement doesn't work out, you can have first option."

Arrangement—what other arrangement?

"You see, the Japanese are going crazy over Italian bikes, and I'm trying to put a package deal together where I'll sell all three bikes to one of those rich collectors overseas," he said. "Then I'm going to tell him that I need to accompany the bikes on the plane to make sure they're handled properly, and I'll be able to get myself a free ticket to Asia."

What is it with Italian motorcycles and their lunatic owners, I wondered as I drove home disappointed once again.

Of course, the bikes never made it to Japan and eventually the Ducati came home with me instead—one year later. I put more mileage commuting back and forth to the gristmill in my pickup truck than I did on the bike itself.

The Morini in the Shed

Being a fan of the Italian underdog, sooner or later I knew that I was going to end up with a Moto Morini. Time marched on, and one day a Morini 500 popped up—450 miles away.

The dance began, and the traditional photo exchange took place, but I just wasn't sure about the Morini. The bike looked okay, but was it really a 500 Sport or a dolled-up Strada?

The only thing to do was see for myself, so off I went, this time in my El Camino. It was early April, and a freak ice storm over the mountains made the trip all the more memorable.

Arriving at a small, broken-down farmhouse behind a giant sheetmetal factory, we went out back to a ramshackle shed that was seriously listing to port.

Leaning on the walls around the inside perimeter were a multitude of derelict Zundapps and Jawas that appeared to be propping the place up! In the middle of the floor (the only place in the shed that wasn't leaking through the roof), the Morini sat on a ragged piece of plywood.

I looked at the photo, then looked at the bike . . . and looked at the photo again. I asked the owner, if in fact, it was the same bike.

"Sure, I took that photo 10 to 12 years ago—just after I bought it new," he confirmed.

Oh great, I drove 450 miles through a monsoon, with another 450 miles back home, and I get this nut case who sent me vintage photos of his vintage bike!

Hours later, after convincing him that it was generously only worth about one-third of what he was asking, I headed back into the storm and returned home with an old, ice-encrusted Morini. I was glad to do so before that dilapidated shed caved in on top of it.

In the end, after recovering from a flu that resulted from being out in the weather all day, the real beneficiary of this adventure was Herm Baver—the Moto Morini importer—who came across a pot of gold of his own (my Visa Gold card, that is) as I diligently returned the 500 to its former glory and searched for all-too-elusive Morini parts.

Don't Ask No Questions

It was then only a matter of time before I landed my first Laverda. At an Italian Motorcycle Owner's Club rally some years before, I lusted over a pristine SF twin and began negotiating with its owner. The bike lived in his living room, and while he indicated he would sell it, he didn't want me to come to his house because he very much wanted to keep a low profile due to his line of work. Gee, this didn't sound so good.

I guess it just wasn't meant to be because we never could come to terms, and at the time I was going through a corporate relocation. But I never forgot that luscious Laverda.

Some years later, I saw an ad for what sounded to be the very same "mint" SF (judging by the mileage and color) that I had longed for years earlier—just two states from where it had previously been.

Off we went again, the chase was on, and soon I found myself in a damp, dark stone garage on top of a mountain, with the very same Laverda. Only now it was sitting on flat tires and its already thin plating was rapidly turning to dust and covered in pigeon poop.

Details were sketchy on how and why it got there, other than something like "Somebody owed somebody something. . . ."

Not interested in repeating the same mistake twice (or learning more), a deal was done but at a price that it really should have fetched years earlier when it was proudly sitting on the Concours field.

The Cannibalized BMW

I once tried to buy back a low-mileage BMW I'd previously sold. I never really intended to part with it, but I was caught at a weak moment. We agreed that should the new owner ever want to sell this beautiful, original pre-toaster tank 750, he'd call me first. A few months later he did, and I immediately went to the bank to make a withdrawal for the same amount I sold it to him several months earlier. Problem was, when we got to his place, the complete exhaust system and turn signals were gone. And he had his sights set on a few more items as well. When I asked him what was going on, he said, "I needed some quick cash, so I sold a couple of bits off the bike. It's nothing that can't be replaced though and shouldn't cost you too much."

Certainly he should know the prices, having just sold the stuff in the used BMW parts market! All I could do was feel sorry for this guy, who obviously had some real problems. I felt even worse about the state of my poor pristine BMW, however.

Miscellaneous Adventures

I was once offered a pair of Velocettes. "Buy either or both," the person told me, adding that I should come back behind the warehouse after midnight and make sure you shut your engine off.

"Come alone, and bring cash."

No, thanks.

Then there was the wonderful experience when I bought my Moto Guzzi SP II. Looking for something to gobble up even more miles, the thought of a long-legged V-twin with luggage just proved too enticing. The search was on. An interesting, untouched example came up some 300 miles from home. Not bad. I could easily do the whole deal in a day.

I worked hard to assure the owner, who seemed somewhat skittish, that I was a serious buyer. I went down with a trailer in tow. After close inspection, I was hooked but wanted to ride the machine first, particularly since I'm 6 feet 4 inches and wanted to make sure that my knees could handle the lowers.

"No, sorry, you can't ride it; how do I know you're not here only for a joyride? I've heard stories about guys who do things like that," he said.

I impressed upon him that I wasn't in the habit of driving six hours with an empty trailer and thousands of dollars in cash in my pocket for the pure fun of it. Finally, he agreed.

"Okay, but you must fully stay within my sight and must ride for no more than five minutes," he said.

At the end of the day the SP II ended up on the trailer, and my legs never proved to be a problem. It was the buffeting off the windscreen that finally made me resell it. It's tough to figure that out in five minutes while you're trying to take a test ride in full view of the owner.

Of course, there have been other truly insane experiences as well. Like the local dealer who was going to have the side covers for my new machine ready the day after delivery because the paint still wasn't dry, only to come up with them six months later—just in time for me to trade the bike back in. He said he just couldn't accept it on trade with the side covers missing!

Here's another one that should curl your hair: My Bimota Dieci arrived via a major, nationally known purveyor of exotica who relied on an independent transport service that just had to drop it off at my place at 5:30 a.m. because that's when they'd be passing through the area. The bike was unloaded in the wee hours, and the trucker headed off into the sunrise. That afternoon I discovered that the serial number on the bike and number on the title didn't exactly match. The dealer's response?

"We had two of them and mixed up the paperwork—just take it over to the local police station and have them confirm the number. Their computer will show that the bike's got a good VIN."

I would have except I still can't get the thing to run right other than at idle. Unfortunately, a Dieci's not the sort of machine you romp around the neighborhood on at 5:30 in the morning to take a final test ride. At least it came with a spare key and an owner's manual for a change.

And let's not forget the infamous KTM adventure with the dealer who literally disappeared during the dead of night—with my $8,000 bank check in hand for a new Duke. That next morning, Saturday, I was waiting for him at the locked door of the dealership with a small crowd that included his staff, his parents, and his girlfriend. We waited a long time, and they finally found him weeks later hiding out in his mother's basement.

After all the proceedings, I got my money back, though no thanks to the importer, who hid himself behind the premise that their franchisee was merely an independent businessman—even though I had a paid bill of sale with a serial number that was registered within their database with my name and address on it for warranty purposes. And they call this a hobby? This required the state attorney general's office to make amends.

Then there are all those wild goose chases after antique cars, old boats, and early outboard motors that I'd like to tell you about as well. But today is Thursday, and this week's issue of the trader paper must have landed down at the store by now, so stand back—the chase is on!

Snowbound

Motorcycle collector Dale Walksler considers factory racing bikes to be the rarest of all motorcycles because so few were produced and even fewer exist today.

"The Harley-Davidson Company manufactured very limited numbers of these specialty machines, which were built specifically for either racing on board tracks or racing on the dirt," said Walksler. "The board-track racers were originally built to race on automotive board tracks and were basically the side show to the car racing."

Walksler seeks out and acquires these rare factory racers, which is how he came to own number 21 SCA 500, the very first of the series.

"We'd have to go back probably 13 years ago," he said. "I received a letter and a photograph from an elderly man in the Buffalo, New York, area. He indicated that he owned the first 1921 Harley racer, which was a large-displacement single-cylinder that ran on alcohol. In the letter he indicated that he had offered to sell his one-of-a-kind bike directly to Harley-Davidson, but they turned him down. This was before Harley-Davidson got their feet in place in putting their museum together in Milwaukee."

The gentleman bought the bike in the 1940s through some motorcycle circles and never raced or even ran it. According to Walksler, the man had owned it for at least 50 years.

"It was in perfect condition," said Walksler. "In the letter he indicated that he considered me probably the bike's most likely next owner. He found me through an article in a motorcycle magazine about my board-track racers collection."

Walksler was living in Mount Vernon, Illinois, but at the time he was on a motorcycle excursion in South Carolina, looking to buy a couple of rare motorcycles.

"It was winter and my driver—One-Eye Roy—and I were in a tractor and trailer," said Walksler. "We came upon an area in North Carolina called Black Mountain. As we crested the mountain, I hear Roy yell, 'Holy Shit!' I looked right next to us and a car was spinning out of control. Roy veered [away from] the truck and, even though the car was spinning wildly, it missed us entirely."

Walklser had the elderly gentleman's letter and a pocketful of cash, so he decided that Buffalo, New York, was not too far away—even in a blizzard—and that an 800-mile side trip was in order.

"I left a message for the man at about 10 p.m. that night telling him we were on our way," he said. "Thinking back on it now, I'm very fortunate he didn't answer the phone and I was able to leave a message. If he had answered, he might have said, 'Don't bother coming, I'm not ready to sell the bike now.'

Dale Walksler and One-Eyed Roy fought a blinding blizzard for 800 miles to buy this Harley board-track racer from a gentleman who had purchased it in 1940. Walksler believes racing bikes like this are the rarest type of motorcycles because so few were built. *Tom Cotter*

"We drove all night through snow and when we arrived in Buffalo the next day, it was still snowing."

When Walksler and One-Eye Roy arrived at the gentleman's house, he was reluctant to let them see the Harley. "Oh, it's at a friend's house in the basement right now," he said.

As the snow outside was getting deeper and deeper, Walksler was finally successful in convincing the man to take them over to his friend's house, where, in the dark, cold basement, sat the nearly perfect 1921 Harley-Davidson board-track racer.

"The bike was well preserved," said Walksler, "but when I was getting ready to make an offer, the man said, 'Well, I'll let you know.'

"So I said, 'Well, you know, we're here and the truck is outside and I've got this money and a letter from you in the truck that you'd like to sell this to me.'

"So we agreed to a price, which was fair, but then he said that he has always wanted a Yamaha four-wheeler."

Hmmm, a new fly in the ointment. Walksler said that he didn't have any Yamaha ATVs in the truck but agreed that if he was able to buy this bike now with the cash that he had, he promised to buy him any four-wheeler he wanted.

In order to buy the bike, Walksler had to pay the owner cash plus purchase a Yamaha four-wheeler—a fair price for the rare and very original racer. *Tom Cotter*

"But I told him that he would have to pick up the four-wheeler himself in Illinois, when he comes to visit his motorcycle," said Walksler.

A deal was struck and Walksler and One-Eye loaded up the Harley in their trailer. Since then, the gentleman has not only visited his old motorcycle in Walksler's Illinois museum but again after the collection was relocated to North Carolina.

"It's a great story about a guy who took great pride in his bike for so many years," said Walksler.

Deals Down Under

The Triumph in the Outback

Chuck Goldsborough was into motorcycles before he got into cars. He started racing motocross as a teenager in the 1970s, then progressed to motorcycle road racing. He raced motorcycles at Summit Point, Road Atlanta, and Mid-Ohio in the early 1980s and returned to race at those tracks again on four wheels when he started his sports car racing team years later.

Goldsborough, from Baltimore, is the founder of the Lexus Racing Team. He campaigned the multicar team of IS 300 sedans in the Grand Am series from 1999 to 2006, giving the brand its first victory, first pole, and both the driver's and team championships. But even though his love of motorcycles was on a hiatus, it never disappeared.

In 1998, he was about to enter the motorcycle world again but this time as a collector.

Goldsborough's friend David Taylor was touring Australia on a motorcycle vacation with some friends. They stopped off at a small motorcycle shop in Launceston to look around when a vintage bike along the back wall caught his attention.

It was a 1928 Triumph Model W and the story the shop owner told Taylor was almost unbelievable.

Back when the bike was new, the original dealer, John King and Son, donated it as the Grand Prize in a charity auction. When the winning ticket was drawn, nobody stepped forward, so the bike was returned to the dealership to wait for the winner to claim it. And it sat and it sat.

The winner never did redeem his or her winning coupon, so the bike took up long-term residence along the back wall of the dealership. For decades and decades. After World War II, the dealership went through several ownership and name changes, yet the bike still sat obediently with an "undelivered" ticket hanging from its handlebar.

When Taylor heard the story, he placed a call to his buddy Chuck back in Baltimore, 17 time zones away.

"Chuck, you'll never believe what I found, man," said Taylor. "It's right up your alley." Taylor recited the story to Goldsborough.

"I asked him to see if it was for sale," said Goldsborough. "He said the man behind the counter would have to ask the shop owner."

One month goes by, then two months go by.

"Finally the motorcycle shop owner called because he was curious about the guy from the United States interested in one of his bikes," said Goldsborough.

As unlikely as it might seem, Chuck Goldsborough from Baltimore, Maryland, purchased this brand-new 1928 Triumph Model W from a dealership in Launceston, Australia, in 1998. The 70-year-old bike was a raffle prize when new but was never picked up. *Chuck Goldsborough*

"Yeah, I'll sell it," said the owner, who also said he would handle the somewhat complicated shipping arrangements of sending the bike halfway around the world.

Goldsborough paid about $5,200 for the bike, a lot when he didn't have much money, but a bargain in today's vintage motorcycle market.

"It took about a year to get all the logistics worked out, but it finally arrived in Baltimore, and I couldn't have been happier," he said.

The Triumph remains in its N.O.S. condition today, complete with its original toolkit, spare spark plug, and the John King and Son dealer decal affixed to the back.

The bike has been used as an authentic guide for several recent Model W restorations.

All in the Family

Australia has yielded rich motorcycle treasures for Goldsborough, who ironically, has never visited the continent.

The story of his second Australian bike began at a cocktail party held in conjunction with the New York Auto Show at the Jacob Javits Center in 2000.

The Triumph is so authentic that the tool bag and original dealer emblem—John King & Sons—are still attached to the rear fender. *Chuck Goldsborough*

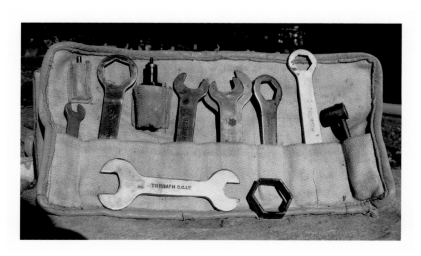

Enough to make a concours judge cry, the original tool set has never been used and remains in its original pouch. *Chuck Goldsborough*

Another Australian motorcycle discovery was the result of a chance meeting during the New York Auto Show, where Goldsborough was displaying his Team Lexus race cars. The gentleman who owned it inherited the AJS from his great-great-grandfather, who had bought it new. *Chuck Goldsborough*

The 1926 AJS had never been restored and still wore its original paint, logos, and pinstriping. Mechanically the bike is in incredible condition for its age. *Chuck Goldsborough*

110

He was attending the show on behalf of Lexus, doing meet-and-greet duties next to his racing sedan during the show.

"I started chatting with this Aussie who actually lived in New York and worked on Wall Street," said Goldsborough. "He told me he had a 1926 AJS that was sitting in storage in New York. He had always meant to restore it, but after so many years and with a grueling work schedule, that was not very likely."

He told Goldsborough the fascinating story of how he came to own the bike. It was bought new in Australia by his great-great-grandfather, who passed it on to his son, who passed it on to his son, who passed it on to his son, who Goldsborough was enjoying a drink with at the New York party.

"It had never been restored but had always been ridden and maintained," said Goldsborough. "When he moved to New York, he shipped the bike over as a family heirloom, but it hadn't moved in at least three years.

"So I said, 'If you ever want to sell the bike, please keep me in mind,' and I gave him my card."

Two years later, Goldsborough received a phone call. The gentleman was ready to sell. For a price of $4,000 the bike was on its way to Baltimore where it would keep Goldsborough's 1928 Triumph company.

The original Olympic tires still hold air, and Goldsborough has been known to ride the bike around his neighborhood, albeit at *very* slow speeds. *Chuck Goldsborough*

The Triumph sits in Goldsborough's house as sculpture but on occasion has also been pressed into duty as the backdrop for the family Christmas card. *Chuck Goldsborough*

He drained the oil and cleaned out the gas tank and carburetor, gapped the spark plug, and the bike fired right up and ran great.

Goldsborough also has a restored AJS of the same vintage, but he prefers his untouched version.

"The original tires look so dry rotted that you're afraid to touch them, but son-of-a-gun, they still hold air!"

The Finest Wine

By Ed Bauer

In October 2008, my digging partner Ken and I took a rare day off of work to hit the farms and woods out near Little Washington, Virginia, pursuing our hobby of looking for Civil War relics with metal detectors. I've known Ken for more than 20 years, but our career paths diverged until about 5 years ago. Ken has four youngsters at home, and his weekends are always filled, as they should be. Me? I'm a part-time bachelor living out of a one-bedroom apartment in McLean with one year to go before retiring and joining my wife, Margo, permanently at our relatively new home just outside of Pinehurst, North Carolina.

Ken and I generally only look for Civil War relics when the weather turns cold and the snakes go into hibernation. There are fewer ticks and less underbrush to deal with. As Ken will tell you, I'm deathly afraid of snakes, but I did bring a baby snake back in dirty clothes this past fall from North Carolina. The little snake lived in my bedroom on the floor staying nice and comfy for a day before I discovered it. I made sure the little guy survived and that it had no friends tagging along. Perhaps a story and lesson on why you don't want to leave dirty clothes on the garage floor, especially when critters are looking for warm and cozy spots.

I enjoy doing the research, largely online nowadays, for leads to sites that I hope have not yet been hit by too many others in the past. But as most relic hunters who have been in this hobby for a while will tell you, "a site is never completely searched out." It takes time and patience, and maybe newer technology, but if you stick with it, you may come up with a unique find.

Instead of hitting our usual dig sites around Berryville, we decided to find a Union campground I had a lead on near Little Washington. It would be a longer drive than our usual trips out Route 7 to the Berryville area, but we felt it was worthwhile to visit a new area and try our luck. Plus we had never hunted around Little Washington before. Also the famous "Inn at Little Washington" was located here. I had not experienced the cuisine but understood food and staff had quite an excellent reputation. We also tend to meet all sorts of interesting farmers and other landowners when out looking for relics. Ken is much better at breaking the ice with total strangers, which usually ends up gaining us permission to search.

I picked up Ken at his home in Herndon and proceeded to head to Little Washington via Route 66. Thirty-some miles later, we stopped on the way at a restaurant in Warrington for breakfast. It was our first time there, as we usually hit the Silver Diner near Ken's house. Suzanne, the waitress who seated us, was friendly, and we began to discuss why we had the day off and where we were headed. Suzanne mentioned that when her family was building a house outside of Sperryville, they found a few old lead bullets, bottles, and other relics. The house is now on what is known as Sharp Rock Winery. Suzanne knew the owners, Kathy and Jim East, and suggested we stop and try their wonderful wine.

Of course, Ken and I were interested. We noted the name of the winery and jotted down the directions Suzanne gave us. I always carry a pen and piece of paper just for instances like this. Since I was driving, Ken bought breakfast, but I suggested that we leave her an extra large tip. We thanked Suzanne and headed on our way. We decided, though, to stick with our primary goal of trying to find the Union camp. Sperryville was another 15 or so miles to the west and we wanted to spend more time digging and less time driving. If successful in finding a virgin campsite, the possibilities would be excellent for locating many interesting relics.

After a few hours of driving around Little Washington and knocking on doors where no one was home, we gave up and decided to give the winery a try. The problem we find with hunting on weekdays is that many people are at work. One rule most of us in the hobby will always follow, including Ken and I, is that we don't trespass onto private land. We have come across landowners who have experienced the other type of relic hunter, the one who leaves a bad taste with the owner and no permission for us.

The winery owners, Jim and Kathy, turned out to be wonderful people. They obviously knew Suzanne and asked why she had not called them lately, thinking Ken and I were old friends of hers. After introductions and promises to not dig within the vineyard, we gained permission and began to hunt the 15 or so acres.

About an hour later and nothing to show but junk, I was walking back toward the tasting room near where Jim was crushing the current harvest of red grapes and glanced into the barn when I noticed a small-displacement red Yamaha motorcycle. It was covered with a heavy coating of dust and a few cobwebs but otherwise looked mostly complete and unmolested. Interested, I proceeded to where Jim was and asked about it. His first comment was that I could have it real cheap. Upon further investigation, I found that the bike belonged to his son, who had bought it about a year ago. He had moved to Charlottesville, Virginia, and had no room for the bike.

According to Jim, the prior owner had it in a barn for about 20 years. After visiting the local Yamaha dealer near Winchester for a new battery, Jim and his son got the bike running. They drove it around the vineyard for a little bit, but that was probably the extent of it. They never titled, registered, or licensed the bike.

Walking back to the bike, I began to think of how I would break the news of a new old motorcycle purchase to Margo when I already had a Harley restoration project sitting in the garage back home. It was not my intention to purchase a used Japanese motorcycle, but all I could focus on was the good deal to be had on my first real barn find.

Ken and I always carry digital cameras to document our historic finds. I grabbed mine and took several photos of the bike, discovering it was a 250cc twin and seemed to be in remarkably good shape.

Ken and I celebrated the find by partaking in our first wine tasting when out relic hunting. Kathy filled us in on the winery and the types of grapes they grew. I was pretty impressed with the quality and ended up purchasing six bottles, four reds and two whites. We thanked Kathy and Jim for their hospitality and letting us search the property.

When I got home that night, I researched the bike online and discovered it was a DS6, either a 1969 or 1970 model.

A week or so passed before I was able to reach Jim to tell him I was serious about purchasing the bike and ask for the price. Without too much hesitation, Jim indicated that for $200 it was mine.

Ed Bauer and his friend Ken were looking for Civil War relics on a Virginia vineyard in the autumn of 2008 when they peeked into a barn and found this complete Yamaha 250. It had been sitting in one barn or another for more than 20 years. *Ed Bauer*

The 1970 Yamaha had only 6,037 miles on it when Bauer discovered it. He bought it for $200 and dragged it home to keep his 1940 Harley-Davidson company in the family garage. *Ed Bauer*

"You have a deal," was my reply. We set up a date toward the end of October, where I would make the 70-mile drive from my place of work just outside Washington.

I have a little trailer inside my Jeep that will carry the weight of a full-dress Harley. The trailer has a male fitting that inserts into the hitch receiver. The front wheel of the motorcycle towing is placed onto an L-shaped support. The back wheel rolls freely. You run straps from the handlebars to the vehicle and away you go. I usually carry this setup in case I come across a distressed rider who might need a tow.

I took off from work on October 30 and headed to Sharp Rock, arriving there around noon. I was driving against traffic and it was great. Jim was waiting. He had cleaned up the bike a little and added air to the tires. That was one thing I was concerned with, since they seemed to be original rubber, and the last thing I needed was a flat tire when under tow. We also removed the rear chain so only the wheel would turn. The bike seemed to roll freely without any noticeable noises from the rear wheel. I wrote out a check for $200 and thanked Jim. My plan was to make it back to McLean before heavy traffic, park the rig near my building out of the way, then head to North Carolina early the next morning.

As the bike had no license plate, I figured I would attach one of those "IN TOW" signs where the tags usually hang. I made one by crafting some heavy cardboard and magic marker. Also, just to be safe and reassured that I was legal in towing an unregistered bike this way, I called the Virginia state police and after explaining my situation to three different officers, was essentially told "happy trailering." I placed a small bicycle lock on the bike just to slow down any attempts at theft. I was all set.

I awoke at 3 a.m. as I usually do when preparing and packing for the ride down. The tow south via I-95 to I-85 at Petersburg and then south on Route 1 around Raleigh to Pinehurst was essentially uneventful. This is a 330-mile trip that I've been making, on average, twice a month for more than a year. Usually there are a few police along I-85 looking for speeders. I did not see one police

Bauer with his cleaned-up "new" bike. He's managed to source a shop manual and some NOS parts from the shelves of an old Yamaha dealer. *Margo Bauer*

car in Virginia or North Carolina on this trip. I couldn't have asked for a better deal. If stopped in North Carolina, my story would have been that I called the state police (without mentioning which) and they indicated I was good to go the way the rig was set up. Fortunately, I did not have the opportunity to recite my story.

There is, of all things, a somewhat new combination Harley/Yamaha dealer just north of Pinehurst on Route 5. I stopped to pick up some two-stroke oil and ended up meeting a gentleman named Sherrill Lee, the franchise dealer.

He was friendly and excited to see the Yamaha. When I told him I didn't know the year it was built, he said there should be a placard on the steering head that indicated the date it was manufactured. I had no idea the placard existed. We looked and discovered it was built in December 1969. Plus Sherrill pointed out the serial number on the frame, which thankfully matched the engine number.

My barn find was a 1970 model. That is the same year I graduated from Mar Vista High School in Imperial Beach, California, a pretty neat connection. To top if off, Sherrill indicated he had a few N.O.S. Yamaha parts sitting on the shelves that might fit my bike.

Of course, now that I mention this, I hope someone doesn't show up at his doorstep and purchase every old part he has in stock. This is my first barn find and the first Japanese bike I've owned in more than 30 years, so please give me a few more months to see what I might need before you bust down his door!

CHAPTER FOUR

Passion Plays

Bikes, Booze, and Broads

David Hansen had entirely different plans for his life. Not that he has any regrets, but he had hoped to play professional football.

"I played football in high school and I was pretty good," said Hansen, 60, of Ventura, California. "I had hoped to play in college and study to become an engineer. I had my whole life planned and had hoped to play football as long as it lasted. I had scholarships to four great schools.

"Then I found out about bikes, booze, and broads, and that was it for me."

It started out innocently enough. Hansen rode a Triumph single-carb 500, which because of his size, he "overshadowed."

"I started riding an English bike because back then Triumphs were held in great esteem, as they still are, by the general populace.

"I never wanted to go the Harley-Davidson route because I saw some of my peers go that route and didn't like the change it made in them. Like a lot of guys who were never qualified to play football, never mind being a tough guy, all of a sudden they were Harley hard guys."

Then he met a gentleman, Lee Standley, who owned a small compressor shop on the other side of town, and he was into Indians.

"I had this N.O.S. Indian front fork I bought and wanted to extend it and put it on my Triumph," said Hansen. "It was brand new and still Army Green.

"So I went to his shop one day with plans to extend the front forks and Lee looked at me like I would probably look at a kid today.

"Well, we can do that, but this part right here is never going to be made again, and it's brand new, and it's called new old stock," said Standley. "They stopped making this part in the 1940s, and it would be a shame to cut it up. I'll do it, but it would be a shame.

"Now, I've got some forks over here that would lend themselves more to what you want, and I'll help you do it if you give me the new Indian front fork. We'll work on it together."

Hansen thought that was a fair trade, so he started showing up at Standley's shop after class and learned how to operate the drill press and the lathe.

"Prior to then, I was one of those guys who was good at taking things apart but not at putting things back together," he said. "He showed me how neat machinery was and how to weld and braze—and also how to sweep the floor and clean the toilet, which was a concept I wasn't familiar with."

David Hansen's The Shop is located on the 101 freeway in downtown Ventura, California. From the highway, the establishment appears to be a Hollywood set for a 1950s Marlon Brando film. *Tom Cotter*

Hansen purchased a factory Indian dealership sign, but the city of Ventura won't give him a permit to hang it in front of his building, so it sits in a back parking lot. *Tom Cotter*

"Lee instilled in me a work ethic that I still have today."

Hansen and his mentor extended the front forks on his Triumph, and the young rider learned something in the process. Then one day he had the opportunity to buy an Indian Scout and trade up from a 500cc to a 750cc machine. He bought it for $200 but soon found out that he was way too large for the bike's frame.

His mentor made him a deal: "If you give me this Scout, I'll give you a basket-case Indian Chief and help you put it together."

So at the beginning of summer 1968, Hansen worked on assembling the Chief. He took the modified Indian fork he had built for the Triumph and installed it on the Chief, and together with his mentor and some repair books, he "muddled through" the engine rebuild.

"By the Fourth of July, I'm riding my 1,200cc Indian and I'm just bitchin'," he said. "I was the cat's ass."

And it went from there. Hansen learned more and eventually rented a small shop on the other side of town. People started finding out about Indians and telling Hansen about them.

"I started to buy them because they were cheaper and cooler than Harleys," he said.

That's when his life took a major change. "My college football coach said, 'You can't ride a motorcycle if you're playing football,'" said Hansen. "On one level, I could understand him completely, but on another level, it was probably time for me to quit because I was going to ride my motorcycle.

"So there went the scholarships and here I am, 40 years later, waiting to grow up."

Hansen's life has revolved around Indians since that time. Today, he owns The Shop, which is right off the freeway in Ventura, California. It looks like an Indian motorcycle dealership because of all the signs. He repairs and restores Indians and Harleys and has thousands of parts in his warehouse for both brands.

He has made some unbelievable barn finds during the past four decades.

Colorado Gold

"It's 1975 and a buddy of mine comes up to me and says he just heard about a whole bunch of Indian parts that a guy wants to get rid of," said Hansen. "He said the guy bought a bunch of parts but only wants to keep the Harley parts and wants to get rid of the Indian stuff."

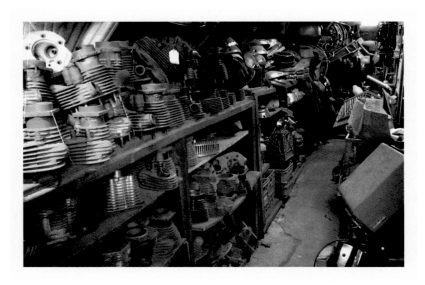

Nearly four decades worth of bike components fill Hansen's parts building. He has purchased contents of old dealerships throughout the United States and even abroad. *Tom Cotter*

Just one of many of Hansen's storage buildings shows some of the treasures he has discovered over his long career as a motorcycle archeologist. Mostly Indians (even the dirt bike) fill the quonset hut, with the oldest bikes in the rear of the building. *Tom Cotter*

Hansen was all ears, and the two jumped into his truck and drove right down to Jefferson, right off the 10 freeway. They walked up to this huge former hangar and walked into what was called Cyclops Choppers.

"There was this huge pile of parts in the center of this gigantic hangar , and they were all for Indians," said Hansen. "On both sides of the pile, there were two-by-four racks of Harley parts: rigid frames, swingarm frames, fenders, and engines—Panheads, Knuckleheads, Shovelheads, and Flatheads."

In addition, trucks would pull up and unload more parts.

"What the guy was doing was as the trucks were coming in with the parts, as they took them off the truck, they would just throw all the Indian parts into the pile. So he made me a deal: I could buy all the Indian parts for $1,000."

While Hansen and his friend were loading the parts in his truck, the man who owned Cyclops came over and told him, "There are a lot more Indian parts where I got these from, and for a 10 percent cut, I'll turn you on to the deal."

Hansen quickly agreed and a few weeks later accompanied the man on a trip to Denver, Colorado, where all the parts came from.

"The old Harley dealer in Denver was Ray Koch and his dealership was on the west side of Colfax Avenue," said Hansen. "But when the river overflowed in the 1960s, it just took his dealership and rolled it into a huge wad of mud and moved it about 20 miles south. I think it was Livingston, Arizona.

"I guess he got enough money from insurance that he quit being a Harley dealer and bought the property where his 'dealership' floated to. He threw a fence around it and called it National Cycle Sales. He concentrated on used bikes, mostly Yamahas, Suzukis, and Harleys, but he didn't have much use for the old Harleys and Indians."

When Hansen showed up at the lot, he said there were motorcycles everywhere. The guy he was with was making a deal to purchase the rest of the Harley parts and probably would pull out another 25 semi-truck loads before he was done.

Almost 40 years ago, Hansen literally unearthed old Harley and Indian parts from a muddy field in Colorado. This Indian motor is from that original discovery and still has Colorado mud caked in its cylinder ports. *Tom Cotter*

Hansen made a deal with Ray Koch to buy everything that was Flathead-powered, whether it was Indian or Harley, for $7,000.

"So me and a buddy hung out in Denver for three weeks that summer and kept loading up rented Ryder trucks and paying for friends to fly in and drive them home," he said. "We probably filled five or six truckloads before we were through.

"The last day I'm there and I'm walking around looking at the property to make sure I hadn't left anything, and I tripped over something sticking out of the ground. It was a piece of a handlebar sticking out of the ground, so I got a pick and a shovel and started to dig around the part. Suddenly I hear glass shatter and thought I must have poked a hole in a headlight."

Hansen cleaned around the handlebar as best he could, then borrowed a piece of equipment from Koch that had a hydraulic arm attached to it. He wrapped a chain around it and the handlebars and yanked out an entire Harley Knucklehead out of the ground.

"I was like a kid with a fishing rod, I was so excited," he said. "I drove back to Ray's office with the bike hanging from the chain and said, 'Look what I found.'"

"Where did you find that, son?" asked Koch.

"I picked it out of the ground right over there," answered Hansen.

"He looked at me and gave me this classic line that I could never make up," said Hansen. "He puts his hand on my shoulder and said, 'Son, I didn't sell you mining rights.' So we made another deal for $2,000 for anything I found underground. So I picked up another 20 bikes.

"They were rusty, but to this day I still have some of those old engines filled with Colorado mud."

A Bigger Truck

Hansen once saw an ad in the January issue of *Cars & Parts* magazine that read: "1907 Indian Twin, 1915 Sears, 1921 Harley Sport, plus parts, $10,000." The ad was placed by Andy Anderson of Springfield, Missouri.

"I had been going to swap meets and knew Andy a little bit," said Hansen. "So I called him and made a deal over the phone. I sent him a $2,000 deposit and told him I'd see him in the summer. So come summer, a buddy and I flew to St. Louis, rented a truck, and drove to Andy's house, which was in an aeropark."

"He had six or seven airplane hangars filled with planes, bikes, cars, you name it.

"So we drove up in this little box van, and he said, 'I don't think this truck is going to fit all the spare parts I'm going to give you.'"

Hansen was confused.

"It's just three bikes and some spare parts, how large a truck do I need?" he asked.

With that, Anderson started opening chicken coops, and there were at least another 25 motorcycles and loads of parts.

"I get on the phone and call some friends and said, 'You better get your ass down here and help us load this stuff up,'" he said. "We wound up taking about 10 truckloads out of there.

"This was an advertised deal that anyone could have purchased. I was just lucky."

The Sheriff's Daughter

One year Hansen and a friend got on their Indians and started riding east in search of old bikes and parts.

"Those were the days when I could leave for three or four weeks and nobody cared because I had guys running the business," said Hansen. "We were taking mostly back roads and wound up one night in Cortez, Colorado. It was a Saturday night and the one bar in town was patronized mostly by Indians from the nearby reservation. We rode up on our Indians and they thought it was the greatest thing ever. They were taking pictures and having a great time."

Well, it happened that Hansen met a girl in the bar that evening.

"She was beautiful," he said. "Her name was Leona and she had on a University of Hawaii sweatshirt. We took a shine to each other, so we were knocking down a few Jack Daniels and Cokes, and the next thing she says is, 'Can I go for a ride?'

"Well, darling, of course you can."

"Remember what I said about bikes, booze, and broads?"

He borrowed his friend's helmet and went for a ride in the country, but when he returned, his friend was mad.

"The bar has been closed for an hour, and I couldn't leave because you had my helmet," he friend said. "The cops are all around here waiting for you.

"You were with the sheriff's daughter."

As soon as Leona got off the bike, the parking lot filled up with police cars. One of the officers stepped out—luckily it wasn't the sheriff—and walked over to Hansen and Leona.

"Leona, you better get home right away, because your daddy's not too happy," said the officer. As soon as she drove off, he gave Hansen some advice. "Son, you need to leave," he said.

"Yes sir," replied Hansen. "We have a hotel room on the outskirts of town, and we'll be gone in the morning."

"That's none too soon, because you don't want Leona's daddy to find you."

They got up early and as promised, departed Cortez before sunrise. They headed up toward Wolf Creek Pass.

"We were two chopper fools and our idea of a rain suit was two garbage bags," said Hansen. "Well, we were up at 10,000 feet and were riding on black ice. It was a bad ride."

They kept riding east and wound up in a little town called Kingsley, Kansas, where they stopped for fuel. As was their custom, they asked if anyone knew of any old motorcycles for sale.

"Well, yeah, if you go down the road and make a right, there's an old Hudson dealership," said a local. "Jerome Fox owns that building and it is filled with old bikes and cars."

So Hansen and his friend followed the man's instructions and son-of-a-gun, there was an old Hudson dealership right where the man said. It was locked and dark inside, but they peered in the window and could see old bikes and cars as far as the eye could see.

"We decided to hang around Kingsley that night," said Hansen, "and were looking for something to do. We went to the VFW hall, which is where everyone hung out, and had a few drinks with the locals. We got along famously with the people, and one of them offered to call Jerome, who said he'd love to meet us in the morning."

Jerome Fox was a huge Kansas farmer and, according to Hansen, one of the nicest men he ever met.

"He showed us everything and wouldn't hear of us staying in a hotel, so we stayed at his house," said Hansen. "Then he asked if we would take a few of his old motorcycles and restore them. So we rented a large truck, loaded up his bikes, and drove back to Ventura."

"Several years later, we got a call from his wife who said Jerome had died and, in his will, wanted us to come and buy all of his motorcycles, of which there were about 40."

Hansen went back there with $200,000 in a briefcase handcuffed to his wrist. Every time they wheeled out another bike, he and the lawyer would decide on a price together, then he would pay them and put the bike into a truck.

"That was in 1985 and we were paying about $7,000 or $8,000 per bike back then," He said. "I had a lot of them pre-sold."

Hansen also bought a couple of old cars from the estate, including a "bitchin' 1933 Pontiac Coupe," but he sold it immediately upon returning to Ventura. "I'd tried to get into old cars, but they are just too much trouble," he said.

"In the age of the Internet, I don't think there are many dumb farmers out there anymore."

Hansen's Philosophy

For more than 40 years, Hansen has come up with hundreds of leads on barn finds. Today, the man who owns 70 bikes, 25 of which are Indians, still follows up on every bike he hears about.

"The only lead you don't follow up is usually the best one," he said. "You need to follow up everything you hear about, especially if it's in the paper and the ad is written a little bit weird. If the ad is in the wrong spot in the paper, follow up on it because most likely nobody else is. Otherwise, the one you miss will be the gold mine."

He has followed up leads about huge stashes of bikes in Mexico City, Venezuela, Iran (they had belonged to the Shah), Iraq, and Lebanon, and he knows of motorcycle junkyards that exist in places where wars are raging right now.

Hansen has been friends with Steve McQueen and Otis Chandler, among others.

Hansen's shop handles complete restorations, maintenance, and parts sales for all Indians and flathead Harleys. He draws customers from around the world. *Tom Cotter*

"Otis would never let me pay for lunch," he said, "so once I arrived at the restaurant early and paid for our meal ahead of time. You had to be ingenious if you wanted to treat the man.

"With McQueen, he was the nicest guy if you were by yourself, one-on-one with him. When he lived in Santa Paula, we'd go out on Friday nights and have pizza, beer, and shoot the shit. But as soon as he was around Hollywood people, he became a star.

"The best thing about McQueen, though, was that he wasn't a Harley guy or an Indian guy. He was a motorcyclist.

"It's been a fun 40 years," he said. "I never thought I'd be lucky enough to do this for so long.

"I tried to retire five years ago but soon realized that this is what I wanted to do if I retired, so nothing changed."

Follow Your Nose

Jeff Slobodian has been involved in every aspect of the classic motorcycle hobby, from rare American and French bikes to European cyclemotors and minibikes.

Growing up in the Philadelphia area, he attended all the local shows and swap meets. He never found it difficult finding cool old machines to buy and credits that to his habit of talking to a lot of people and asking a lot of questions.

"At shows, there is great stuff to be found, but you've got to walk around and stop along the way to have conversations with other enthusiasts and the vendors," said Slobodian.

"Once I heard some guys talking about this bike that was 5 miles down the road from where I lived. It actually belonged to the son of a lady who my mom knew." The woman's son had his grandfather's old Excelsior motorcycle stored in the basement, where it had been for 30 years.

"'We're tired of it down there,' she said when I spoke with her. 'He thinks he's going to restore it, but he never will. Why don't you come over and buy it?'"

This was music to Slobodian's ears.

When he went over to the woman's house, he discovered a complete machine with an Excelsior racing cylinder head installed.

"It was perfect," he said. "But I told her it was a shame it was missing the speedometer. She said for me to check out the barrel in the corner, that maybe it's in there. Inside that barrel was a brand new racing Mesinger seat that was in perfect condition, a different rear hub for racing, and the original floorboards that had been removed.

"It had everything needed to make this into a racer."

When Slobodian tried to buy the bike from the woman's son, though, he said it wasn't for sale. Slobodian told a friend about it, who tried for the next 15 years to buy it, but he was also snubbed.

"For all I know, it's still down there," he said. "But the amazing thing is that it was just 5 miles from my house."

Another bike he discovered while looking at an outboard motor collection was 10 miles from his house. In the corner of the garage was a 1906 Wagner motorcycle, an unusual bike where the motor actually exhausts through the frame by using some abnormal plumbing.

"It wasn't for sale, but I liked the Wagner design," he said. "So when I was at the Davenport, Iowa, show afterwards, I found a 1905 Wagner in the swap meet and decided to buy it. It was only a frame and a motor and was missing the forks, wheels, handlebars, brakes, and most other items.

"Everyone was amazed that I would pay $3,000 for just a motor and a frame." His friends told him he'd never put it together, but he surprised all the critics. Within six weeks of his purchase, he had acquired every part he needed for the bike, including two extra frames. He restored the bike. It made quite an impression on a friend who was visiting.

"I love that bike," said his friend. "I'd like to buy it."

Slobodian said he wasn't interested in selling the Wagner but told him there was another one just 10 miles away.

"You're kidding me," his friend said.

Slobodian and his friend went over to the outboard motor collector's house to see if the Wagner motorcycle was for sale, but the owner declined.

"But I might trade it for something," he said.

Several more years went by. Slobodian's friend called and asked if he thought the 1906 Wagner might still be there.

"Of course it is," he said. "He asked me if I minded if he tried to buy it, and I said, 'Go for it.'"

His friend loaded a Harley into the back of his pickup truck and made one more attempt to acquire the Wagner. The trade worked.

"He got a great '06 Wagner, which still had original paint, to my memory," said Slobodian.

Slobodian tired of motorcycles, and when he moved from Pennsylvania to Ojai, California, he thought he would be leaving his motorcycle hobby behind. For a long time he did.

"In Pennsylvania, I brought my very original 1912 belt-drive Harley to a meet," he said. "I bought it out of a guy's garage where it had been for 30 years, and his father owned it before that. At the meet, there were five others just like it."

When he moved out West, he became passionate about different types of two-wheelers: cyclemotors and velomotors, or, as we call them in the United States, motorbikes.

Many Americans know of the Whizzer motorbike, which is often on display at antique car shows. But Slobodian wanted something more unique than a Whizzer.

"They made so many Whizzers," he said. "If you wanted a Whizzer tomorrow, any condition or color, I could find you five of them. They are that easy to get.

"I got into motorbikes because there is always something you've never seen before that is still available, and sometimes brand new," he said. "I've had at least 15 motorbikes from the 1950s that have only been ridden once or twice.

"My bikes are not really rare, but they have great design."

Slobodian fell in love with the intricacy of European motorbikes, which he says are much more unique than American counterparts like the Whizzer. *Tom Cotter*

Once Slobodian was communicating with an eBay seller about a clutch. Near the conclusion of the phone call, he mentioned to the seller, "What else do you have?"

"He said he had this Motorwheel Powerbike that he was getting ready to list on eBay," said Slobodian. "So I said to him, 'Why don't you just sell it to me instead?' He said he wanted $800, and I said OK.

"Powerbikes were made in Saginaw, Michigan, about 50 miles from where I bought this unit. It had never been run. It still had the hardware in little stapled envelopes with the instructions. It has a 2¾-horsepower engine, and it goes 35 miles per hour, faster than you'll want to go."

Slobodian explained that the Powerbike motorbike attachment adapted easily to almost any bicycle. All a home mechanic needed to do was unbolt the rear fender and rear wheel and bolt on the Powerbike.

"It included a centrifugal clutch, coaster brake, kickstand, muffler, taillight, and fender, all built into one bolt-on unit," he said. "You kick-started it like a Maytag.

"The guy I bought it from had it in a shed, where it had been since 1948. It belonged to his father, who, as a kid, had it taken away when his father found out he had it."

Slobodian bolted the unit to a restored 1948 Western Flyer, making for a very proper, period-correct piece.

"I liked it so much, I bought a second one."

Another motorbike Slobodian bought on eBay was powered by a 1953 Rex engine. It was mounted to a 1970s Schwinn tricycle.

"The guy mounted it on there just to have a place for it," he said. "It had never even been started. I took off the cylinder and saw the oil to be crystal clear, not even a spec of carbon dust. I took it apart and the piston rings were perfect and shiny. Brand new."

A storage unit houses Slobodian's future motorbike restoration projects. He scours eBay and motorcycle flea markets for motorbikes, minibikes, and parts that most hardcore motorcycle collectors would bypass. *Tom Cotter*

133

Jeff Slobodian tired of restoring rare old motorcycles and now restores motorbikes. He found this brand-new 1948 Powerbike and installed it on a restored 1948 Western Flyer bicycle. A similar bike just sold at auction for $14,000. *Jeff Slobodian*

Slobodian threw away the trike and mounted the Rex motor on a period-correct German 1953 Meile bicycle. When completed, he parked the bike in the showroom of his Ojai-based custom cabinet shop.

"A guy came in to order a wood case and became interested in the bike. He said, 'I have no interest in bikes at all, but I'll take this one and that one,' and he paid a lot of money for them.

"This in a bad economy."

One of Slobodian's most recent purchases is a minibike.

"I was at a swap meet and walked past it four or five times before I walked up to the seller and said, 'Nobody is going to buy this,' and he said, 'You're probably right.'

"I don't even want to tell you how ridiculously cheap it was."

The minibike intrigued Slobodian because it was homemade and fabricated out of a bicycle. He fell in love with the red frame and green 1953 engine.

Slobodian needed to install a new recoil starter on the engine, but where could he find something from a company that went out of business in 1953? He walked into an engine-repair shop that had been a dealer for the brand when they were new. The man pulled a brand-new recoil starter off the shelf that had been there for 55 years.

Slobodian installed this brand-new 1953 Rex motorwheel on a period-correct Meile bicycle, both made in Germany. A man walked into his cabinet shop in Ojai, California, and after admitting he knew nothing about motorcycles, fell in love with the bike and bought it. *Tom Cotter*

"My friends all asked, 'What the hell did you buy that for?' But now they all look at it and can't believe how cool it is. I bet I can get $3,500 for it when I'm done. It's homebuilt and homebuilt stuff is cool.

"Stuff that's never been found is cool. One out of every 10 people knows where something cool is.

"Once you've built 10 or 15 full-size motorcycles, it gets to be like going to work on the Ford assembly line. It doesn't matter what make or model, they all have the same engine and transmission. It gets boring.

"In Europe, with these little motorbikes, you could find a different bike everyday for the next 30 years and you would never even scrape the surface on what was available in Europe and Russia."

The Madman of Marin County

By Somer Hooker

Most people collect bikes because they love them. Not so with George Disteel. He collected them because he HATED them! There is a reason. Disteel lived in the San Francisco Bay area in the 1960s and 1970s working primarily as a carpenter. He had an unusual appearance: long flowing beard, ill-fitting clothes, and a patch over his eye. He had cataracts and was probably trying to strengthen his eyes by using one at a time. He also had an affinity for things mechanical: rifles, cameras, medical equipment, and motorcycles.

He would go into Sears once a month and buy a rifle. One day, federal agents came by to find out what was going on. He looked at them and said, "If it's legal for Sears to sell them to me, why isn't it legal for me to buy them?" Perplexed and with no answer to his question, they left him alone.

He especially liked motorcycles with unusual motors, such as Cammy Nortons, Velocettes, Moto Guzzis, Brough Superiors, and Vincent HRDs. He

This haunting photo of Disteel ran in a local San Francisco Bay–area newspaper. The reclusive fellow hunted down and purchased all the Vincent motorcycles he could find to prevent other young men from dying on them as had happened to his own son. *Somer Hooker collection*

would take them out on the porch of his small house and display them. There were various anecdotes of people who were taken inside to see him pull back a cover to display some brilliant piece of machinery.

George had one son. His wife had died in childbirth and George was left to raise him. His son rode motorcycles with the typical disregard of youth. Unfortunately, one day, he was high-sided while racing a Vincent Black Shadow on the street. Disteel was left alone in the world and swore a "Vin"detta against Vincents. He vowed he would take them off the road.

Although Disteel looked like a vagrant, he was shrewd. He had acquired land and cash. When bikes came available, he would buy them and stash them, sometimes with friends and sometimes in shops. One guy remembers going into a dealership and seeing five lined up. When he inquired, he was told they belonged to Disteel. Marty Dickerson, the famous Salt Flats racer, tuner, and Vincent dealer from Southern California, remembers his encounter with Disteel, who showed up at his shop one day driving an old hearse. He struck a deal for the bike and they drug it into the back of the hearse. Maybe this was a symbolic farewell.

Disteel lived in his car for a while. His eyes had gotten too bad to ride motorcycles anymore. The semi-blind man could still be seen driving his car up

Just one of many Vincents that George Disteel horded in barns and sheds throughout the San Francisco Bay area in the 1960s and 1970s. When Disteel died, this Vincent Touring Rapide and all the other bikes were brought out of hiding and auctioned. *Somer Hooker*

and down the steep grades of the Bay Area, as well as Mount Tamalpais. Unable to work as a carpenter anymore, he took odd jobs. For a while he worked in San Rafael's Boyd Museum. He lived in a 1952 Hudson in the parking lot. It was packed with junk. He was packing junk in every nook and cranny in the museum. After a skinny-dipping episode, he was out of there.

Disteel moved to a salvage yard and started working as a night watchman. One day the owner noticed Disteel pushing a Vincent into an abandoned panel truck. Disteel then began to cover it with rags and boxes, finally closing the doors. Later the owner watched Disteel build a small shed without doors. The shed was going to become a tomb for the bikes! Once again Disteel found himself asked to move on.

Disteel moved on to a flophouse. There were still sightings of him riding his bicycle at high speed with a knapsack on his back and his long beard flowing over his shoulder. Sometimes a dog's head would be sticking out of the pack looking like it was navigating for Disteel! Finally one chilly day in November 1978, Disteel stepped out on the steps of the hotel where he was living at that time and dropped dead from a heart attack.

Initially he was classified as a "John Doe." Soon his properties were discovered and the premises investigated. One chicken shed yielded cameras, rifles, tax liens (!), and motorcycles, lots of motorcycles. About 17 were pulled out. There were parts and motors mixed in. This may have only been the tip of the iceberg. One person once reported having seen more than 20 Vincents in one spot. Dealers were known to have been employed by Disteel to acquire the machines to "get them off of the road" for him. One can only wonder what some had done when faced with the dilemma of suddenly having a garage with four or five Vincents in it, the only "heir" being the state. For years I heard rumors of individuals who had a few Vincents that had allegedly been Disteel's. Of course, no one would ever stand up and say where they acquired them.

The state hired Butterfields auction house to auction off his estate. The assets would be held in trust for seven years should a rightful heir step forward. There were about eight Vincents in there. Some were original; some were tired. All were sold.

Charlie Taylor had a business north of the city then. He specialized in Vincent repair. He would park at the end of the auction stand and insert one of his business cards in the new owner's hands.

"I couldn't believe the prices they were fetching," he said.

Even the non-running bikes were selling for close to $2,000—high prices for these machines in 1978. As is typical at an auction, prices rose near the end as the crowd realized it was do-or-die time. The last Shadow across the block had a lot of holes drilled in it. Arlen Ness figured if he was going to get one this would have to be it. It was hammered down for a little under $2,000.

54 San Francisco Chronicle ★ Thurs., Jan. 26, 1978

Joe Craviotte of the auction firm prepared the motorcycles for the Saturday sa

A Classic Collection of
Motorcycles on Auction

Eighteen classic motorcycles from the estate of Marin county eccentric George Disteel will be auctioned off Saturday at the Butterfield and Butterfield warehouse at 1625 Pine street.

The collection includes seven hard-to-find Vincents, two German DKWs, two Moto Guzzis and a prewar Velocette.

Disteel, a retired carpenter, dropped dead on a Tenderloin sidewalk last November. He left no will and he has no

known relatives.

His son was killed on a motorcycle many years ago. As a result, officials said, Disteel began buying up motorcycles and hiding them in several barns in Marin and Sonoma counties so others would not be killed riding them.

The auction will be from noon to 2 p.m. Saturday. There will be a review from 9 a.m. to 5 p.m. tomorrow

A short newspaper article from the January 26, 1978, edition of the *San Francisco Chronicle* telling readers of the upcoming auction of Disteel's motorcycles, including seven Vincents, two DKWs, two Moto Guzzis, and a Velocette. *Somer Hooker collection*

This Black Shadow, purchased at the auction and restored, was sold at the Butterfields Auction to chopper builder Arlen Ness, who later resold it. *Somer Hooker*

Years later I was in the Bay Area and heard that a guy had some of Disteel's old bikes for sale. He had acquired them at the auction. One was a shabby but complete and original Black Shadow. The other was a remarkably complete and original Red Rapide showing only 5,000 miles.

Yeah, I should have bought them. Now I'll just keep my eyes peeled for sheds with no doors, thank you.

The Million-Mile Harley

"Every day I meet the most incredibly interesting people at the Wheels Through Time Museum," said curator Dale Walksler. "Some have interesting motorcycles, some have interesting motorcycle stories, and some have both."

Walksler remembered one particularly busy Saturday when one young man, who seemed shy, was hanging around the front counter.

"I could tell he wanted to talk to me," he said. "And because I'm always anxious to talk to anybody, I said, 'Can I help you?'"

The young man, Lee Miller, 36, of Hickory, North Carolina, said yes, and proceeded to tell Walksler about his granddad's Harley-Davidson.

"I've got some photographs," said Miller. "The old bike has been sitting on our front porch for 40 years. It's at our family home place outside of Granite Falls, North Carolina."

The grandfather, W. L. Klotz, was born in that house, lived in that house, and died in that house, according to Miller. Miller's mother, JoAnn, remembered as a little girl when her father used to ride his prized Harley. But her son, Lee, even though he is 35 years old, had never seen the bike run.

"The last time I rode on it, I was probably eight or nine years old," said JoAnn Miller. "He would [give me a] ride to the store on it. I'd sit on the front of the seat and hold onto his wrists."

"He bought the bike in 1952 and rode it that year and in 1953," she said. "After that, North Carolina had a law that you had to have insurance on motorcycles, so he parked it because he couldn't afford insurance on both a car and a motorcycle."

Young Joann Klotz-Miller with her father, W. L. Klotz, in the late 1940s. Joann said she was eight or nine years old when her father gave her the last ride on his prized Harley. *Klotz-Miller family collection*

"Lee had some interest in the bike," said Walksler, "and people had been coming by the house for 10 or 15 years trying to buy it, but it was a family heirloom and was not for sale. He showed me two pictures of the bike sitting on the porch. It was a great-looking 1949 Panhead, and I thought it was extremely cool."

Miller also showed Walksler some of his grandfather's original paperwork for the bike, including the sales contract. It was signed on October 11, 1952, and committed Klotz to make six payments of $49.46 each and a final payment of $44.54 for the used 1949 Harley, serial number 49EL3353. Klotz financed the $346.30 purchase though Kilbourn Financial Corporation of Milwaukee, Wisconsin.

"So at some point in our conversation, I mentioned to Lee that he should bring the bike over to the museum so we could take a look at it," said Walksler. "Maybe we could even get it running."

"You're kidding me!" said Miller.

Walksler assured him he wasn't kidding and handed him a business card. "Call me sometime and we'll get that thing running," he said.

That was on a Saturday. The following Wednesday Miller was on the phone and wanted to know if he could bring the Harley over on Friday.

"I told him it was a great idea and that I would have my video crew record it for one of my Time Machine shows," he said.

"Lee showed up at about 5 p.m. with his mom, JoAnn.

Barely visible after a half-century of resting on the front porch of his home, W. L. Klotz took his Harley-Davidson off the road when insurance in North Carolina became mandatory in 1953. *Klotz-Miller family collection*

Before being put in hibernation, Klotz, a mechanic, most likely drained the fuel and lubricated the cylinders.
Klotz-Miller family collection

"We gave the bike a pretty thorough 5-minute evaluation, unloaded it from the trailer, and brought it into the shop. We had it running in 15 minutes and had it perfected by the end of the evening."

Within a week, it was operating well enough that Walksler said you could have hopped on it and ridden it anywhere, if you were happy with riding it on old tires.

"The saving grace was that the carburetor and gas tank were dry, so apparently old W. L. drained them before he parked the bike," said Walksler. "It was a huge time savings to us in getting the bike revived again.

"The bike was incredibly straight and hadn't been damaged. A lot of times bikes are put up when they are on their last breath, maybe with a blown transmission or a blown rod, or a bad ring. This was a case where a perfectly good motorcycle had been parked on a porch for 40 years while W. L. raised his family."

Walksler said that most people would take a bike like this Harley and completely restore it, but he said a bike in this condition deserves to be preserved in its original condition.

"In today's world, barn finds have a lot more interesting stories to tell than restored machines," he said, "because all those stories are still attached to the bike.

Even though the bike was under cover on the porch, all the plated cast pieces became badly pitted. These are accessory lights mounted on the front fenders. *Matt Walksler*

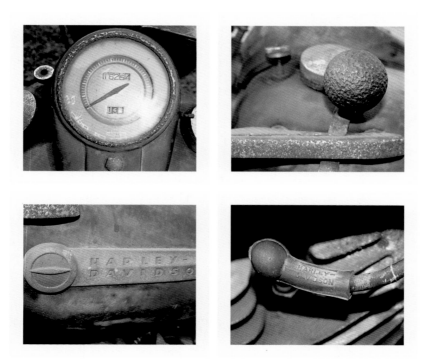

The bike is 100 percent complete and includes many original parts and accessories that are often tossed in the trash during restoration. *Matt Walksler*

Klotz purchased the 1949 Panhead used for $346.30 in 1952. As can be seen in the photographs, the bike was fully accessorized with leather saddlebags, custom lighting, and chrome guards. After just a few hours of fiddling, Klotz's old Harley fired up and was ridden around the parking lot of Dale Walksler's Wheels Through Time Museum in Maggie Valley, North Carolina. Walksler said that with new tires he would consider the bike reliable enough to ride across the United States. *Matt Walksler*

"I've seen hundreds of before-and-after photos, but personally, I'd rather see the before pictures and never even see the finished product."

According to JoAnn, they had discussed fixing up the bike for years, but her father was always worried that his grandson, Lee, would get hurt on it. When her father died in December 2007, they knew the time was right to get it running in honor of Klotz.

"When I was a little girl, I rode a million miles on that bike when it sat on the porch," she said. "I never doubted that it would run just as good as it did when I was a little girl.

"When Dale got it all fixed, he told me to crank it. I told him, 'There's no way I have the power to crank up that bike.' But Dale said, 'Your daddy is going to help you.'

"I know he's smiling down on us now."

You can see Dale Walksler's four-part video on reviving W. L. Klotz's 1949 Harley Panhead by going to the website www.wheelsthroughtime.com and clicking on Dale's Blog.

Same Bike, Different Basement

By Zack Miller

I think it's possible, when young, to have a motorcycle experience so affecting that it remains with you the rest of your life. A sort of two-wheeled first kiss. The world shifts, tilts, and a general longing transforms to a specific desire.

I think this happened to me when I was 12. We had a visitor in our garage that summer, a 1970 Ducati Mark 3 D. It belonged to Bruce, a friend of my father's and something of a rock star, at least in my eyes and by the standards of east-central Iowa. Tall, thin, with long hair and stylish '70s clothes, he variously arrived at our house in a Pantera, a Continental Mk III, or a 4-4-2 reputedly "set up for drag racing." Bruce owned stereo shops and music stores. He went target shooting with, not one, but a pair of nickel-plated .357s. It was hard to believe my father actually knew someone this cool.

I don't recall when the Ducati arrived or why, but I do remember seeing it for the first time, centered in the only open space in our otherwise crammed

Though sold and titled as a 1970 model, this Mark 3 D was likely built in 1969. Some Mark 3s exported to the United States had the Scrambler tank and tall bars rather than the "coffin" tank and clip-ons worn by their sportier European-spec brothers. *Zack Miller*

146

two-stall garage. Dad explained that Bruce bought it and immediately had it modified before ever riding it. I could see a velocity stack, a matte-black megaphone exhaust, and a special gold paint job. I could only imagine the trick bits that must have been hidden away inside the engine. Apparently the diminutive Duc was so mind-bendingly fast that it scared the bejesus out of Bruce the first time he gave it a hard twist. Now the demon was cooling its heels in our garage. What luck!

My dad rode it only a few times over its short stay with us, preferring the relative refinement and quiet of his old AJS twin. Madness, to my thinking. But then he also thought the Pantera "rode like a lumber wagon." For my part, I logged hours in the saddle, sitting in our garage and imagining myself blowing down the road at supra-legal speeds, a Phil Spector–wall of megaphone sound in my wake.

The Desmo, as Dad called it, went away as unexpectedly as it had arrived, recalled by Bruce and gone forever for all I knew.

Time sped on and so did I, first aboard a Honda CL160 and a short-lived Kawasaki triple while still in high school, then astride a further succession of Kawasakis while in college in the early '80s. But like a first crush, that little Ducati never quite left my mind. For years, I had a recurring conversation with my father:

Me: So, do you think Bruce still has that Ducati?

Him: That Desmo?

Me: Yeah, the Desmo.

Him: Maybe. Why?

Me: Think he'd sell it if he had it?

Him: Maybe.

Me: Why don't you ask him next time you talk to him.

Him: I haven't talked to Bruce in years.

Me: A good excuse to touch base. "How's the wife? Do you still have a wife? A Pantera? Do you want to sell that Ducati?"

Him: Yeah, I should call him.

Repeat every few months for a few years.

Then one day, unbidden and out of the blue, the old man calls. "I talked to Bruce the other day."

"Bruce who?"

"Which Bruce do you think?"

"Cool Bruce?"

"Yeah. Bruce with the Ducati."

"Does he still have it?"

"Yep. Been parked in his basement for 15 years."

Fifteen. Years. Unbelievable. How could anyone own something so cool, so exotic, and not have ridden it for fifteen years? It was like being married to an

Italian supermodel but sleeping in a separate bedroom every night. I couldn't comprehend it. I knew this machine deserved better.

"Does he want to sell it?"

"He said you should call him."

Give me that number.

I called, skipped the how's-the-wife-and-Pantera niceties, and quickly got to the point.

"Dad says you'd be willing to sell the Ducati."

"Sure."

"How much do you think you want for it?"

It must be fast, the speedo needle is wound past 100 and lodged on the wrong side of the pin. The bike showed only 3,105 miles when purchased, the additional mile has been logged rolling around various basements. *Zack Miller*

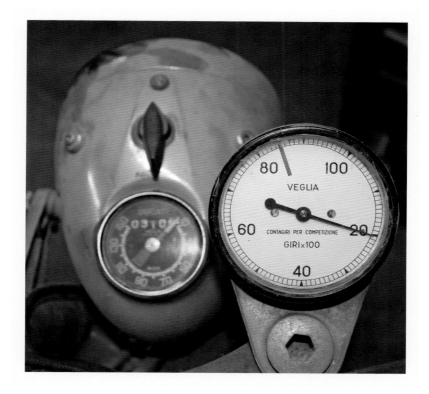

This Veglia tach is a very desirable period accessory. Note the 8,500-rpm redline. Stratospheric for the day, courtesy of Ducati's desmodromic valve actuation. *Zack Miller*

"Well, I'll sell it to you for the same price I offered it to your dad."

"Okay. So, how much was that?"

I couldn't believe the number. It must have been the price offered my dad in 1975 or something when the Desmo was a five-year-old, weirdo Italian thing that 11 people in all of Iowa had heard of. In the summer of 1988 the asking price was a killer deal. I confirmed that I'd drive to Iowa from Minnesota to retrieve it that weekend.

Bruce lived in a tidy ranch-style house, and, just as Dad had reported, the Ducati was tucked away in a corner of the basement. The bike was thick with dust but showed a scant 3,105 miles on the odometer. It still wore the megaphone exhaust and velocity stack I remembered, and it had a lovely little Veglia accessory tach mounted atop the triple tree. We horsed it up the steps and rolled it into the back of my truck.

The legendary Desmo-single powerplant that so captivated my 12-year-old imagination. Yes, that's genuine 1970s-era grime. *Zack Miller*

Twelve-year-old Nate does his best steely eyed impression of what the old man must have looked like all those years ago. *Zack Miller*

Beaming, I hit the road back to Minnesota. I felt like I had a pickup bed full of Krugerrands. People passed me on the highway staring at the Duc with what I imagined to be considerable envy ("My God, Madge, that young buck has a 350 Desmo in the back of that truck!") but was probably closer to pity ("Poor bastard. Do you think that's a motorcycle under that grime?").

Once home, the Desmo was rolled into its new basement lair, where a bit of probing and prodding revealed it to be basically sound and largely unmolested, save for some fool having bobbed the rear fender a couple inches—seemingly with a bow saw—for God knows what reason.

There the Duc sat while I finished a slow, ground-up rebuild of a Ducati Pantah. In the mean time I went back to school, got married, bought a house, rolled the Desmo into that basement, changed jobs, had a kid, finished the Pantah, had another kid. Imagine the hands of a clock spinning wildly around the dial like in some silent-movie representation of passing years and you'll begin to get a sense where this story is going.

Fast forward a bit further still, and I find myself talking to Tom Cotter about this book.

"You know, Tom, I have a story I think I'd like to write for your book."

Kindly, he agrees to let me.

So, I'm driving home from work one day thinking about this story, the story of a very special Ducati left to molder in some dude's basement for fifteen years. Still shaking my head in disbelief my mind wanders back to the summer of 1988 when I rescued it. 1988. Twenty years ago. My reverie is stopped dead in its tracks. Twenty. Years. Unbelievable. How could anyone own something so cool, so exotic, and not have ridden it. . . .

No. Don't even ask. Not for sale.

The Beeza in the Bedroom

By Ken Gross

Years ago, I lived in sunny Sydney, Australia, where nearly every sparkling morning signaled a motorcycle day. I was content with my trusty old Vincent Rapide and my new 750 SS Ducati, but I still read the weekend cycle classifieds. One Saturday, there was a brief but tempting three-line ad for a BSA Gold Star.

Britain's famous 500cc "Goldie" was one of the most coveted 1950s racing motorcycles. BSA stood for Birmingham Small Arms, one of England's top armaments suppliers. When the company wasn't waging war, it built sporting motorcycles. Temperamental, hard to start, difficult to ride well, and wickedly quick, the beautiful "Beeza" was a bike men lusted after but only a lucky few could own.

Surely, there couldn't be any harm in looking.

The man who answered the phone said I was his first caller. He directed me to an address in Sefton, a working-class neighborhood in Sydney's western suburbs, located a few miles past an urban sprawl of factories and light industry.

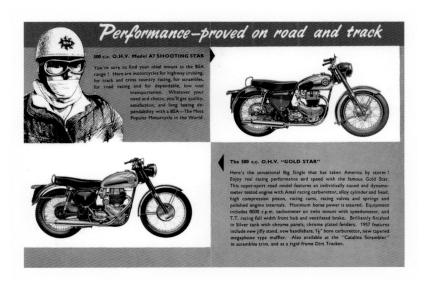

Listed in a BSA advertisement, the Gold Star featured an Amal racing carburetor, alloy head, high-compression piston, racing camshaft, and 8,000-rpm tachometer. *Ken Gross collection*

The street's brick, semi-detached row houses all looked alike. Many numbers were faded or missing, so it took a while to find number 63. Walking up a neatly tended path, I was excited to see the bike. At the door, John Hearne, a trim-looking man in his 20s, introduced me to his strikingly attractive young wife, Fiona. She smiled shyly, looking strangely pleased to see me. He was cool, almost as if he weren't interested in selling his motorcycle.

Even though there was a garage tucked behind the house, we headed straight inside and into a small back bedroom. I couldn't figure it out. Once inside, I saw why. There, between the double bed and the wall, stood the prettiest Gold Star I'd ever seen. The chrome sparkled, the black enamel shone, and the glittering wheels set my heart pounding. I waited, wondering what would happen next.

"We're living here with me mum and dad," John admitted. The grim look on Fiona's face told me all I needed to know about that arrangement.

"We're planning to use the money from the sale of the BSA as a down payment for a place of our own," his wife volunteered. Glancing sideways sharply, John frowned at his wife, as though she'd betrayed a confidence.

Ken Gross's son Jeremy, age 9, having fun on his dad's BSA Gold Star when the family lived in Australia from 1976 to 1981; Jeremy is now 39. Gross bought the bike out of a young couple's bedroom, where it had been stored, so they could buy a house. The bike had been restored before Gross bought it. *Ken Gross*

To break the awkwardness of the moment, I asked if he'd start the bike. He was proud to comply. After maneuvering the immaculate machine through the kitchen to the back porch, he skillfully found the compression point. Tickling the big Amal Grand Prix carburetor until pungent fuel dripped past the float, John retarded the ignition, raised the valve lifter, and kicked down smartly on the starting lever. The bike settled into a fast but very even idle with that characteristic spitting sound common to well-tuned BSA singles. He looked up and grinned. I smiled back.

"Nice," I said.

"Too right," he replied, using the Aussie vernacular for "You bet."

Fiona left us for a moment. "Look, I never intended to sell this bike," he sighed. "Still don't really want to. I bought it in a basket five years ago. It's taken me all this time to rebuild it. I'll show you the bills, the used bits, and all the receipts. Spared no expense, I did."

His words came faster and faster. "Me brother's a speedway champion and he helped. You'll see from the logbook," he said, handing over a battered green packet, "I'm the sixth owner. The machine spent most of its life on the Isle of Man. You know, where they run the TT."

I gave the bike a quick going over. It was perfect. The classic 4-gallon BSA Clubman tank had been replaced with a 5-gallon Lyta aluminum racing tank, and an Eddie Dow finned side plate had been added.

There wasn't one burred bolt. The machine looked better than the day it had rolled out of Birmingham in the summer of 1961. Bargaining on the basis of flaws would be a waste of time, an insult to the painstaking work John had done. We both knew it. This motorcycle was special.

"Are you sure you want to sell it?" I asked, suddenly torn between wanting the motorcycle and hating to see him give up all the work he'd done.

"I have to," he replied sadly. "And I've got to get every penny of the asking price."

Fiona came back and stood looking anxiously over his shoulder. We were soon joined by her beamy, fierce-looking mother-in-law. She, too, wanted to see how we were getting on.

There was no need to ride the bike. I knew it was right. "I'll give you what you want," I said, "and I'll give you something else. I'll promise if I ever sell this motorcycle, you can have the first chance to buy it back."

He was silent for a moment, obviously disappointed that I'd decided so quickly. He sighed, nodding. Fiona squealed and hugged him. The deal was done.

As I wrote the deposit check, my hand trembled. Driving home, I felt strange. The happiness I'd expected to feel in discovering the perfect Gold Star was tempered by what the sale meant to John Hearne. He'd traded one kind of freedom for another. It seemed a curious bargain.

A few days later, John and Fiona appeared at my lock-up garage, the BSA carefully tied down in the bed of his Holden Utility pickup. We unloaded the machine with the reverence military pallbearers show a soldier's coffin. He took a few minutes to show me the starting drill and to say good-bye.

Sitting on the bike for the last time, he caressed the clip-on bars and the fuel tank as a lover would. "It's easy to start," he said, as he demonstrated the complicated drill. When the Goldie fired, he shouted over the loud idle: "Keep the revs between 1,500 and 2,000. There's no way you can get a proper tickover [idle] with a GP carbie. It's geared high, so slip the clutch a little in first. With this sprocket, mate, you can top 115."

John smiled bravely as he packed up his truck, but I'm sure I saw the hint of a tear. Fiona stood still, sensitive to the solemnity of the moment. She silently took his hand. When they left, I turned to the bike and tried unsuccessfully for an hour to start it.

I owned the Goldie for three years. That BSA had its own special aura: aloof, elite, forbidding. I never registered it, preferring to start it up only very occasionally, and riding it at vintage bike meets. It's odd, I suppose, but I never really felt as if it were truly mine.

After returning to the States, I succumbed to an overwhelming temptation to buy an old Ferrari. To afford it, I had to sell my motorcycles, including a Velocette Venom bought sight unseen from England, along with the Ducati and the Vincent.

Before advertising the "Beeza," I kept my promise to John Hearne, and I sent him a letter.

"If you'd like your Goldie back," I wrote, "you can have it for the price you sold it to me. I'll split the cost of crating and shipping it to Australia. I've hardly used it. I'd like you to have it again."

Two months passed. He didn't reply. I tried phoning unsuccessfully. Finally, I sold the Gold Star to Chris Wimpey, a California photographer.

In the years since, I wondered if John Hearne's new house brought him the satisfaction his classic motorcycle so obviously provided. I wondered why he hadn't responded to my letter. Long after the bike was sold, I still somehow expected to hear from him. There was no completing the circle.

The bike's new owner created a poster of the BSA. Preserved on a dramatic black background, the Gold Star's cool perfection recaptures the moment I first saw it in John and Fiona Hearne's bedroom.

And that's the way I like to remember it.

Birth Year Beauties

By Larry Edsall

For Ron Adler, it started when the bicycle he was given wasn't the bicycle he really wanted.

Adler was the fifth of five children and his mother said they simply could not afford the brand new banana-seat Schwinn Stingray bicycle her youngest son wanted. However, she said she was willing to take the money Adler was getting from collecting and returning Coca-Cola bottles and put a copy-cat bike on layaway at the local Sears store.

Adler remembers the Sears bike cost him $53.90, less than half of the $110 he would have needed for the real Stingray. But it really didn't matter because he went to work to make his bike look like a real Stingray. In fact, by the time he was finished, his bike looked even better than a real Stingray. The youngster did such a good job modifying his bike that he sold it for more than that real Stingray would have cost.

Some four decades later, Ron Adler is still collecting and modifying and restoring bicycles. But his interests have grown up. His focus has turned to

Ron Adler has been collecting motorcycles for decades. His yard in Rye, Arizona, not far from Phoenix, has at least 10,000 motorcycles scattered across a couple of acres. *Larry Edsall*

Although it may appear that the thousands of bikes are just scattered randomly over the acreage, owner Adler (pictured) seems to know where each and every bike and part is located. Hondas are the most popular make at Adler's yard, with two 300-foot-long rows dedicated to the brand. *Larry Edsall*

motorized two-wheel vehicles. He buys, sells, repairs, and restores bicycles, motorcycles, and cars, but especially motorcycles, and he has some 10,000 motorcycles and who knows how many motorcycle parts covering almost every square inch of the two-and-a-half acres of his All Bikes yard.

All Bikes is located at Rye, Arizona, a wide spot on the road that leaves the desert floor near Phoenix to twist and turn as it climbs to the northeast, up through the Mazatzal Mountains, and then down into the Tonto Basin before climbing again, toward the base of the Mogollon Rim.

Rye is a dozen miles south of the resort community of Payson but has neither an official census count nor a post office (although it did have a post office from 1884 until 1907). You see, Rye has some history.

Named for the wild cereal plants found growing along what would become known as Rye Creek, Rye was a crossroads for nineteenth-century expeditions into the Arizona territory, including General George Crooks' campaign against the Apaches. Rye also served as a safe haven for those fleeing the area's long-running Graham-Tewksbury feud, a cattlemen versus sheep herders battle also known as the Pleasant Valley War. Whether feud or war, this fight over rangeland served as the inspiration for Zane Grey and many other early authors of western fiction.

With his long hair and beard—he's not gray, he insists, claiming the color is "chrome"—Ron Adler looks like someone who might have lived in Rye in the 1800s, or maybe he fulfills your mental image of the famed Lost Dutchman, who prospected for gold a few miles south of Rye in the Superstition Mountains. In a way, Adler *is* mining. He's mining old motorcycles.

Today, Rye is made up of a few businesses on either side of Arizona Route 87. All Bikes is just east of the highway, on Garvin Drive, a block-long street that also serves the Rye Creek Bar and Restaurant, Hunter Auto Sales, the Rye Trailer Park, Park Ministries Bible Fellowship, and Garvin's Towing and Impound, an Arizona Department of Public Safety vehicle storage yard.

Drive into Rye and what catches your eye is a hillside that glistens as metallic shapes reflect the bright Arizona sun. At first glance, All Bikes appears to be a final resting place for thousands of motorcycles and bicycles, along with a few old cars that overflow an aging, double-deck car transporter.

However, All Bikes is not a final resting place. Everything is for sale. Everything, that is, except for bicycles, motorcycles, cars, and trucks built in 1954.

Ron Adler was born in 1954. His personal passion is collecting vehicles from that year. His prized possession is a 1954 Adler, a German motorcycle that was a "basket case when I got it, a rust bucket," he said.

But over the course of four years, Adler lovingly restored the 200cc bike. Now, he's found another—this one a 250—and he has begun its restoration process.

These art deco bikes are 1964 German DKWs. Adler purchased this pair from Parker, Arizona, and actually rode one back to Rye, a distance of about 175 miles.
Larry Edsall

Born in 1954, Adler has a penchant for collecting cars and motorcycles manufactured during that year. Here a car hauler loaded down with 1954 cars and trucks towers over their two-wheeled companions. *Larry Edsall*

Adler is German for "eagle." In 1880, Heinrich Kleyer of Frankfurt-am-Main began importing bicycles from the United States, bicycles he sold as Herolds. By 1885, he was manufacturing bicycles, and soon typewriters as well. He supplied wire wheels to Carl Benz and Gottlieb Daimler for their earliest automobiles. Before long, Kleyer was producing cars. By 1928, only Opel and BMW were building more cars in Germany than Adler.

Adler's last new car model was produced in 1937. The company did not resume automobile production after World War II. Its dealer network was incorporated into Volkswagen's, and Adler's motorcycle designs were given to BSA in Great Britain as part of the war reparations, though Adler continued to build its own line of motorcycles until 1957. It also continued to produce office equipment until 1957, when it was folded into Grundig, which later became part of Olivetti.

Not long before the company that shares his name ceased motorcycle production, Ron Adler was born in Los Angeles and later lived in Las Vegas, where his father taught culinary arts at a vocational high school. When Ron Adler was 19, he moved to Tacoma, Washington, to help an older brother who was going through a divorce.

Adler opened a bicycle-repair shop in Washington. Friends soon asked him to work not only on their human-powered two-wheelers but on their motorized ones as well. Adler started working on motorcycles not long after he started modifying bicycles. He got his first motorcycle, a 1957 Mustang, when he was 14 years old. "It looked like a little Harley," Adler remembered. He bought the Mustang with money he earned on his paper route.

160

While still in high school, he started working in automotive body shops, learning, he said, "from the old guys." Perhaps he did not learn quite quickly enough. Asked if he's ever sold anything he now regrets, he thinks all the way back to a 1957 Studebaker Silver Hawk he bought while in high school and to a 1952 Stude he acquired for spare parts. Adler destroyed the Silver Hawk's engine, and his father reacted unhappily when he discovered the oily mess in the driveway. "He made me sell both cars," Adler said, recalling that he ended up scrapping the vehicles for $35 each.

Adler still likes the old ways he learned from the old guys. He said the closest he's gotten to a computer is his Etch A Sketch. He doesn't work on modern machines with their computer controls but sends those potential customers to shops with the right equipment. Meanwhile, he gets a lot of referral work from motorcycle shops that don't know how or don't want to be bothered dealing with things like carburetors. For example, he's working on a 1970s-vintage Indiana moped for a customer who came to him because a motorcycle shop told her parts weren't available. But Adler either has them or has found them.

Adler's bike shop in Washington grew into a succession of dealerships, at first selling Triumph and BSA motorcycles, and later various Japanese brands. Then, in the mid-1980s, he traveled to Arizona to help build a house for his sister in Strawberry, a village northwest of Payson. He fell in love with the area and in 1988 bought property beside the highway in Rye.

Way back then, his collection of bikes, motorcycles, and cars filled eight semi trailers. Through the years, Adler has bought out the inventory of nearly two dozen bicycle or motorcycle shops that were going out of business. He goes to swap meets, including those at Sturgis and at Bike Week in Daytona, and to motorcycle auctions. He buys, sells, trades, and sometimes arrives at All Bikes to find bikes that have been left at his gate by people who figure their old bicycle or motorcycle will find a good home among so many others.

And they do. Adler has taught his son, Jason; his only full-time employee, Teresa Barnes (she started by answering the telephone but pestered Adler to the point she's become the mechanic-on-duty); and a succession of part-timers who help him with bicycle and motorcycle repairs and restorations. He also does automotive work and has found a niche of sorts creating "rat rods," very drivable vehicles that marry modified and customized old car bodies to Chevy S-10 or Ford Ranger frames with disc brakes and air conditioning. He also works with local schools to teach mechanical skills to students, including those with physical and mental disabilities.

While he can teach them how to do repairs and restorations, he has yet to find a way to share his uncanny ability to know where pretty much every bike and motorcycle and every part is located around the All Bikes grounds.

To most people, All Bikes may look like little more than rows and rows of bicycles, motorcycles, and parts. But Adler knows where everything is, to the point that he'll send someone down one of the narrow paths between the rows, shouting to them to go another three or four feet, then stop, turn to right or left, look down, and sure enough, they'll be looking right at the bike or part they need.

All Bikes is open Wednesday through Sunday, from 9 a.m. to 5 p.m., unless the weather's bad. Since nearly all the work is done outdoors, or on an open porch, the place is closed when it rains.

Adler's customers come from all around the nation and the world. He gets a lot of tourists, including Europeans. Many are on their way to the Grand Canyon or Four Corners. Some are just curious. Some are more serious. For example, a German bike dealer had Adler restore and export four Honda Mini Trails, which, it turns out, fit nicely on a shipping pallet.

Some people stumble upon the place as they make their way from Phoenix to Arizona's cooler high country. Many stop in out of curiosity but end up telling a friend who ends up becoming a customer.

Some have been customers for decades. For example, a man from Wisconsin had Adler build a chopper-style bicycle for his son. Now, some 30 years later, he has him doing another one, this time for his son's son.

Adler also becomes a customer by word of mouth. For example, someone told him about a barn that was going to be torn down, but first the owner had to get rid of the vehicles stored inside. Adler bought them.

He has sold parts to the crew that restores Jay Leno's vehicles. Steve McQueen bought an Indian Scout from Adler more than 30 years ago and McQueen's brother has continued to be a customer.

Adler also has bought bikes with celebrity. He has the trike used on *The Munsters* and the 125 Honda that Dick Van Dyke rode through an episode of *The Dick Van Dyke Show* until Mary Tyler "Oooooh Rob!" Manning thought it was too dangerous. Adler admits, however, that the motorcycle's title papers, with Van Dyke's name, are probably worth more than the bike itself.

Adler's oldest vehicles are two wooden-wheeled bicycles that date to the 1800s. One is a Jill. The other was brought to him by a 93-year-old woman who said she'd bought the bike 43 years earlier at a yard sale, hauled it through three moves, and finally wanted its long-broken wheel repaired. Adler loved the bike, and when he learned the woman had no heirs, he convinced her to sell it to him but made sure she retained "visitation rights."

Adler's oldest powered bike is a 1915 Matchless motorcycle.

"What year were you born?" is the way Adler greets many visitors, who immediately are pointed toward bikes from their birth year.

Birth-year vehicles are Adler's passion, though he also pursues vehicles from their last year in production and has a fondness for quirky ultra-compact micro cars.

In addition to his namesake motorcycles, he has other 1954-model two-wheelers, including a 1954 Harley-Davidson Panhead he's restoring, as well as more than a dozen 1954 cars and trucks—from a Studebaker wagon to a Ford pickup, from a pair of Chevrolet sedan deliveries to a Ford Crestline Victoria, and from a Mercury cab-over-engine truck to a Super White Power bus. He's also collecting vintage 1954 Arizona license plates, which the state allows to be used on 1954 models.

He got a lead on another 1954 Stude on New Year's Day 2009 when a husband and wife from the Phoenix area stopped at All Bikes to see if Adler might have a driver's-side door for a 1958 Chevrolet Impala. Adler didn't, but he had a friend who restored a pair of 1958 Impalas and might know of a source for such a door. Adler and the visitor talked about cars they'd owned, sold, and still own. The visitor had more than a dozen and needed to get rid of a few, including a 1954 Studebaker sedan. Phone numbers were exchanged.

While he covets 1954s, Ron Adler's wish list is topped by the car that bears his family's name. He thought he had a deal to trade an Indian motorcycle for a 1934 suicide-door, front-wheel-drive Adler, only to learn the car's owner sold it to someone else before their trade could be consummated. Adler's still looking.

Horse Trading

When a friend of Al Kelly's realized he liked old motorcycles, she piped up. "You know, my father-in-law has an old Harley," she said. "It hasn't moved from the barn since the 1960s."

"What's he doing with it?" he asked.

"Oh, he never sells anything," she said.

Kelly had heard those words before in his quest for old motorcycles, so a week later he went to the gas station owned by the woman's father-in-law. It was a Flying A station, and the gentleman, Bob, was a nice man in his 60s.

Kelly said he had heard from Bob's daughter-in-law that he owned an old motorcycle.

"Yeah, I still have my old 1949 Harley Hydraglide," said Bob.

Bob's motorcycle was originally a police bike. His brother-in-law bought the bike at a police auction, and then Bob bought it from him. Bob was a part of a group of guys who rode their Harleys in the 1950s and 1960s. As the guys aged, most them parked or sold the bikes. Bob's was stored in the rear of his huge Flying A station.

The bike was sitting in the rear of a large service center and was covered with a blanket. The bike probably hadn't been moved in 20 years.

Kelly asked Bob if he would consider selling it.

"Ah, shit, nobody has ever made me a good offer on it," said Bob. "I've been offered $2,000 for it, but it's got to be worth more."

Kelly looked at the bike, and it was in nice shape. Kelly said, "I'm interested in it. I'd say it's worth between $6,000 and $8,000. I'll pay you a fair dollar for it."

Bob said that price was fair, but that because he and his wife had enjoyed so many good times on the bike, it would be hard for him to sell it. "I was hoping to start enjoying it again and maybe take my grandchildren for rides on it up at our lake house," said Bob.

Grandchildren? Kelly's brain was working overtime. "How many grandchildren to you have, Bob?"

Bob told him four.

Kelly said, "I'll be right back."

A little while later, Kelly came cruising back to Bob's Flying A station in a 1951 Chevy Deluxe Coupe that he owned.

The Chevy is a barn find as well. Kelly's brother Ken's next-door neighbor was a landscaper who had mowed an elderly woman's yard for years. Once, he ran out of gas for his mower and asked the woman if she had any gas he could borrow. She said he could find some in the barn. When he went into the barn, he found a 1951 Chevy under a pile of army blankets. The car's last inspection sticker was from 1963.

Ken (left) and Al Kelly proudly show off their new acquisition, a 1949 Harley-Davidson Hydraglide. Al traded a 1951 Chevy Deluxe Coupe that he had just restored plus $2,500 for the bike that had been stored in the rear of a New Jersey gas station for 30 years. *Kelly family collection*

"The car was really clean and only had somewhere around 35,000 and 40,000 miles on the odometer," said Kelly. The landscaper eventually sold the car to Kelly. "I bought it immediately. It was forest green in color and had a beautiful interior."

"Wow, look at that beauty," said Bob.

"Listen, Bob, when you mentioned the lake house and the grandchildren, I thought of this car," said Kelly. "You can put all your grandchildren in this car and take them all to the lake at the same time. This way you don't need to just take one at a time.

"I'll tell you what, Bob. I'll trade you this coupe plus $2,500 for your Harley."

Bob thought about it. He considered the good times on the Harley but also his advancing age and his desire to spend more time with his grandchildren.

"Other people had seen my bike and tried to buy it," said Bob, "but they all wanted a bargain.

"Yours is the first fair offer I've received for the old bike. Let's trade."

Bob wound up with a cool old car to ride his grandchildren around in and Kelly got a special Harley-Davidson by offering a fair, realistic deal.

Interestingly, now, about 15 years after the trade, Bob still owns the Chevy and Kelly still owns the Harley. And they are both still happy.

The Time Machine

Dale Seymour has been a bike guy for almost five decades. The Trumbull, Connecticut, resident had a 1947 Indian while he was a senior in high school. He developed a real appreciation for the brand, but the responsibilities of life and a career in law enforcement made motorcycles a part of Seymour's past. At least for a while.

Indian motorcycles were built in Springfield, Massachusetts, not far from Seymour's residence in Suffield, Connecticut.

"I was out of it for a while," he said, "and decided I needed an old Indian again.

"I found a guy who was selling [one]. I met him through his father, Leon Gresky, who interestingly had been an Indian dealer in Enfield, Connecticut,

Dale Seymour had been a motorcycle collector and Indian enthusiast for many years but stumbled across this Indian totally by accident. A carpenter working for Seymour mentioned that he had an Indian at home in his garage. *Dale Seymour collection*

The bike was purchased by carpenter Bryan Barnes in 1955, who rode it until 1963 when the registration sticker on this plate expired. The Indian sat in this spot from then until 1984. *Dale Seymour collection*

just nine miles from the factory. He was a dealer until 1953, when production of the traditional Indian ended."

Seymour bought the bike in the early 1970s from Gresky's son, J. R. He fixed it up but called Leon Gresky near the end of the restoration to inform him that the motorcycle he purchased didn't include a speedometer, and if he knew of any around, he'd appreciate it. Well, former dealer Gresky just happened to have a new-old-stock speedo—still in the box and wrapped in tissue paper—that he gladly sold to Seymour for just $5.

He restored the bike and proudly mounted one of Connecticut's first motorcycle vanity plates on the rear. The plate read, "Chief."

Seymour had the Indian motorcycle bug bad. Many years ago, as a Hartford, Connecticut, police officer in the early 1970s, he pulled over an Indian rider by the name of Phil Maciag.

"Officer, what was I doing wrong?" Maciag asked nervously.

Seymour told him he had done nothing wrong, but he only pulled him over to tell him about the Indian Welcome Home Rally that was scheduled for the upcoming July weekend in Springfield, Massachusetts. Seymour was on the committee of that event. Maciag left with a smile on his face and he and Seymour became friends.

Eventually Seymour bought another Indian but soon decided it was time to let someone else enjoy them. One January he loaded the two of them onto an open trailer and dragged them down to Atlantic City, New Jersey, for the annual classic car auction and sale. Seymour purchased a booth space, then sat back and waited to see if any of the antique car enthusiasts had interest in buying his two-wheeled classics.

Before he left for Atlantic City, he had a carpenter, Bryon Barnes, come over to his house to make some small repairs. Seymour soon discovered Barnes' nickname was "Biker." Biker Barnes inquired about the two Indians on the trailer. "Oh, I'm bringing them to Atlantic City to sell them," Seymour explained.

"I have an old Indian at home," said Barnes.

"Great. If I don't sell my bikes, maybe we can go riding in the spring," said Seymour.

"Well, I don't ride anymore," said Barnes. "But maybe you'd like to come over and see it sometime. I keep it in the barn behind my house."

Seymour (left) and longtime owner Bryan Barnes with the bike after it was removed from the Connecticut barn. After this photo was taken, Seymour loaded it on a trailer and brought it to a coin-operated car wash, where he sprayed away 25 years worth of grime. *Dale Seymour collection*

The bike had only been ridden 13,980 miles when Seymour purchased it in 1984. He continues to ride the unrestored bike today, most recently to the Fairfield County Concours in Connecticut. *Dale Seymour collection*

When Seymour visited Barnes' barn in the late 1970s, it was like traveling back in time. The Indian had been parked in that spot since 1963. Barnes' helmet and goggles were still sitting on the seat, and the 1957 license plate with the 1963 registration sticker was still in place. The odometer listed only 13,980 miles.

Barnes purchased the Indian in 1955 from Freddy Marsh, who was born in 1900 and lived to be 102 or 103 years old, according to Seymour. Marsh was once an Indian factory team racer and reputed to be the oldest motorcycle dealer in the world.

"At the time, I was not very interested in buying another motorcycle," said Seymour. "But over time, the more I thought about it, I thought it would be fun to own."

Barnes was not interested in selling.

"And don't keep bugging me," Barnes told Seymour, "or else I'll never sell it to you."

This was clearly frustrating, but Seymour decided to use the tried-and-true method of barn-finding stewardship: become friends with the owner. As anyone in a professional sales career knows, you must sell yourself before you can make the sale; everyone wants to do business with a friend.

"I'd stop by his house once in a while and visit him," said Seymour. "But I'd never mention the bike. Eventually, in 2004, Barnes called and said, 'OK, I'm ready to sell you the Indian.'"

Barnes told Seymour how much money he wanted for the bike, and Seymour thought it was too high. But after some friendly negotiation, Seymour agreed to a price that both considered market value. He was pleased.

Seymour and his friend Ron Cross went to pick up his new purchase. "Ron is an old car and bike enthusiast and owned a trailer," he said. "He used pliers to get the caps off the tire valve stems. And believe it or not, the original tires held air!"

Because the barn was so cramped, they removed the bike's saddlebags and windshield in order to make it easier to remove.

"We strapped it onto the trailer and went directly to a self-service car wash," said Seymour. "We probably spent $5 just washing off the years of accumulated dirt, dust, and sawdust.

"From a distance, suddenly it looked great, but up close you could see lots of chips in the paint."

Seymour decided to bring the Indian to Phil Maciag's motorcycle shop (the guy he had stopped with his patrol car many years ago). "I told him I didn't want to restore the bike but just to leave it as-is from the exterior," said Seymour. "He probably had the bike for one year. Having a restored bike was not of interest to me. There are lots of restored bikes around, but there aren't many unrestored bikes around."

Maciag was the right guy for the job. He owns a motorcycle shop that specializes in British, Japanese, Harley-Davidson, and Indian motorcycles, and according to Seymour, has enough Indian parts around his shop to construct several bikes. Maciag started performing motorcycle tune-ups and repairs for his friends behind his house when he was in college. Eventually he opened a shop.

"At the time, you could buy old bikes and parts very cheaply, so Phil bought lots of them and kept them," said Seymour.

Maciag flushed and cleaned the gas tanks and replaced the pistons, rings, valve guides, valves, wiring harness, coil, plugs, plug wires, cap rotor, battery, chain, sprockets, horn, and tires.

Corrosion in the gas tanks has continued to plague Seymour several years into his ownership. In the fall of 2008, he proudly rode his Indian to the Fairfield County Concours d'Elegance in Westport, Connecticut, and entered it in the preservation class. At the conclusion of the show, the bike failed to start because of the fuel tank issue and was hauled home in the back of Seymour's son-in-law's pickup truck.

He promises to continue riding the Indian when the gas tank issue is solved by Maciag, but he also promises to never make the bike look better than it does now.

CHAPTER FIVE

Speed Freaks

The Crocker Trio

G lenn Bator has been in the motorcycle industry for many years. He was "discovered" by the late Otis Chandler, who found that the home contractor was restoring vintage bikes to a very high standard.

Starting off as a part-timer with Chandler's museum, Bator eventually became the general manager and head restorer who purchased about 80 percent of the bikes for Otis and restored seven or eight himself.

"I was living in Palm Springs when I met Otis," said Bator, 51, of Ojai, California. "I was selling a 1957 Sportster because of a divorce and had consigned it through the Rick Cole Auction. Before the auction, I was down on the display floor wiping down the bike and Mr. Chandler came up to me and introduced himself. It didn't make any difference to me, because I had never heard of him before.

"He said, 'I'm going to buy your Harley tomorrow in the auction.' I thought that was kind of crazy, because anyone could buy it."

Chandler wound up buying the bike just as he was getting into his motorcycle phase.

"He went through phases," said Bator. "He was into the classic cars, then muscle cars, and then bikes. Mine was one of the first bikes he bought.

"He liked my work, so he asked if I would consider doing some restorations for him on the side. Eventually they hired me in-house and I was involved in all restorations."

Bator tells the story of the restoration of a 1934 Packard Bohman & Schwartz town car that had been owned by singer Eddie Cantor. Bator and his wife were still assembling it as it was being loaded onto the trailer en route to Pebble Beach.

"We won, but nobody knows that the door handles weren't bolted on and were falling off as the car was approaching the awards stage," he recalled.

Since leaving Chandler's museum, Bator has been brokering rare motorcycles to buyers around the world. Because of his contacts, he often hears of bikes before they are advertised.

Two Crockers

Finding one Crocker motorcycle in your life is a big deal. Finding two is amazing, but finding two with consecutive serial numbers is nearly unbelievable. Bator did just that, and he credits his finds to luck and good timing.

"Al Crocker used to work for the Indian Motorcycle Company in Springfield, Massachusetts, in charge of design and production of some of Indian's high-performance bikes in the 1920s and 1930s," said Bator. "After a few years, he spun off from Indian, moved to California, and became one of the only motorcycle manufacturers to come out of Los Angeles."

Crocker produced about 64 of the handmade V-Twin bikes, making them among the rarest and most desirable collector bikes ever built. Bator caught wind of one in Italy that was for sale, but it was too expensive.

"At $200,000, it was priced out of the market," he said. "But a year went by, and suddenly with the price of rare bikes going through the roof, the price began to sound more reasonable.

"I have a friend in Italy, Alessandro Altinere, who is also in the vintage motorcycle business, and we communicate back and forth. When you couldn't buy a Crocker for less than $250,000, I told him to please help me buy the bike."

Bator received photographs and decided the bike was worth flying to Italy to buy, so he flew to Rome and drove to Milan.

"This was all kind of stealthy, because the man who owned the bike was a diplomat and somewhat secretive," he said. "I couldn't just go over there, hand him a check, and take the bike; it had to go through channels.

"I met a gentleman who actually restored the bike, and his wife would act as my interpreter. We turned down this little alley, which was like a foyer, that was completely surrounded by garage doors. This one big bodyguard-type guy rolled the bike out. I saw the quality of the restoration and knew I was going to buy it.

"Then the bodyguard's phone rings and he hands it to me. It's the diplomat who was calling in from Switzerland. We spoke about the bike for a few minutes, but there was no negotiation. I knew if I offered him $1 less, it would have been an insult, and the sale would have been called off."

Bator agreed to the amount of money, but it had to be paid to a Swiss bank so the money would be "buried," as Bator recalled.

Bator's friend Alessandro helped him with the crating and shipping of the Crocker to Bator in California.

"As soon as I received that bike at home and was starting to get the word out that it was available, I received a phone call while I was driving up to the Half Moon Bay motorcycle show," said Bator. "The caller said he was a meter reader in Colorado and read the meter for an old boy who [now] has become a friend of mine. He had four motorcycles in a barn he wanted to sell.

Collector Glenn Bator received a call from a utility-meter reader from Colorado who told him about several old motorcycles in the barn of an elderly gentleman along his route. What got Bator's attention was when the man mentioned the brand Crocker. *Glenn Bator*

"So I asked him what they were. He said, 'Well he has a 1950-something Ariel Square Four, another Ariel in pieces, and a Harley-Davidson XA military bike' (which was a knock-off of a BMW).

"So far the bikes he has told me about are interesting but nothing to jump through hoops about. Then he says, 'And a Crocker.'"

That got Bator's attention and he promised to call him back after the weekend.

When he returned home Monday, he called the guy and asked him to send pictures right away. When they arrived, they were low-quality snapshots.

"He hadn't moved anything in the barn to get a better image," said Bator. "It was just snap, snap, snap.

"But I could tell that the Crocker engine was mounted in a British frame, which turned out to be a Triumph military chassis. And it had an Ariel Square Four gas tank attached.

"I'm thinking, 'Man, this bike is cool. I really like it.'"

Al Crocker sold complete motorcycles, but he also sold engines, which could be mounted into nearly any frame, mostly for racing purposes, so the fact that the engine was not in a Crocker frame didn't upset Bator.

None of the photographs showed the engine serial numbers clearly, so another batch arrived the next day.

Crocker numbered his engines first by the year, 39-, then by the engine size in cubic inches, 61-, followed by the production number, 106, so the serial number was 39-61-106.

"That was a familiar number, but I couldn't remember where I had seen it before," he said. Then he went into his garage and looked at the Crocker he had purchased from Italy and the engine numbers read: 39-61-107.

"Unbelievable. Obviously this was meant to be."

He called the meter reader in Colorado and asked how much the elderly gentleman was asking for the four bikes. He gave Bator a price, and there was no bickering.

"OK, you've got a deal, and I'll give you a 10 percent finder's fee on top of the price," said Bator.

"Now, I know anytime you do a deal like this over the phone, it's not secure until money changes hands. Anything can happen.

"The meter reader told the old man about the deal, and the price went up another $15,000, which was not too surprising, considering how quickly I agreed to the first price.

"I said, OK, I'll buy them, but he has to handle the sale because I'm loading up my trailer and leaving for Colorado at the crack of dawn, so I'll be there ASAP."

Bator called a friend and the two drove all night long, arriving at the man's doorstep in a record 22 hours. Bator bragged that he only received one speeding ticket on the drive.

When they arrived at the man's house, they walked out back to a barn where the motorcycles were stored. He discovered that the meter reader was also receiving a BMW motorcycle from the old gentleman, so in addition to Bator's 10 percent commission, his meter-reader's salary was being supplemented quite a bit.

"You could tell this old guy had lived there for quite a while," said Bator. "Beside the barn he had a garage and a trailer where he lived. He also had a big-block Corvette lying in his yard, which I am still trying to buy.

"He was into motorcycles many, many years earlier and told me he had owned other Crockers. He told me he bought this engine, number 106, from California in the 1950s without a frame, so he actually built the bike himself from a single-cylinder Triumph frame.

"This engine was listed in the Crocker Registry as 'unknown,' so I really unearthed a desirable piece of history."

Bator purchased the bike and brought it home. He rode both of them and shot photos of the two consecutively numbered bikes next to one another. But even though he tried, he couldn't sell them as a pair.

Bator couldn't believe his good luck when he discovered that the Crocker engine number of the Colorado bike—39-61-106—was only one digit off from the Crocker he had recently purchased from Italy, 39-61-107. *Glenn Bator*

The beautiful black Crocker from Italy was sold to the gentleman who owns the Solvang Motorcycle Museum in Solvang, California, and the barn-find Crocker was sold to a man from Kansas.

The Crocker in the Bathroom

Bator's next Crocker story concerns a racing Crocker that had been owned by Sam Parriot and raced on the Muroc Dry Lakes in the 1920s, 1930s, and 1940s.

"Al Crocker and Sam Parriot were friends, and Sam would race Al's single-cylinder bikes," said Bator. "Usually the twins were for street use and either could be ordered as engines alone to be installed in midget racers or whatever.

"So I found a complete Crocker racing bike with Sam Parriot history."

Bator would go to the Hollywood shop of Bud Ekins once in a while to visit the dynamic man. His shop was always in shambles, but his multifaceted career was stellar.

"Bud was a man's man," said Bator. "He was a hard drinker, a hard smoker, and a hard liver. But if there was someone in the world you wanted to be like, it was Bud.

This is the son of the man who shoehorned the huge V-Twin Crocker No. 106 motor into the small World War II-era Triumph frame, which had been designed for a single-cylinder motor. When Bator purchased the bike, it had not been moved in at least 25 years. *Glenn Bator collection*

Two Crockers that likely hadn't seen each other since they were manufactured in Los Angeles nearly 70 years earlier. Sadly, the bikes were purchased by two different buyers, so who knows when they will meet again. *Glenn Bator*

"Bud was Steve McQueen's stunt double in many movies, including many of the driving scenes in *Bullet* and the motorcycle jump scene from *The Great Escape*. He was ridden hard and put away wet, but he lived in an era of McQueen, Garner, Von Dutch, and when he wasn't involved in movie production, he was messing around with old bikes."

Ekins was an ex-factory rider for Triumph and won the Catalina Grand Prix motorcycle race. He was also an avid collector of vintage bikes who worked out of a small, cramped shop with paper over the windows so pedestrians couldn't see what was going on inside.

"There was just this old Budweiser Beer sign out front that said 'Bud,'" said Bator. "Inside he had old cars and bikes. In the early years, Bud had the best collection of vintage bikes, bar none. He did some restorations, but many of them just sat in racks.

"You'd go to his shop and there would be crap everywhere. Once I was wandering around looking at old bikes and looked into an old bathroom in the back of the shop that had been used as a storage closet. It was basically a junk room, and on the floor I noticed an unusual chassis.

"I asked Bud, 'Is that a Crocker single frame?' and he said, 'That's not just any Crocker, that's Sam Parriot's Crocker.'"

Ekins went on to explain that Parriot raced Crockers on the dry lakes and was a friend of Al Crocker. The bike in the bathroom was Parriot's speedway bike.

"The last time he raced it, the engine locked and he flew through the time traps at more than 100 miles per hour," Ekins said. His body was gliding over the dry lake and the bike was bouncing topsy-turvy on the ground. It was a famous newspaper photo in the day.

"I asked Bud what the story with the Crocker was, and he said that it had been sitting there for well over 10 years. It had been dropped off by Sam's son, Buddy, and left here for him to fix up because of the crash damage decades earlier. He straightened and repainted the frame but hadn't touched the rest.

"I asked if he minded if I contacted the Parriot family, and he said, 'Go ahead.'"

Bator found out that Buddy Parriot was also dead, so he was left to deal with the grandchildren.

"I started sleuthing around and found Sam's heirs," he said. "It turns out that Sam once owned much of California's City of Industry. He also used to race Kurtis race cars on quarter-mile ovals and held the very first license ever issued by the NHRA.

"I was able to appease the dozen or so Parriot grandchildren and bought the bike. I had to give each many thousands of dollars, but they were happy."

Bator was surprised that none of the grandchildren had the least bit of interest in their grandfather's fascinating history. One of them even gave Bator a scrapbook with many of their grandfather's newspaper clippings inside.

Bator took the frame that Ekins had repaired and resurrected the race Crocker.

"It was definitely the rarest Crocker single you could own," he said. "This was 15 years ago, and when I sold it, I got $50,000. Today you couldn't touch it for $150,000."

The Hillclimber Chronicles

A t what point does passion become obsession? When does a small collection of interesting artifacts take over a life and become the reason to live?

Dale Walksler has struggled with this issue for 40 years, since he innocently purchased his first Harley-Davidson at age 15. Since then, motorcycles have become woven into every fiber of his life.

Walksler currently owns about 300 motorcycles, nearly every one of them with a unique story of discovery. His collection is housed in the Wheels Through Time Museum in Maggie Valley, North Carolina, but which may be moved to a new home in Arizona by the time you read this.

We will list several of Walksler's more interesting discoveries over the next few pages, but if you need to know more about his collection, please go to his website, www.wheelsthroughtime.com.

A Career in the Making

At age 15, Dale Walksler competed on his high school wrestling team and liked hot rods, but motorcycles attracted most of his attention.

"A high school wrestling buddy of mine worked at Renfrow Tires where I lived near Mount Vernon, Illinois," said the 55-year-old. "Behind the tire store was an old building and a house. I looked inside the building and remember seeing an old Harley in there, and there was an old Harley three-wheeler sitting in the backyard."

The young man knocked on the door of the adjacent house and asked if the motorcycle in the building was for sale. The owner said it was and a deal was agreed upon for $250. Walksler was now a motorcycle owner. He wheeled his new purchase—a 1952 Panhead—over to the tire store and began fiddling with it.

"We got it started and I rode it home," he said. "I immediately decided to fashion this bike into some kind of cool custom, not a chopper. I pulled off a lot of the stock components and put a springer front end on it."

One of Walksler's other wrestling buddies bought a Harley of his own: a Flathead 80. It broke almost immediately, so in frustration, he sold it to Walksler for $90.

"Now I owned my bike, which was disassembled, and this other bike," he said. "I was approached by a guy who needed a ratchet-top, which is located on the top of the transmission, so I sold the part off the $90 bike for $125.

"And I said to myself, 'This is what I want to do for the rest of my life!'"

Eighteen months later, he went back to the house behind Renfrow Tire and purchased the trike that was still sitting in the weeds for $125. The three-wheeler was a rare Police Servi-Car. Today, nearly 40 years later, he still owns it. "I have it out in the trailer," he said. "I made a chopper out of it."

The Rare DAH Hillclimber Number 1

In 1971, Walksler was a student at Western Illinois University. When he wasn't hitting the books, he was out scouting for old motorcycles and motorcycle parts.

"I had a conversation with someone in Macomb, where I was going to school," he said. "This guy said if I go down the blacktop road for 7 or so miles, that's where John Alexander lives. Alexander had a Harley shop that burned down in the 1960s, so I was told he stuffed the contents of his dealership into his barn."

So Walksler jumped on his motorcycle—a Honda 90—and cruised down the blacktop road for 7 miles. He came upon a farm where an older guy was raking leaves. Walksler, who had hair down to his shoulders as so many students did at the time, climbed off his bike and walked up to the gentleman.

"I'm looking for the guy with the old motorcycle parts," said Walksler.

"That would be me," the man said. This was John Alexander.

Alexander looked Walksler over skeptically. "He asked a number of questions before he invited me into the barn," said Walksler.

Once inside, Walksler realized this was like Disneyland for a motorcycle enthusiast. Motorcycle parts were strewn about, having been placed there 12 to 13 years earlier. Some of the items had been burned, but most were in pretty decent condition.

Walksler was able to purchase the contents of the barn for $500, which he borrowed from his dad. The purchase included a number of parts that he could not identify.

"Some unusual gas tanks had some fire damage on them, but I could still read the Harley-Davidson name very legibly," he said. "There were also a number of unusual handlebars among the parts.

At the time, no Harley-Davidson history books existed that could help Walksler identify the unique parts, so he just loaded them into a tractor-trailer truck and transported his newly acquired stash to Chicago.

"During my summer break from college, I ran a little bike shop called Hog Parts," said Walksler. "I sold used motorcycle parts and fixed some bikes, but I also drank beer and chased girls.

"Within the following year or two, a terrific book by Maurice Hendy was published. . . . While leafing through that book, Voila!, I discovered the handlebar and the gas tank that I purchased from Mr. Alexander's dealership inventory. They both had the DAH designation, which meant they had been built for one of only 20 factory hillclimb racers. How they ever made their way to a small Harley shop in Macomb, Illinois, nobody will ever know."

In 1975, Walksler was restoring an old Daytona racing bike and needed some information. He sourced a fellow from Long Island named Gene Baron.

"He shared with me information I needed for the bike I was building and he told me what he was working on," said Walksler. "He said he needed old hillclimber handlebars like the ones I owned.

"Knowing I would probably never find a DAH racer, I traded the handlebars for a particularly rare cast-aluminum oil tank I needed."

Fast forward to 1992. Walksler had now been a Harley-Davidson dealer for 14 years and had already restored several dozen old motorcycles (and through all these years, bikes, and parts, he still owned the DAH gas tank). Because the bikes that this tank fits are so rare, he realized that it was unlikely he would ever own one of these racers.

"One day I received a call from a friend, Steve Hunzinger, who is one of the premier motorcycle restorers in California," said Walksler. "He was actually doing some restorations for me at the time. Steve told me about a friend of his who had a DAH 750 that was totally disassembled. He told me his friend was getting older and he wanted to sell it."

The next time Walksler went out to California, he hunted down the old man who owned the DAH and examined the parts. There was something familiar about his bike's handlebars.

"I recalled in the hard drive of my life when I had that small bike shop near Chicago," he said. "The business was run out of this crappy old house I owned and I knew when I sold it the building would be demolished. I was on the second floor, which was strewn with boxes and parts, and I remember picking up those old DAH handlebars and punching holes into the plaster walls with the open end. Every time I hit the wall, I was packing plaster into the handlebars.

"When I picked up the handlebars almost 20 years afterwards, I looked in the end and they were packed with plaster! They were my old parts!"

Walksler purchased the basket-case DAH and contracted with his friend Hunsinger to do a complete restoration on serial number 30 DAH 510.

The Rare DAH Hillclimber Number 2

Within 90 days of his purchase of his rare DAH racer, Walksler received a call from an old associate who lived in California, Gary Copeland. He called Walksler to see if he knew anything about old hillclimbers.

"Yeah, a little, what are you looking at?"

"I know this old lady, and she has a bike called a DAH," said his friend.

"Oh, that's a good one," said Walksler. "Is it for sale?"

"I could probably talk her into selling it," he said.

"Count me in," said Walksler. "How much?"

"Probably $5,000," said the friend.

"Count me in," said Walksler.

Walksler was elated about this hopeful purchase.

A week goes by. Then 10 days.

"I'm on my way to Davenport, Iowa, for the big swap meet," he said. "I'm driving a big truck and Gary calls me up on my bag phone. Remember before cell phones, we used to have those huge telephones in a bag. He says that he's on his way to buy the motorcycle. I said, 'Great! I'm on my way to Davenport. When I get back on Monday, I'll send you the money. But hey, before you hang up, what's the serial number?'

"He says to hang on, because he's driving. A moment later he comes back on the phone and says, '30 DAH 509.' It was then that I realized I had two sequentially numbered hillclimbers."

Walksler sent Gary the money and arranged for the bike's transport to Illinois. When it arrived, it was completely intact and in good condition except for the gas tanks, which had been painted in purple metalflake. That would normally be a problem except that Walksler never throws anything away. Remember those parts he purchased out of John Alexander's barn back in 1971? That original painted gas tank that sat in his parts bin for more than 20 years now sits on DAH 509.

Walksler explains how significant the discovery of the two hillclimbers was: "The factory built 20 750 hillclimbers in 1929 and 1930, during the height of the Great Depression," he said. "These were built for one specific reason: to win on Sunday and sell on Monday. These were development bikes designed to win races and give Harley-Davidson substantial traction in retail sales during a very struggling era."

Walksler explained that races consisted of brands from the Big Three—Harley, Indian, and Excelsior.

DAH 509 was acquired from a woman in Northern California. She was the widow of the man who purchased the Harley in the late 1940s to ride as a "cut down."

"A cut down is not a chopper or a bobber but is an early machine that is cut down to lower it and shortened in order to make it a hot rod motorcycle," said Walksler. "It was the hot ride in the north of Hollister, California, and made famous by a guy named Finigan Spear, who built three or four cut downs.

"The DAH is actually a factory cut down and didn't need further modification. This particular bike was sold by the factory at the conclusion of its racing days to Dudley Perkins, who was the second-oldest Harley dealer in the country. He bought it for $300 and stored it in his basement until this woman's husband bought it.

"Apparently he would zip around town and evade the police and do all the things that hooligans did in those days. When he died, the bike went into storage, and my friend Gary bought it. That's how I got it.

"Going back and looking at what I consider is the rarest type of motorcycle in the world, in my opinion it would be either those built in extremely low quantities for racing or one-of-a-kind prototypes developed by engineers, of which only a small handful survive in the world.

"Getting back to the hillclimbers, it's interesting to note that when Willie G. Davidson [heir to the company's founder] contracted bronze sculptor Jeff Decker to develop the consummate piece of artwork for the lobby of the new museum in

If only this paint could talk! Harley built only 20 of the 750cc hillclimbers between 1929 and 1930—in the midst of the Depression. Walksler purchased this gas tank in 1971 and was finally able to use it 20 years later. *Tom Cotter*

One of two consecutively numbered factory Harley-Davidson hillclimber motorcycles Walksler has on display in his Wheels Through Time Museum. He purchased this one from a widow in Northern California whose husband intended to modify it into a bobber. *Tom Cotter*

Milwaukee, he chose a DAH 750 hillclimber. It is nearly three times the size of the actual model, which Harley does not own an actual version of."

Walksler has the two hillclimbers on display in his museum, one restored and the other left in its as-found condition.

184

The Race Engine in the Trailer House

In 1995 or 1996, Dale Walksler was driving to the West Coast in a truck pulling a trailer loaded with old motorcycles. He stopped in Phoenix to visit his uncle who owned a trapshooting range with a campground. It was an area where people from points north—Montana, Wyoming, the Dakotas—would spend their winters.

When he pulled into the campground, one of the guests took a particular interest in Walksler's motorcycles on the trailer.

"We started to talk and I quickly realized he really knew his motorcycles," said Walksler. "He was from Montana, and somewhere during the conversation, he said, 'I know where one of those Harley-Davidson racing engines are that has three numbers.' I said, 'Very interesting.'"

"He gave me his card with all his contact information, and we decided I'd get hold of him in the spring or summer when he returned back home.

"You know how business cards can somehow get lost in your truck or on your desk? Well, I lost this man's card for two years. When I put my hands on it, I gave him a call. Fortunately, he remembered our conversation of two years earlier."

Walksler asked the man if the engine was still available.

"It's 100 miles away," said the man.

"I'll be glad to pay for your gas and time to check if it's still there," said Walksler.

The man called Walksler several days later and read the engine and casting number, CA9. Walksler realized instantly that the engine was a rare Banjo Twin-Cam two-cylinder racing engine, one of only four in the world. He realized he was on to something really big.

A short history on Harley's twin-cam engine: The company used racing as a test platform for new technology. Between 1914 and 1919, often what appeared on the track one year would be utilized on street bikes the following year. In 1919, Harley developed the twin-cam engine, realizing the design would probably never be used on the road; this design was strictly for racing. The engine was raced in limited numbers from 1919 until 1922, when an industry-wide hiatus on two-cylinder design was put into effect because they were deemed too fast and too dangerous.

The rare engine was owned by Monte Chapburn, and it was for sale. Walksler agreed to buy it and booked a flight to Montana. It was a cold May morning, and Walksler drove his rental car on the interstate into the middle of Montana, then turned onto some country roads.

"Dew was on the ground and the grass was 3 feet tall," he said. "I pulled into a compound type of area with a barn and a house trailer. I knocked on the door, and an old man answered. This was Monte. I peered into the door and saw an interesting sight; the engine was sitting right next to the door, right next to a matted area where apparently Monte and his dog slept to stay warm. The area was completely matted with dog hair. I don't think Monte bathed very often."

It turns out that Monte paid just $4 for the engine back in 1940, knowing it was special. At one point, he was a rider and a collector as well.

Walksler and Monte talked and talked. They went out to the barn to look at other things, but when they talked about the engine, the price went up somewhat. But the deal was sealed and Walksler drove out with the engine.

These were pre-9/11 days, when airlines weren't nearly as strict with carry-on luggage as they are now.

"I covered the engine with burlap and duct taped it to one of those little chrome luggage carts and carried it right onto the airplane!"

Two years after purchasing twin-cam engine number CA9, Walksler met Jim Davis at the Daytona Hall of Fame breakfast. At 101 years old, Davis was a celebrity of celebrities and signing autographs even though he was very old and had poor eyesight.

"I brought a photograph along with me of Jim racing the famous Dodge City Twin-Cam motorcycle," said Walksler. "He signed the photo for me."

Walksler (center) is all smiles as he takes possession of this ultrarare Harley Twin-Cam racing engine. On the left is Monty Chadburn, who bought the engine for $4 in about 1940 and owned it until it was sold to Walksler in 1996. *Dale Walksler collection*

Engine No. CA9 sits in a showcase at Walksler's museum. It had originally been raced by the famous Jim Davis for the Harley factory team. *Tom Cotter*

"I tried to keep the conversation going, so I asked, 'What was your favorite motor?' meaning, in 1950s terminology, 'What was your favorite motorcycle?' He said CA9 and wrote it down on a piece of paper. That's when I discovered that I owned Jim Davis' CA9 racing motor.

"In his long racing career, that's the single engine that stuck out as the best."

The Curious Tale of the Beauty and the Beast

By Ken Gross

As a young motorcycle enthusiast, I'd heard a lot about the Vincent, Britain's quick and cleverly designed post–World War II superbike. I knew the big-for-their-time 1,000cc British-built V-twins came in three basic specifications: the basic Rapide, the wickedly fast 125-mile-per-hour Black Shadow, and the rare, stripped-down racing model, the legendary Black Lightning.

I vowed one day I'd own a Vincent, but by the time I could afford one, prices had gone way, way up. At long last, I was able to buy a 1952 Series C Rapide from a Vincent restorer named Charlie Taylor. Although it wasn't a concours bike, it didn't matter. It ran like Jack the Bear, and I rode it everywhere, thrilling to the distinctive rap of its two-into-one exhaust, marveling at its quick acceleration, and delighting in the recognition accorded me by other riders, even Harley guys. When I was transferred to a job in Sydney, Australia, the Vin went along, and I commuted to work on it on many a sunny day.

When people saw it, they would say, "A Vincent! Is it a Black Shadow?" And I'd have to say "no." Even though I'd fitted the massive 5-inch 150-mile-per-hour speedometer (Vin diehards called it a "clock") from a Shadow, my bike was just an entry-level Vincent.

Returning to the United States, I sold everything in my garage in 1981 to buy a Ferrari 275GTB. I forgot about bikes for a while. Then I read a magazine article about Vincents, and that got me thinking. I called Charlie, who said he'd heard about a 1952 Black Shadow in Texas that had been modified, with many parts drilled out for lightness. It seems this bike was one of two with nearly consecutive serial numbers (8714 and 8716) owned by two brothers, Mal and Jim Thompson, and it had been drag raced for years, then placed in storage. Jim died, and Mal wanted to restore his bike. To afford that, he'd have to sell 8716.

The Shadow (at last, I'd have one!) was in rough shape. We learned it had been stripped of some parts, stolen, presumed lost for a time, and eventually recovered. The no-quibble price was $10,000, and the understanding was that Charlie Taylor would restore it. I didn't hesitate, after I learned the bike's story.

And here it is, as Mal told it to me, and wrote it many years ago in *Texas Iron* magazine:

"It was over 80 degrees and raining. The forecast was for rain all the way home. My brother Jim and I had talked a trucker into letting us ride 'suction' behind his rig so that the rain wouldn't sting our faces so badly. It was already dark as we left the city lights of Fort Worth for our home in San Antonio. We didn't relish this 270-mile trip in the rain, at night, but God, we were happy. We were riding two brand new Vincent Black Shadows. Thanks to our father, William Clifton Thompson, for financing the bank note. Jim had traded in his Ariel Square Four and I my Harley 45 at Gene Fasig's Indian Shop for 'The World's Fastest Standard Motorcycle.' Jim was 23; I was 17." (For the record the receipt from Fasig's shows the original price was $1,334.52, with tax.)

"Now, it's 39 years later," Mal continued. "Mother, father, and Jim are gone. Today as I ride that same bike, rebuilt to its old glory over those same Texas roads, I think about all those years in between. The years of drag racing, the more than 300 trophies we won, and the pact that Jim and I made to store the bikes forever, or until they were worth something (whichever came first).

"I glance down at the speedometer as I crack the throttle and it jumps past 60. Sixty-eight rings a bell in my mind. There used to be a tach there. We had the redline at 6,800 rpm. The tach is gone now. So is the smell of nitro and burning rubber, and the engine drones quietly instead of an ear-splitting staccato from the twin, tuned, 2-inch pipes. We never won any money in those days, just trophies. We did it 'just for the fun of it.' The best time for this bike (on fuel) was 145 miles per hour in 8.5 seconds."

It's obvious that Thompson's Vincent was highly modified for drag racing. Before he restored the bike, it won more than 300 drag racing trophies. *Herb Harris collection*

Catherine Jennifer Anderson, the daughter of Mal's neighbor, posed for a photo on Mal's restored Vincent. *Herb Harris collection*

Mal Thompson always credited his dad for his racing success. His father was born in San Antonio. In 1913, he rode an Excelsior motorcycle from San Antonio to Corpus Christi, Texas, more than 150 miles on dirt trails. As Mal later wrote, "His lifelong friend, Otto Leoloff, was a couple of days in front in a horse-drawn buggy depositing cans of gasoline along the intended route. Dad missed a couple of pickup points and ran out of gas. He tried to borrow some from a local farmer who of course, in those days, had none. He did have some 'white lightning corn squeezings' that he claimed 'really burned' when you put a match to it. Dad figured 'what the heck,' and poured it into the tank. Much to his surprise, the engine fired up, ran cooler, and had much more power. Eureka! The first use of alcohol in an internal combustion engine."

The senior Thompson later worked as pit manager for the Indian Motorcycle Racing Team. Don Johns, Indian's top rider at the time, was a five-time world champion quarter-mile dirt tracker.

"What no one else knew," said Mal, "except Don and Dad, was that while everyone else was about 4:1 [compression ratio] on gasoline, they were at 7:1, burning alcohol."

After service in World War I as a motorcycle courier, the elder Thompson remained overseas. Moving to Newcastle-Upon-Tyne, England, he became the works manager for the NUT Motorcycle Company. An avid sidecar racer, he met Winifred Ann Simeson, a young English lass, who later became his wife.

She was an enthusiastic racing sidehack passenger—possibly one of the first ladies to do so.

After NUT went out of business in 1946, William Thompson moved his family home and set up a British bicycle shop in San Antonio.

"Many Americans didn't like the idea of skinny-tired British bikes back then," Mal recalled. "This was the classic case of being 30 years too early with the perfect idea."

Thompson converted the bike shop into a machine shop and small foundry, where both his sons worked for a time.

In 1955, Mal Thompson fulfilled a childhood fantasy. He became an aviation cadet in the U.S. Air Force. With the help of their very mechanically adept father, Jim's bike, 8714, was stripped down and converted into a full-on Black Lightning. Mal wrote, "Jim was a fairly good mechanic. I was mediocre in this respect, as I was totally involved with fulfilling my dream of becoming a fighter pilot."

Extensively modified, with nearly every external element drilled for lightness, Mal's bike, 8716, became sort of a "Super Shadow." The brothers called Jim's Vincent, the much-modified pseudo Lightning, *The Beast*. And 8716, its virtual twin, was known as *The Beauty*.

Mal and his ex-wife (striking aerodynamic pose) lived in a nudist colony, hence this Vincent beauty shot. *Herb Harris collection*

191

1952 VINCENT "BLACK SHADOW"

PURCHASED NEW BY OWNER, MAL THOMPSON, 5 MAY 1953. CONVERTED TO A NITRO BURNING DRAGSTER IN 1956. RACED FROM 1957 TO 1960. BEST TIME IN THE ¼ MILE WAS 145 MPH IN 8.9 SECONDS. IN STORAGE 1961 TO 1989. RESTORED BY MAL THOMPSON

After he restored his Vincent, Thompson made this sign and displayed it with his bike at vintage bike meets. Few motorcycles have enjoyed a more colorful life than Thompson's Black Shadow. *Herb Harris*

But by 1960, the Thompsons' racing days were "pretty much over. The 'Lightning' was already in storage," Mal said, "as back in 1960, we had chased off all motorcycle drag racing in Texas. We always won. They always lost. It got to where Jim and I had only each other to run against. It wasn't fun anymore. Through the years, Jim turned the engines over at fairly regular intervals to keep the parts oiled. These 'crank-throughs' were usually done after I called him from wherever I was with the Air Force. The first thing we discussed on those calls was always, 'How are the Vincents?' never 'How are you?' or 'How am I?' That came later."

After Jim died, Mal returned to settle his brother's estate. Sadly, the unthinkable had occurred.

"Imagine my horror and disbelief," he later wrote, "when I found out that the two bikes, along with a Rapide that we had acquired from Bobby Harper, were not in storage as we had thought. They had been stolen! A couple of guys had been stripping parts [off them], and then they took the whole bikes. With the help of a lot of people, the bikes were recovered.

"I won't go into the details," Mal wrote, "except to express my heartfelt thanks. First to my wife, Jody, for buying a *TV Guide* featuring a picture of Jay Leno with his arm draped around the rear wheel of a Shadow (I dropped Jay a line telling him of the theft); second to Jay for calling me and giving me some names and phone numbers of people he thought could help find the bikes; to Dave Rosenfield (one of the names Jay gave me for suggesting writing to *MPH* [the Vincent Owners' Club] magazine; to the editor, John Webber, for printing the story; to the reader in Houston who called me and told me where they were; and finally to Union Cycle Salvage (in Houston) who, when they found out that the bikes were in fact stolen, accepted the loss and turned them over without a squabble.

"I was torn between my pact with Jim never to sell them—a pact which he lived up to until the day he died, even though he needed the money—and my need to accomplish something with what I had left. I decided," Mal continued, "that the most logical thing to do, considering my limited finances, was to sell Jim's bike, which was still in one piece, [along with] the leftover parts from Bobby Harper's bike, a pair of Rapide cases and fork blades that Jim had picked up through the years, and restore my bike 'the Lightning,' to its original Shadow configuration."

And then those old racing habits surfaced.

"Well, not exactly original," Mal wrote. "I figure that if there is a life in the hereafter, Dad will be watching! So this one's for you, Dad. I had my engine mechanic, Mike Parti, go with your Lightning cams (still good), Ian Hamilton's pistons (shimmed down to a little over 9:1), and Bobby's rear head ported out to 1¼ inches to closer match your 1⅜ths front head. I'm using modern 32-millimeter carbs and I found your 'booze' (an alcohol additive, we think) helps offset this 94-octane unleaded gas. So, we still have the fastest street Shadow around.

"Due to my [motorcycle] recovery notice in *MPH*," Mal wrote, "I had a lot of bids on the bikes. I sold—not to the highest bidder—but to people I thought would appreciate, restore, and ride them. I hope that someday we can get 8714 and 8716 sitting next to each other in all their restored glory. That would only be fitting, as they sat next to each other, silent (*sic*), for all those years."

Mal described letting go of the bike in poignant terms. "I shipped the Shadow to Ken Gross," he wrote. "I crated her in a used BMW crate. Not a good way to go, I thought, but I couldn't find anything else to put her in. I cannot explain how I felt the day I took her to the freightline. I do know that my heart was trying to jump in my mouth but couldn't get past the lump in my throat. The tears in my eyes blurred my vision as I patted her on the tank for the last time. I tried to tell her in my own way that she would have a good home. After all those years of riding her and the 142 trophies she won for me, it was not easy to let her go."

Mal Thompson ended his fascinating Vincent story back where he started. "Now, on her sister machine, I ride the Loop around San Antonio, then pull

Beautiful women seem to be attracted to this particular Vincent; here is Ken Gross with his wife Trish Serratore, taken at Christmas in 1991. *Ken Gross collection*

off on a side road. I pull into the cemetery and taxi up to the gravesite for the dedication of Jim's memorial plaque. As I sit here with the engine idling, I think this trip down memory lane is over, but somehow Jim will hear this engine and approve."

If you're wondering what happened next, here's the rest of the story:

Charlie Taylor restored 8716 for me in 1989 and 1990. When Charlie tore the engine down, he indeed found high-performance Vibrac rods, high-compression 9:1 pistons (which were replaced with 7:1's), MkII Lightning cams, polished internals, and evidence that the heads had been extensively ported. The mileage on the bike was about 21,600, much of it, we know, from the engine's extensive crankshaft runout, in quarter-mile intervals. I rode the bike sparingly for a few years. There was additional work needed and Maryland Vincent specialist Ken Bell finished the job in April 1994.

Not long after that, I decided to build a '32 Ford highboy, and that effort required that I sell virtually everything I owned on two or four wheels. Somer Hooker, a knowledgeable Tennessean who deals in fine motorcycles, brokered the sale of my bike to Rick Nash in Bloomfield Hills, Michigan, and Rick in turn sold 8716 to Jerry Sibley of Vail, Colorado. Jerry and his wife have used *The Beauty* extensively, as it should be. They brought 8716 to the Vincent 50th

Anniversary event in England, rode it on the famed Isle of Man, and have attended three Vincent National Meets, one as far away as Vancouver, British Columbia. Jerry said he "likes things to be original," so he's made an effort to fit genuine parts, bringing the bike up to a very high standard today.

Sadly, Mal Thompson fell on hard times in 1999 and had to sell the remaining Vincent. With Somer Hooker's assistance, *The Beast* (8714) passed to Herb Harris, a noted Vincent enthusiast who runs the Harris Vincent Gallery and owns several rare Stevenage-built bikes, including the famous ex–Rollie Free Bonneville record-holder Black Lightning. "8714 was offered to me," Jerry Sibley said, "and I didn't buy it at the time. I wish I had."

Mal died in December 2005. Herb Harris' 8714 was featured in a *Robb Report Motorcycling* article a few years ago. If you'd like to hear a recording of the ripping exhaust sound of *The Beast,* accelerating hard, click on www.harrisvincentgallery.com

Vincent owners like Jay Leno, Herb Harris, and Jerry Sibley will tell you "there's nothing like a Vincent, and there never will be." I agree. Today, both *The Beauty* and *The Beast* are owned by two consummate Vincent enthusiasts, and the twin Shadows are frequently and enthusiastically ridden.

I know Mal Thompson would be pleased.

The $200 Puzzle

John Ennik was 15 years old in 1980. The car-crazy kid was a high school sophomore and after school worked in one of the many Volkswagen specialty shops that were sprinkled throughout the Berkeley, California, area where he lived with his parents.

A mechanic at another San Francisco Bay–area VW shop made an offer to Ennik.

"For the princely sum of $200, I could purchase every motorcycle and part he had," said Ennik, now a vintage race specialist for the prestigious Phil Reilly and Co. in Sonoma County. "The package included a cool-looking Suzuki motorcycle, which ran, and enough parts to probably build two or three more bikes. There were frames and engines and forks and wheels and gears all for $200."

He scraped together the money from his part-time job and bought the whole pile.

"I knew nothing about the bike, which turned out to be a T-10 X6 Hustler," he said. "And I was unable to obtain a service manual at the time, so I just kind of messed around with it when I got it home.

"I discovered that it didn't have any baffling in the exhaust system at all, so it was one of the few vehicles that I've owned that my parents wouldn't let me start up after the sun went down because the neighbors would complain."

Motorcycles have always been popular in the Bay Area, and for a time, a number of enthusiasts had the 250cc, two-stroke Hustler when that was the hot bike to own. Eventually, though, most of those riders traded up to quicker 400cc four-cylinder bikes, as well as BSAs and Ducatis.

Ennik was able to determine his Suzuki was a production racing bike, which, he said, means "it has a fanatical blueprint."

"When I bought it, I had no idea, but it is very modified and ported so there is almost no torque. So I burned the clutch out in it fairly quickly because below 3,000 rpm, there is nothing coming on, and it really doesn't come on until 5,000 to 6,000 rpm. But the porting really seems to start working at 7,000 rpm, when it makes a strange strangled sucking noise.

"That's when the tach starts swinging upward crazy fast."

Ennik was a beginning rider at the time, so the Suzuki was a thrill ride when it was running well. It did take some practice to get it moving without damaging the clutch, though. He would aim it in a straight line and twist the throttle a little bit, trying to get it through a couple of gears. It turned out to be a real handful to ride around town, however.

"I was just massacring the thing." So the last time the clutch burned out, it was pushed into his parent's garage and forgotten.

The racing bike with unknown racing heritage: John Ennik's T-10 Hustler has changed little since he traded $200 of his hard-earned cash for the bike in 1980. For nearly 30 years Ennik has tried unsuccessfully to learn about the history of this bike. *Tom Cotter*

When Ennik went away to college, the bike bounced around from storage spot to storage spot.

"I tried to get the pieces to fix it up, or at least get information about the bike, but I wasn't very successful," he said.

Ennik would visit dealerships and repair shops, but he wasn't able to find out anything about his rare bike.

"The dealers were concentrating on the new models and just kind of blew me off. They just weren't very interested, and parts weren't available, so it continued to sit."

Not surprisingly, as it was moved from location to location, Ennik's treasure trove of extra parts got whittled down, some of it thrown away and some parts sold.

"I decided the bike was like eye candy, so I decided never to get rid of it," said Ennik. "The look is just so classic that I always thought it was something I could one day mount on the wall."

Ennik had a friend who was computer savvy and told him he'd look up the motorcycle online to see if there was any information on the Web. They ultimately found a website that had photos and lots of technical data, but it was all written in Swedish.

"This was the first written information I ever found on the bike," he said. "But at least it showed proper ignition timing and spark plug gaps and those kinds of things."

Another website discovery revealed that a longtime Suzuki dealership, Crooks Suzuki in Cumbria, England, had raced a team of similar Suzukis at the Isle of Man races to a fair amount of success.

In 1996, 16 years into ownership of his Suzuki, Ennick was still trying to figure out what he owned. It was then that he became re-energized in his two-wheeled possession. At the time, Ennik was employed on an Indy Lights racing team, and a fellow teammate was really into motorcycles, which got him fired up all over again.

"So my friend says, 'I've got to see it, I've got to see it,' so we went over to see it," said Ennik. "The bike had been stored at an estate where I used to live but I hadn't been there to see it in more than two years. We literally had to uncover it, removing old furniture and debris that had belonged to other tenants who had lived there.

"So we got the bike out, and he really got on me for not having done something with it all these years."

When eBay began, Ennik was able to occasionally pick up spare parts and often called and spoke to the sellers to see what they knew of his model.

"I'm more interested in the process of making it correct right now," he said. "I want the correct factory pieces on the bike rather than be in a hurry just to get the bike completed.

"With this bike, any time I've tried to short-cut something or do a rush job, it has always come back to bite me."

These days, Ennik is trying to find the correct seat for his Suzuki because he physically doesn't fit on the bike with that seat in place.

But if his intention for the bike is as an interesting ornament, why does he need a seat that is correct for his body?

"I've actually ridden it around under its own power a little bit lately," he said. "I haven't done that in a long time."

"It got me thinking that it might be fun to race it in vintage motor-cycle races."

Almost 30 years after buying the bike, Ennik's relationship with the unique Suzuki is in its third beginning.

A Beast of a Harley

As hard as it might be to believe, once upon a time, motorcycles were faster than dragsters in the quarter-mile. It was in the early 1950s, and Wally Parks' new National Hot Rod Association (NHRA) was still in its infancy. During those early days, bikes offered a power-to-weight ratio superior to even the hottest drag cars of the day.

One person who was particularly interested in keeping bikes in the fastest-time-of-the-day category was a young speed demon named Chet Herbert.

Herbert was born in Arizona but grew up in Southern California. His parents had hoped he would pursue a career in the music industry and bought the youngster a trumpet. Herbert quickly tired of the trumpet and traded it for a motor scooter. His life has been in the fast lane ever since.

Herbert traded up from the scooter and eventually rode a Harley on which he terrorized the streets of Los Angeles in the mid-1940s.

California hot rod pioneer Chet Herbert was the fastest man in the world in quarter-mile drag races in the early 1950s with this bike known as *The Beast*. Tom Cotter

"I heard about a guy who worked at a Harley dealership who was selling the fastest bike on the street," said Chet Herbert, 80, and still operating speed shops in Santa Ana and Chino, California. "So I bought it, but I started to change it more for racing.

Herbert was a tough competitor, but soon after purchasing the Harley, his toughness would be tested. In 1948, he contracted polio, which left him paralyzed from the chest down. He was just 20 years old. From a racing standpoint, it took him out of the saddle, but from a development standpoint he never wavered. Herbert began to develop and engineer parts for bikes and cars from his wheelchair.

"It kind of motivated him to become an innovator," said Herbert's son Doug, who followed his father's love for speed and became an NHRA Top Fuel driver. "He's never been afraid of anything; he just goes after it.

"He was in the hospital for a long time and started to read about how the Germans were using nitromethane to power torpedoes. He knew when he got out of the hospital, he had to get his hands on some of that stuff."

The 1947 Knucklehead motor was mounted on a Harley VL frame because the single-loop design was lighter and more aerodynamic than were Harley's later twin-loop designs. *Tom Cotter*

No other car or bike could touch Herbert's Harley in the early 1950s. Here an article in a 1950 issue of *Cycle* tells of the bike's nearly 130-mile-per-hour run at the Santa Ana, California, drag strip. *Chet Hebert collection*

From his wheelchair, Herbert continued to modify the motorcycle he could no longer ride. It was coined *The Beast* by track announcers because of its ungainly appearance. The 1947 Knucklehead used a VL frame and front forks because they were lighter and more aerodynamic than other frames. But it required fish-plating, which was steel plates welded at crucial points so it wouldn't twist with all the torque off the line.

"I used a pre-1933 Harley-Davidson frame because it was a single-stringer frame," said Chet Herbert. "It was better for racing than the double-stringer frames that later Harleys used."

Herbert's Beast rode through the traps at 103 miles per hour once at the Santa Ana Drags with a rider he no longer remembers. Some more modifications and another rider, Al Keys, and *The Beast* was clocked at 121.62 miles per hour, the fastest any vehicle had ever accelerated through the quarter-mile to that point.

It was July 1950, and Herbert was ready to set another record but knew it would take more than pump fuel to accomplish this task. His crew members mixed up a concoction of alcohol, water, castor oil, and the German torpedo trick—nitromethane—and filled the bike's homemade gas tank using rubber gloves to avoid being burned by the potent mixture in the event of a spill. The fuel was fed to a huge pair of carburetors that had come off an Offenhauser midget race engine.

The Beast had already been ridden to 128 miles per hour at the El Mirage dry lake, but Herbert was seeking domination on the paved quarter-mile.

When rider Ted Irio mounted *The Beast,* he held on tight. The bike had no clutch or starter, so it was kick-started on a stand, which was no easy task, since it had a 13:1 compression ratio.

Eyewitnesses that day remember that even though Irio started off in second gear, the bike's rear tire wouldn't stop spinning and ultimately caught fire as it left the line. Irio had to back off on the throttle until the tire stopped spinning, then slowly accelerate as it gained traction.

The Beast fishtailed all the way down the drag strip and spectators from the stands were treated to a record-shattering run of 129 miles per hour. But the fans were also confused because all they saw was a cloud of dust at the far end of the strip.

Irio was going fast, so fast that he couldn't stop *The Beast*. He went on a wild cool-down ride, catapulting end-over-end until he finally came to rest, thankfully unhurt, in a pile of dirt far beyond the finish line.

Speed secret? This antique door knob acts as a shift knob on this otherwise single-purpose racing machine. Could it have been Herbert's secret of success? *Tom Cotter*

The bike sits patiently waiting for its restoration to be completed in son Doug Herbert's North Carolina race shop. The younger Herbert is restoring his father's old racer as a tribute to his dad's career. The engine and transmission have already been rebuilt. *Tom Cotter*

The Beast was rebuilt and continued to race at drag strips and dry lake events until Herbert decided to sell it.

"I raced it for a couple of years but decided to put it up for sale in 1952," said Herbert. "I put an ad in one of the cycle magazines for $1,500. At the time I was really getting away from bikes and getting more into cars.

"This rich kid from Chicago called me and wanted to buy it. He and another rich kid with a hopped-up roadster had a bet with each other. The kid with the roadster said, 'You get any kind of motorcycle, and I'll blow your doors off in the quarter-mile.' So the other kid bought my bike and the bet was called off. That roadster would have been lucky to go 105 miles per hour, and *The Beast* would go 25 miles per hour faster."

The senior Herbert continued to develop speed parts. He bought a lathe from Sears and began grinding his own camshafts for cars and motorcycles. He invented the roller cam and lifter setup, which have been used by racers ever since.

"Once people realized how much horsepower those roller cams produced, there were 50 people lined up at his door to have custom camshafts ground," said Doug. Herbert also started the Zoomie Header business.

Herbert opened a speed shop that operates to this day but never stopped building fast cars. He built numerous dragsters and Bonneville streamliners that continued to set speed records for decades.

Through a lifetime of success, though, he never forgot his first bike, *The Beast*. Son Doug tracked it down and bought it back.

"It was in terrible shape and all disassembled," said Doug. "It sat around his shop for a long time before I asked him if I could restore it.

"I took it last summer [2008]."

Today *The Beast* is in Doug Herbert's race shop in Lincolnton, North Carolina, going through a slow and thorough restoration.

"I want to restore it in my dad's honor and display it in my showroom," he said. "And I'd like to bring it to the drags and let people see a bike that was once the fastest thing on wheels. It's not very often that they get to see such an early bike."

CHAPTER SIX

Rare Birds

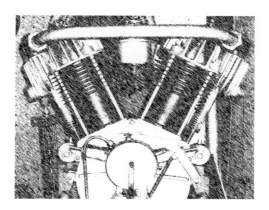

The Curtiss Parallax

Dale Axelrod became interested in Curtiss motorcycles years ago. It's actually a dual fascination for Axelrod. He loves old motorcycles, but he also loves vintage aircraft. The retired diving instructor and paramedic from Middleburg, Florida, explained how his two passions are contained in this one bike.

"Just like the Wright brothers, who went from building bicycles to airplanes, Glenn Curtiss went from building bicycles to opening a bicycle factory, then motorcycles, and finally airplanes. Interestingly, it was Alexander Graham Bell who talked Curtiss into becoming involved with flight.

"The Wright brothers also built bicycles, but I've never found one. That's why the Curtiss motorcycle is so interesting to me."

Glenn Curtiss was an early aviation pioneer, who later was actually in competition with the Wright brothers.

"The Wright brothers always criticized Curtiss for sneaking out and watching them fly their early airplanes and stealing ideas," he said. "While they were alive, there was bad blood between them, but when they died, the government merged the two companies to form the Curtiss-Wright Corporation.

Well before that merger, though, Glenn Curtiss manufactured very interesting motorcycles, ones that used engines designed for aircraft. But we're getting ahead of ourselves.

In 1992, Axelrod attended an Antique Motorcycle Club of America (AMCA) swap meet in Harmony, New Jersey. He had spread the word to his friends about his interest in a twin-cylinder Curtiss, but because of the bike's rarity, he didn't really expect to hear about one anytime soon. So when his friend came up to him at that swap meet and said there was a Curtiss frame for sale, he got excited.

"There are so few of these bikes left," he said. "Four, five, maybe six twin-cylinder bikes remain in the world. I paid $500 for a rotted 1907 frame and an original-paint gas tank."

He retained the tank, but the frame turned out to be for a single-cylinder engine, so he built that bike up with a proper engine that he already had and sold it to support his twin-cylinder project.

"That bike is beautiful," he said. "It got third place at a big show."

Over the course of many years, Axelrod kept collecting other parts for his main project: leather handlebar grips, a leather seat, and a tool bag. He even found a 1907 motorcycle license plate.

Collector Dale Axlerod is fascinated with Curtiss products, especially because founder Glenn Curtiss built both motorcycles and aircraft. According to Axlerod, probably fewer than six twin-cylinder Curtiss motorcycles—like his original-paint 1907 pictured here—exist today. *Dale Axlerod*

"And I found a period leather V-cog drive belt, which had been sitting in a guy's flooded basement," he said. "So I dried it out and [now] display it on the handlebars at shows."

But the discovery that Axelrod is most excited about is the engine he discovered—a twin-cylinder Hercules originally built for a dirigible.

"I looked for probably 15 or 20 years for an engine like this," he said. "They built so few of them. They are a terrific engine that was manufactured near the south end of Lake Keuka, part of the Finger Lakes region, in Hammondsport, New York.

"I had heard about an aviation collector in Kansas City who had a Hercules engine. I had heard it was a four-cylinder, but it turns out that it was a two-cylinder, which was even better.

"At first he wouldn't sell, but we kept talking, and finally he told me he'd take $20,000 for it. I bought it without ever even seeing it. I wouldn't have taken $100,000 for it after I bought it.

"I was told the engine was N.O.S. (new old stock) when I bought it, but it had a bent connecting rod in it when I received it, so it was locked up and wouldn't turn over."

Axelrod collects Curtiss motors like this 1904 twin. Curtiss' motors were called Hercules from 1902 through 1905, but they changed to the Curtiss name from 1906 to 1910. *Dale Axlerod*

A 1908 Curtiss Roadster twin. These motors could have been purchased for use in motorcycles or dirigibles. Because of their rarity, Curtiss motorcycles and engines are extremely valuable today. *Dale Axlerod*

Axelrod explains that the Curtiss engine was of the I.O.E., or intake-over-exhaust, design similar to early Harley-Davidsons. Also called a pocket-valve design, a small lobe was used to open each cylinder's exhaust valve, but the intake valves used an atmospheric system. The intake valves were opened and closed by engine vacuum.

"Harley struggled with the pocket valve, but they could never make it work properly," said Axelrod. "They eventually gave up the design."

So Axelrod had all the major components—engine, gas tank, small accessories—but he was still missing a frame. It turns out that he had a friend with a correct Curtiss frame in his basement, so Axelrod went to look at it. He discovered it was still wearing its original paint.

"Great! All the Curtiss motorcycles 1908 and older were painted black, so now I had an original black frame, original black gas tank, and many other original parts in their original finishes," he said.

This was quite a discovery, according to Axelrod. "Think about what people rode on 100 years ago," he said. "It was all deeply rutted dirt roads from the wagons that traveled on them. Motorcycles got beat to pieces in those days. To have no dents or rust on the sheetmetal gas tank or fenders is amazing."

Axelrod took six or seven years to restore the Curtiss. Even though he didn't paint any of the major components, he did paint, plate, and polish many of the smaller bits. He takes great pride in the fact that he does all the restoration work himself, even nickel plating nuts, bolts, and other hardware to resemble the original finish.

"I only make what I absolutely have to," he said. "I want to keep it as close to original as possible. For instance, I still need a battery and a fender, but I won't resort to making one. I'll just wait and hopefully one will turn up at a swap meet."

Now, except for the fender, the Curtiss project is basically completed. Axelrod takes it to motorcycle meets and rides it around the field. He is deservedly proud of his rare machine.

"There is only one other original-paint twin Curtiss in the world that I know of," said Axelrod. "It belonged to a member of the San Francisco Motor Club, and when he died in 1926, his son donated it to the Club. It's been sitting in the clubhouse ever since."

Its rarity means the bike's value must be substantial. "I wouldn't take anything less than $250,000 for it," he said. "One sold at auction a few years ago for $160,000 and most of it was remade with new parts. The good news to me was that I was able to buy a box of authentic Curtiss parts that were taken off that bike."

For Axelrod, it's all good.

The $50 Ariel

Russ Aves is an amazing fellow. The retired wine bottler houses a small collection of amazing machines in his well-equipped workshop in St. Helena, California, including a 1932 Ford three-window coupe that he hot-rodded 50 years ago, a 1940 Buick four-door convertible, and his daily driver, a Chevy-powered 1940 Ford pickup. But it's the 1950 Ariel motorcycle that drew us to his shop.

Aves purchased the Ariel in 1956 or 1957 from his brother-in-law for $50. "Rudy needed some money and I gave him $50 for the motorcycle," said Aves. "I was probably supposed to give the bike back to him as soon as he had enough money to buy it back from me, but he never asked for it back, and I never offered.

"He got it in boxes, and I just inherited that pile of boxes. Apparently the previous owner had tried to convert it to some kind of chopper, but the engine let go before he had a chance to ruin the frame. A connecting rod came right out the bottom."

Rudy had the Ariel for only about eight months, far less than the amount of time that Russ has owned it.

"It sat in the corner of my shop for, I'm ashamed to admit, probably 30 years before I started to restore it about 12 years ago," said Aves. "Even though it was still in boxes, I had plenty of time to fix some little things and do some of the custom work I had to do."

When he decided to roll up his sleeves and get serious with the Ariel's restoration, the first thing he did was build a proper service stand. Ever the inventor, Aves fabricated a stand out of an old barber's chair. With a simple pump of the foot, he is able to raise or lower the bike to a proper height to work on it. It can rotate 360 degrees with ease.

Aves had never restored a motorcycle before, but that didn't cause him to hesitate. He tore into the project with the intention of completing everything himself except for the upholstery and pinstriping. Soon after he acquired the Ariel, he was offered a job at Northrop Aircraft in El Segundo, California.

"There, I met some of the guys in the machine shop who were motorcycle guys, and they reground the crankshaft and welded up the case all properly, all on Northrop's dime," he said.

The bike was missing a few items, such as the proper fenders, headlight, and crash bars. Aves was able to locate the proper parts by attending swap meets and he even made a couple of trips to Coventry, England, to meet with original suppliers who actually made the parts for Ariel.

"I'd go on trips and eventually I'd meet Ariel people, and I was able to gather the parts and pieces I needed," he said.

Aves did nearly everything on his bike, including paint and even the chrome plating. When he removed the knee pads on the side of the gas tank, the original red that had not been bleached from the sun was clearly evident. He compared paint samples at an auto paint store, where it was a dead match with the Dodge pickup truck color from the special edition, Little Red Wagon.

"On the chrome plating, my dad was in the auto accessories business, and we had the ability to chrome plate parts ourselves," he said. "So as was done when it was new, I chrome plated the gas tank before painting parts of it."

Aves explains that the most unique component of the Ariel is the four-square, four-cylinder engine.

"This style of engine uses two crankshafts," he said. "Each connecting rod has two pistons attached and they are connected by a common bull gear on the side of the case. Each crankshaft rotates counterclockwise. It was a design that they developed in something like 1931 in the smaller 500cc engine, if I remember correctly.

"As it grew to this 1,000cc engine, 250cc per cylinder, the problem of the rear cylinders running quite hot [worsened]. With four cylinders and only two exhaust pipes, there was no good way to get those hot gases out of there.

The Ariel sits among future projects at Russ Aves' farm in St. Helena, California. The $50 bike was totally restored by Aves, including the chrome plating. *Russ Aves*

A proper Ariel speedometer was a challenge for Aves to locate, but the correct Smiths instrument was eventually found. The bike has been ridden just 35 miles since restoration. *Russ Aves*

"[Later] Ariel developed a four-pipe system that [helped] the problem. Gosh, I was so sorry that I didn't install that four-piper on my bike. But these things make the greatest sounds. It was a sound of a little four-banger that had [rarely] been heard on a motorcycle before.

"The bike had a nice little rumble that was just phenomenal."

The two services Aves contracted out to someone else to perform were the pinstriping and the upholstery.

The pinstriping was done by a policeman from Bodega. He laid the tasteful stripes on the Ariel and also had striped Aves' '32 Deuce Coupe years earlier. But the seat is a sore point.

"I had the original seat with that small-grained leather," he said. "I was so pure when I was restoring that bike that I actually sent that seat back to England to have it reupholstered so it would come out just right.

"It came back with all my original leather gone and just this kind of crappy leather covering it now. It's authentic, but it's just not like the leather it had on it."

Since he's an old hot rodder, Aves is most impressed with the 1,000cc twin-crankshaft engine design and exhaust note. *Russ Aves*

The bike was quite well-equipped for the day. It has a horn, an air pump, and a small toolbox mounted to the frame. Aves tells of an interesting piece of trivia: that Ariel was originally in the bicycle business and the company invented the adjustable-spoke wheel.

"Bicycles had been using wooden wheels and wires, and they came up with a nipple-and-adjuster arrangement," said Aves.

The finished Ariel has scored a number of trophies since it's been completed. Most of his wins have been at concours events throughout California. One first place came in Oregon. Aves pointed out his perfect-condition, period-correct California motorcycle license plate, something he had to remove for the Oregon show.

"You'd better have Oregon plates on it if you hope to win in Oregon," he said. "They'll never let a California bike win in Oregon."

Hunting for the Barber

Motorcycle collections come in all shapes and sizes. During the course of writing this book, I've met motorcycle enthusiasts who are proud of their one-bike collections and multibike collectors who own a number of examples of either one brand of bike or of several brands. These are the collectors who often have either their garage or basement full of bikes, parts, and equipment, often with a well-equipped shop. They often perform their own repairs and restorations and are known as motorcyclists among their peers.

The rarest category is the collector with a huge stash of bikes in a huge facility. These collections can have hundreds of bikes and may be private or open to the public. Some have no employees and others employ a staff of technicians. These museums are often the life's work of either an individual or a group.

It is that last category that we will discuss in this section. The Barber Vintage Motorsports Museum, housed in a fabulous facility in an unlikely location outside of Birmingham, Alabama, is a monument to the hard work and passion of its founder, George Barber.

Barber was born into a dairy farming family that supplied the region around Birmingham with milk, ice cream, and other dairy products for generations. His free time was occupied by his passion for sports cars and motorcycles. In 1989, he began to collect bikes and by 1995 opened his still-growing collection to the public in a converted dairy barn. The collection grew, and now, as a 501(c)(3) foundation, Barber made a huge investment in building a purpose-built museum with an adjoining road-racing circuit (check it out at www.barbermuseum.org).

I caught up with the museum's director, Jeff Ray, and the technical advisor, Brian Slark, since they are responsible for most of the museum's motorcycle acquisitions. They shared with me the fact that being a large museum with many resources to purchase bikes has its advantages but also its disadvantages. I talked with Ray and Slark about some of the more unusual acquisitions they have made on behalf of the museum and their philosophy on buying.

"When we first got serious about buying motorcycles, sellers would see us coming and think, 'They're with that dairy farmer down in Birmingham; he'll buy anything,'" said Ray, who has personally acquired between 800 and 850 motorcycles for the Barber Museum. "When I first started buying bikes for the collection, I wanted to make sure everything was purchased as an investment, so if everything went terribly wrong, Mr. Barber wouldn't lose his ass."

Ray grew up in Birmingham, a typical Southern kid who loved cars and bikes.

"When you grow up in the South, you get a bicycle when you are 6 years old, then when you are 9, you get a mini bike," he said. "I got a little Honda 70 when

I was 12, and my mom would give me 50 cents on a Saturday morning and say, 'Don't come home unless you are bleeding.'

"Those were good times, and when you turned 16, the bike went into the basement or behind the garage, and you got your first car."

Ray still has the Honda 70 he got when he was 12 and is currently restoring it.

At the Barber Museum, they have what they call "patient money" when they are on the trail of a bike.

"The difference between a collector and a museum is that the collector enjoys the bragging rights of motorcycle ownership," he said. "He enjoys having guests over and taking his buddies into 'the shrine.'

"He needs to have a certain motorcycle now, so he can show his friends what he has accomplished."

Ray explains that museums must take an entirely different view on motorcycle acquisitions.

"I've had to wait on bikes that we've wanted," he said. "We take the longer view and look at it as a long-term investment. Sometimes I'll watch bikes sell but for more money than I was willing to pay. I'll wait, and either one of two things will happen: either my idea of value will catch up with the sale price, or the sale price will come down to my idea of value.

"I've got an Indian racer that I saw sell twice in 10 years, but I finally got it."

Slark is a Brit with a lifelong fascination with all things two-wheeled. He added that there is a close network of enthusiasts within the hobby.

"It's a small community," said Slark. "When you get into the real collectible motorcycles, the ones that are really expensive, the slice of the pie that can afford them gets smaller and smaller.

"There are a handful of people who can afford them, and everyone knows who they are. Those bikes don't get advertised, but when they become available, we're on the mailing list."

Ray travels the world to look at bikes and collections, although these days, he is more selective about his travels.

"There was a time before the Internet when I would come into work in the morning and have 100 motorcycle offers on my desk that had come in that day's mail," he said. "Of those, there might be only 9 or 10 that we might be interested in.

"I've bought as many as 30 bikes at one time, or the entire contents of a garage, in order to enhance or sweeten the acquisition."

Ray and Slark shared many motorcycle barn-find stories with me during my visit and brought a different perspective to the art of motorcycle barn-finding than the average enthusiast normally encounters. With all the discoveries they have made, the stories could easily be published in a book by themselves, so I've culled that list down to what I thought were the most interesting for you to read.

14,000-rpm Wall-Hanger

Honda's first serious attempt at Grand Prix racing was with a model called the RC161, an exotic factory racer that had an incredible power-to-weight ratio as well as some flaws. The bike debuted at the 1961 Isle of Man TT and struggled. The 250cc four-cylinder double-overhead-cam motor produced an ample 35 horsepower but was not very durable. The Superhawk-type frame was not rigid enough and the bike handled poorly. As many as eight RC161 Hondas were built, and four or five were campaigned by factory riders at Grand Prix events.

"Honda won't confirm the numbers for us, but it looks like additional powerplants were produced for the eight bikes that were built," said Ray. "Our researchers have told us that because these engines were so fragile and compli-cated, no fieldwork could be performed on them, so basically you had to replace the motors for almost any reason."

Slark said the RC161's unreliability occurred because the motors were being strung so tightly. "These were conventional engine designs, but they were turning 14,000 rpm, which was astronomical compared to anything else out there," said Slark.

The tuning process was so complicated that even a regular task such as adjusting the valves became a service best performed at the factory. Silver solder was required to fill up the "adjustment bucket," then was honed down to achieve the correct clearance.

Maintenance issues aside, the bike was the hottest thing on the track. Only world champion–caliber riders were given the opportunity to race the RC161. Riders like Mike Hailwood, Tom Phillis, Jim Redmond, and Luigi Taveri put the RC161 through its paces during the 1961 season. Even though the bike dominated many races, securing the manufacturer's and 250cc world titles for Honda, it wasn't the blowout Honda had expected.

After campaigning the RC161 for the 1961 season, Honda introduced its second-generation Grand Prix racer, the RC162, which was less complicated and more reliable.

But what was Honda to do with the 8 RC161 bikes it had constructed, along with the 20 or so engines that were lying in a warehouse?

Honda gave the year-old bikes to loyal racing teams in Southern California and told them, "Here are some bikes. Take some of your best riders and go out and campaign them. Understand there are no parts available, so if you break something, you'll have to cannibalize another bike to keep it running."

"We found out that three or four RC161s were delivered to American Honda at the end of the 1961 season," said Ray.

"We discovered that one was written off at Riverside in 1964 when it slammed into the hay bales, then slid down the track."

Slark's friend Tony Murphy attended a Honda Fun Day in the 1960s at Riverside Raceway where manufacturers had displays and offered demonstration rides.

"He was told by one of the Honda engineers to go out there on one of the RC161s and don't be afraid to rev it. When Murphy asked how high, the engineer said, 'It doesn't matter, 17,000, 18,000, whatever.'"

When the RC161s were used up, Honda had instructed teams to literally destroy the bikes by throwing them into the Pacific Ocean, according to Slark. One display bike was built of spare parts and presented to American Honda, where it sat in the lobby of the company's California headquarters for years. It was later donated to the Henry Ford Museum in Dearborn, Michigan.

Honda's RC161 was the company's first successful 250cc Grand Prix racing machine. The bike on the right was discovered hanging over the bar at the California home of champion rider and team manager Kel Carruthers. The bike on the left was assembled with spare parts the museum acquired. *Tom Cotter*

Ray and Slark decided that the Barber Museum needed an RC161 for display, since it was such a significant bike in Honda's racing history. In 1994, they tried to buy the one that was donated to the Henry Ford Museum, but it wasn't for sale.

About that same time, folks within the motorcycle-collecting community were recognizing that the Barber Museum was quickly becoming the "Steward of Motorcycle History" within the United States, so many of them openly assisted Ray and Slark in obtaining desirable acquisitions.

"We were finally being seen as a museum not looking for contributions but acquiring bikes the old-fashioned way," said Ray, "by writing a check."

One of the people taking notice was motorcycle racing legend Don Vesco. "Don was a guy I had always heard about as a kid for his land speed record attempts, aerodynamics, bodywork, fairings, windscreens, things like that," said Ray. "To me, Don was the Carroll Shelby of my generation."

One day Vesco called Ray and asked if he was interested in an ex-Works Honda.

"Which one is it?" asked Ray.

"It's the RC161," said Vesco. "It's here in Southern California, and it is currently contracted to a broker, but that contract is about to expire. If you are interested, I'll give you a call when the contract is free and clear."

A couple of months went by and Ray hadn't heard from Vesco. Then one day the phone rings.

"The sale didn't go through," said Vesco. "Would you like to come and see the bike? It is expensive."

The Honda's English-made Smiths tachometer could register up to 18,000 rpm. The rev limit for the RC161, though, was "only" 14,000. *Tom Cotter*

Ray hopped on a westbound flight and met up with Vesco. They drove to El Cajon to the house of Kel Carruthers. Carruthers deserves a book all by himself, having been the 1969 250cc World Grand Prix champion and Isle of Man TT winner in 1969 and 1970 on a Benelli. After retiring from active racing, Carruthers became a team manager and engineer for a young Yamaha rider who showed promise, Kenny Roberts. Roberts won three consecutive 500cc world championships and gave Carruthers much of the credit.

Carruthers was born and raised in Australia, where his father ran a small motorcycle shop. Later he became a Honda dealer in his home country.

When Honda was looking to dispose of its retired inventory of RC161 race bikes in 1961, one bike was sent to Carruthers' father, who prepared it for his son to campaign on the Australian circuit. The young Carruthers went on to win five national titles—some 500 races—with the bike and even ran it on some dirt tracks.

"When the engine blew up with a broken crankshaft in 1968, the bike was retired," said Slark. "But they kept it running and competitive longer than any of the other seven RC161s. Australians are famous for being innovators and keeping things running. In their remote location, they have always been forced to improvise."

When Carruthers retired from active riding, he moved to El Cajon and built a house in the desert. On the wall over the bar, he mounted the single bike that he had won more races on than any other, the RC161.

"Kel wasn't home, but when Don told me about all the components that came with the bike, including factory service tools, it got my attention," said Ray. "But I told Don that with the substantial amount of money we were talking about, I'd need to meet with Kel, get the bike down off the wall, and see it run. I told him I couldn't commit to that kind of money while looking at the bike from a ladder."

Vesco agreed that he would contact Ray when Carruthers was back in the United States so he could arrange for another trip west.

Four of five weeks later, Ray flew out again to meet with Carruthers.

"Kel was a very interesting gentleman and we talked for quite a bit," he said. "We walked into the garage and the RC161 was already sitting there.

"'Would you like to hear it run?' he asked. I said, yes sir. So he fiddled with the carburetor for a few moments, rolled the bike about 10 feet, and bump started it right in his driveway.

"There he was, sitting in his driveway revving up this racing bike at 9,000 rpm just to warm it up."

Ray had done research and discovered that the weakest component on the bike was its crankshaft. Not wanting to risk damaging it, he told Carruthers he had heard enough. "Let's look at what else you have," he said.

Also in Kel Carruthers' possession was this 1973 Yamaha TZ350. Finnish rider Jarno Saarinen won the 1973 Daytona 200 on this bike. Saarinen was the first European to win the race. *Tom Cotter*

When Jeff Ray of the Barber Museum asked Carruthers what else he had, he pulled out Saarinen's racing leathers and the helmet that he had worn at Daytona. For Ray, that closed the deal. *Tom Cotter*

Carruthers started pulling blankets back that covered boxes with a spare engine, boxes of parts, tooling, and at least one extra crankshaft.

"I realized this was a nice little stash," said Ray.

"It was going to turn into one of those deals where if you keep asking, 'Well, what else do you have?' the deal was going to get sweeter."

"You know, I have another bike you might be interested in," said Carruthers, as he went toward the corner of the garage and pulled a blanket off another racing bike. Ray's mouth fell open.

It was the 1973 Yamaha TZ350 that Carruthers' teammate, the brilliant Jarno Saarinen, rode to win that year's Daytona 200, becoming the first European to win that race.

"Kel rode the sister bike to Saarinen's Yamaha to second at Daytona that year but decided that because his teammate's bike won, it was more significant," said Ray. "So he kept it all these years.

"All of a sudden, my antennae goes up. 'What else do you have?' I asked Kel."

Carruthers walked over to a closet and produced Saarinen's racing leathers.

"Suddenly I've put together a package deal for a couple of the most significant racing bikes of their time," he said. "This wasn't your typical barn find, but at more than $200,000, it was more expensive than a dozen of your average barn finds."

Indian Burial Ground

Before the days of email, Ray would most often receive his leads via snail mail, usually a letter and a few photographs. One day he got an interesting hand-written letter from a gentleman in Charlotte, North Carolina, who said that he had 41 Indian motorcycles to sell, all four-cylinders of various years between 1934 and 1940.

"That was when four-cylinders were all the craze, and a nice one would knock you back about $45,000," said Ray.

"Can you tell me about them?" Ray asked the man.

"You've got to come and see them," said the man.

"Can you send me photographs?" Ray asked.

"You've got to come and see them," repeated the man.

Ray realized that a trip to Charlotte was in order, and with 41 motorcycles to inspect in one day, Brian Slark would need to accompany him.

"Brian is a good sounding board when it comes to appraising bikes," said Ray.

So they packed up their motorcycle inspection equipment, which consisted of a penlight, two disposable cameras (today he uses digital), notepad, several pens and pencils, gloves, and some wet wipes, "Because you never know how much dirt you're going to run into."

They planned to make a day of it. They hopped a flight from Birmingham to Charlotte. They still remember that NASCAR legend Bobby Allison was also on the plane. They took the first flight out in the morning and planned to return home on the last flight that evening.

"We figured that would give us nine hours on the ground, adequate time to analyze the bikes with a first-blush inspection," he said. "Unless the bikes are super, super cheap, we first make a survey trip, then a second trip after we've done additional research on the bikes back at the museum.

"If a seller is in a hurry to close the deal, he's scaring me. Most of the time there is something wrong."

The two touched down in Charlotte (surprisingly on time), rented a car, and drove about 45 minutes, following the gentleman's directions.

"We were expecting that with a collection that large, we would be arriving at a rural area with a large barn or at least a Butler Building," said Ray. "What we didn't expect was a subdivision of perfectly manicured homes on two acres of land. We passed the house the first time, figuring we had the wrong address. When we pulled into the driveway, we were convinced the bikes were probably stored off site. As we walked toward the door, we noticed that not one blade of grass was out of place, and we noticed a privacy fence stretching across the back of the house.

"We knocked on the door and a wonderful lady met us," said Ray. "She could have been my second-grade teacher. She invited us in for tea and coffee. The house was very formal, like out of *Better Homes and Gardens* magazine.

"Her husband comes in and we all shake hands. He was in no hurry, so we allowed him to chitchat for a while until I looked at my watch. 'Sir, we only have seven-and-a-half hours until our flight home. We really need to look at the bikes.'

"So he said, 'Let me get the key. Meet me next to the garage.'"

Ray and Slark walked outside, where the man emerged with a claw hammer, which turned out to be the key. He used the claw to pull nails and spikes out of the fence so they could walk into the backyard.

"I could just imagine the agreement he and his wife formed years earlier," said Ray. "From the back of the house forward to the street would be hers, and from the back of the house to the property line was his.

"It was like Jurassic Park back there."

"I remember he had mentioned an old car he was restoring when we were drinking tea," said Slark. "When I saw it in the backyard, it had a 6-inch-diameter tree growing through it. It was an old Dodge Brothers car, and it was total junk."

Both their hearts sank a little bit as they noticed a shed in the backyard that was leaning and ready to collapse. Then they saw row upon row of blue tarps, the type you buy at Home Depot.

"Those are the frames," said the man.

"What frames?" asked Ray as his heart hit bottom. Then the man started to tell his story.

He had been an airline mechanic and engineer who became infatuated with Indian motorcycles. He bought dozens of them, but instead of repairing, restoring, or riding them, he completely disassembled them.

Each frame had been sandblasted and magnafluxed, then stored on a rack outside. He did the same to the next bike, and the next bike, and so on. Many had been there for more than 15 years.

"It was like a time warp," said Slark. "Who knows when he bought his last bike, five years or ten years ago, but he talked about them like he bought them yesterday.

"When he pried open the doors to the shed, there were wooden racks full of magnetos, crankcases, carburetors, everything in order like a vault."

Next to the shed was a collapsing lean-to, which was entered by crawling on hands and knees. Inside were rows of crankshafts, stacked up like firewood and completely rusted. There were brand-new engine cases that he had castings made of, but they were never finish machined, so they were stacked on shelves unmatched.

"The fenders were all stored in the lean-to, in the shed, or outdoors. All had been sandblasted and left to the elements," said Ray. They were completely rusted.

"I noticed that he had tried to categorize the fenders with a felt-tipped Sharpie, and you could actually still read some of the numbers through the rust," said Ray.

"In his mind, he was sitting on a gold mine worth at least $1 million," said Slark. "He was looking for somewhere between $35,000 and $40,000 for each bike, which at the time would have bought you a mint-condition Indian."

Ray and Slark realized this trip was a mistake and began planning an exit strategy, which is politically sensitive when you represent a museum.

"The last thing you want to do is to disrespect someone or leave in such a way that the person has a bad impression of the museum and tells his friends," said Ray. "It destroys everything you work for.

"You have to politely tell the person that you are not interested in making the purchase but that you appreciate their time. We definitely don't want to tell him that we are going to think about this opportunity, because the saddest part is when they make three or four phone calls to your office after you leave. . . . 'What is the problem?' they ask.

"In this case, if he had properly cared for the 41 Indians, they could have been quite valuable. The worst thing he did was to take them apart.

"We told him that the best opportunity for him was probably going to be with a parts dealer who could come in and make sense of all the components. We didn't get offered a second cup of coffee, but we did make our flight."

A Widow's Harley

About 15 years ago, Ray got a phone call from a woman who said her next-door neighbor in Pensacola, Florida, had just visited the Barber Museum and recommended she call.

"I have a Harley-Davidson that I think needs to be in your museum," the woman said. "My husband passed away about one year ago, and it has been sitting in our living room, leaking oil, for years. Out of respect for him, I kept it here since he passed, but now it's time to say good-bye to it."

Ray asked what year the bike was and she said a 1913.

"My neighbor said it should be worth $10,000," she said.

Ray said he would see her Thursday.

Thursday morning came, and Ray and his wife decided to make a day of it, so they dropped their son and daughter off at school and hit the road in the museum van for Pensacola, about four hours away.

"I took the van because if there was anything to this story, I'll want to take it back today," said Ray.

True to her word, the Harley was sitting in her living room with a pie pan under it to catch the leaking oil. It was an unmolested 1913 Harley with just the right amount of genuine patina.

Ray asked her the story behind the bike.

"My husband always wanted this motorcycle, which belonged to his uncle," she said. "His Uncle Frank was a Harley dealer in Denver, Colorado. He was also a racer, but this was his personal bike that he rode around on. When my husband was growing up, he was mesmerized by the bike, so in the 1970s, before his Uncle Frank died, he gave the bike to his nephew.

"I have some old photographs."

Ray said the photographs show an older gentleman standing next to the bike in overalls.

"The bike had new tires on it, so I was told that they were changed in order to give Uncle Frank one last ride on the bike before he gave it to his nephew, who was living in Arkansas at the time," said Ray.

To Ray, this was a no-brainer.

"I know your neighbor said the bike was probably worth $10,000, but I'd like to offer you $15,000 for it," said Ray. "I work in a small circle of people, and the last thing I want is the reputation that I beat up on a widow. In actuality, the bike was probably worth $20,000 at the time.

"I was ready to write her a check and asked what else she might have that would be important to document the history of the bike for the museum. She dug around and found an old Harley-Davidson sweater and some more photos of Uncle Frank on a race bike.

"I asked her about the race bike, and she said she had that too. Do I want to see it?"

This was turning out to be a better day than Ray had hoped for.

"It's just an old bike he used at the dealership," she said.

She led Ray out into the garage. Next to the dryer was the frame. Here was the front end; there was the front wheel. But Ray was getting confused.

"The gas tank mounted in the frame, more like an Indian than a Harley," he said, "and the handlebars were high bars, not racing bars. Plus the front forks had been welded on by a blacksmith."

In unrestored condition and still wearing its original paint, this 1913 Harley-Davidson Model 9-B was purchased out of the living room of a woman's home in Pensacola, Florida. Her husband had owned it for many years, but when he died, she decided it was time to clean house. *Tom Cotter*

"Everything was taken apart properly, with all the hardware still in place, but there was a missing piece to the puzzle."

Ray pulled pieces from here and there and dry-fitted the bike together right there in the garage. The rear wheel had a Goodyear Racing Tire mounted on it, but he noticed the frame was slightly "tweaked" to one side.

Then she said that the sidecar was in the corner.

Sidecar! Now it all made sense; the high handlebars, the tweaked frame, the lowered gas tank.

"It was a Flexi sidecar, which meant that the wheel cambered over in the corners to aid in handling," he said. "The frame was offset to one side to allow the rider to sit lower in the frame for a lower center of gravity."

But where was the motor?

"It was so greasy and grimy that I had some men carry it into the backyard," she said.

There, underneath a wash bucket, sat a Harley V-Twin engine, number 366 M.

"The M motors were very, very special," said Ray. They denoted it was a race engine and that it was built for a sidecar bike.

"So I asked her, 'How much for all this?' She gave me a price and I said I would pay her double.

"I was so giddy I couldn't stand it."

It turned out that Uncle Frank would often race the bike in as many as six classes in one day, even as a single-cylinder. Ray explained that he has photographs of one cylinder made inoperable by removing the connecting rod.

"When he got back to the museum with the van that evening, we lined up all the parts in the parking lot," said Slark. "It was like a giant jigsaw puzzle."

The bike was eventually documented and reassembled but not restored.

"As a restored bike, it would be beautiful but not historically correct," said Ray. "As an unrestored bike, it's like a snapshot in time. It will be preserved."

Rhode Island Red

Doc Batzler has an annual all-day party over at his Daytona house in conjunction with Bike Week in February. Batzler is a former Indian racer who was known for racing his hand-shift bike on dirt ovals. Jeff Ray is lucky enough to be on the invitation list to the famous annual brat cookout.

"Doc introduced me to Woody Peckham, so we chatted for a little while as we were eating Doc's brats," said Ray. "Woody was probably in his 80s and was a very colorful character. We exchanged phone numbers and went our separate ways.

"About a month after Daytona, I got a letter from Woody with a photograph of an old Indian. It was a 1912 TT two-speed, and he wanted to know if I might be interested in it for the museum.

"I said, 'Sure, when can I come down to look at it?' He told me anytime, but it wasn't in Florida but at his family home place in Providence, Rhode Island."

Ray said he'd be glad to fly up there anytime, but Peckham admitted that he didn't fly, he only drove.

So they made arrangements to meet in Rhode Island, in the town of Riverside, on a certain date in the near future. Ray flew to Providence and was met by Peckham, who had just driven up from Florida, at the airport. They rode together out to a peninsula near the Atlantic Ocean.

"The area was probably very high-end at some point in time, but it had seen better days by the time I got there," said Ray. "The homes were all turn-of-the-century and we drove to one at the end of a dead-end street. I instantly noticed a wooden shed that had about 10 plastic tarps draped across the roof."

Peckham had arrived there earlier in the day and had removed the Indian from the shed and it was sitting in the driveway. Alongside the bike was a spare motor, an acetylene headlight, and an acetylene generator.

"For what he was asking for the Indian, I'm ready to shake hands on the deal right then," said Ray. "But something told me to keep my mouth closed."

Because Ray didn't jump at the offer, Peckham walked into the shed and returned with another headlight, a toolbox, and a dry-cell battery tube from about 1906 or 1907. Ray decided that if Peckham was going to keep sweetening the pot, he'd wait to see how sweet the pot was going to get before committing to the package.

"He came out with a nice spread of parts, and I finally said, 'Mr. Peckham, you have a deal. But tell me, what's in the shed over there?' I'd like to look in that building."

Peckham explained that his father and his uncle had been mechanically inclined. Both before and after World War I, the brothers did machining and motorcycle and car repairs out of that shed, which had originally been just 10 feet by 10 feet in size. Ray believed the building was about 25 feet by 15 feet when he was there.

The Peckham brothers were not officially Indian dealers, but Peckham Indian became well known in the community. Their original 10-by-10 building had a powerbar that ran across the rafters and operated machines like drill presses and lathes. It was originally operated by a steam engine that sat outside the building.

"When I got there, parts and pieces were mounded up all over the floor, like they shut down the business in 1940 and walked away," said Ray.

"I offered him a few thousand dollars for the pieces in there, and he accepted but wondered how I would get everything back to Birmingham.

"I asked him if we could make an appointment to meet in Rhode Island again, and I would bring the museum's 24-foot trailer and a couple of volunteers to help load. When we returned, we also brought along Doc Batzler, who was curious about the discovery. We worked all day loading that trailer.

"We were definitely overweight, with about 12,000 pounds loaded in that trailer. And there was still more to load. I asked Woody if we could make another appointment to take out the rest, and he agreed.

"All the parts we removed had a slight rusty patina to them, so we called the load Rhode Island Red."

About six weeks later, the crew arrived again with the 24-foot trailer in tow. Batzler joined them for a second time, enthralled that underneath garbage were piles of genuinely good Indian parts.

"As Doc was shuffling around the trash, he discovered a trapdoor on the floor of the original 10-by-10 building," said Ray. "This was the only floor in the building that was concrete; all the rest were dirt floors.

"We opened the hatch and went inside. This was the Peckham brothers' parts room. It turned into an archeological dig, where all the wooden shelves had rotted away, but the floor was stacked with pre-teen and early teen Indian components."

Ray said that Batzler literally sat on the floor with a cat litter scooper, digging into the pile of disintegrated boxes, and coming up with rare parts.

When they returned home, they did a survey of their acquisition. Among hundreds of parts, they had a set of 101 racing alcohol cylinder heads, an overhead-valve conversion, lots of magnetos, and five or six engines. The museum took what they thought they might need and traded with Carl Sorensen, a parts dealer from Florida, for a 101 Indian Scout.

"We got what we needed, so he came up with a U-Haul, delivered the Scout, and took back thousands of pounds of Indian parts," said Ray. "He also invited me to join him at a big vintage motorcycle meet in Eustis, Florida, which I did."

When Sorensen opened his flea market booth, Ray couldn't believe his eyes.

"Carl had a 25-foot flatbed trailer with about 25 percent of the parts we sold him," said Ray. "When he pulled in, it was like a gorgeous 16-year-old girl walking into an all-boys school. It was still dark out, but guys had their flashlights out that Friday morning, and they began rummaging through the parts.

"The Eustis crowd is all about originality and not restoration, so Carl brought them a wealth of hard-to-find and unobtainium parts.

This 1912 Indian was pulled from a ramshackle shed in Providence, Rhode Island, along with literally tons of spare Indian parts. It is displayed at the Barber Museum in as-found condition. *Tom Cotter*

"One guy I remember needed fender stays for his Indian. These are just simple metal rods with a loop on one end and an eye on the other. He took out of his bag two rusty and bent pieces off his own bike and matched them up. 'How much?' he asked. Carl told him $100. I didn't know if the guy was going to haul off and punch him out or what, but instead, he reached into his billfold and paid Carl for what was the Holy Grail to this man. This happened over and over that weekend.

"By the time that weekend was over, Carl's trailer was still loaded with parts, but he had easily made twice as much money as the value of the 101 Scout he traded to us."

This was an eye-opener for Ray, who found out that this was the first virgin stash of serious Indian parts that had surfaced in a long time. And now, 12 years after, Sorensen is still selling some Indian parts he has remaining.

The First Black Shadow

A Canadian enthusiast heard about a guy who hoarded Vincent motorcycles and parts. The Canadian sought out the man and made a deal that he could pick, choose, and purchase pieces from the 11 various basket cases the man had in his barn in order to assemble one complete Black Shadow. On the way home after picking up the parts, a friend who had helped him load the pieces onto his pickup truck was reading the owner's manual. He read that engine number 696 was the first Black Shadow engine built.

"Shit, isn't that the engine you just bought?" he said to his friend.

By the time they arrived at his home, his friend offered to trade him straight-up a mint restored Black Shadow for the basket case pieces and engine number 696.

He turned down the offer.

Many years later, the basket case was still in baskets.

"He had done a little bit of work on the bike but had lost interest and pursued a sale," said Somer Hooker, a Vincent guru from Nashville who desired the engine for the first Black Shadow. "I was interested in the bike, but another guy had already said he would buy it.

"Fortunately, I knew the buyer well enough to know that he seldom followed through on his promises. I sent a letter to the seller, saying that if the other guy bails out, I'm a player."

Many months later, Hooker received a phone call from the seller, who told him that, in fact, the purchaser had bailed out.

"Would you like a deposit right now?" Hooker offered.

Since Hooker lived in the South and the seller lived in Canada, the actual exchange of money for a pile of mismatched Vincent parts and the rare engine took place, appropriately enough, at a motorcycle race at the former Bryer Motorsport Park in Loudon, New Hampshire.

"It was in 1992 when I brought the bike home, but on the way I dropped off the engine with a specialist in Connecticut," said Hooker. "I brought the rest of the parts home, but I wanted to have the engine restored by a pro.

"A problem erupted when the engine builder decided to move to California halfway through the project."

The engine builder was living part-time in California, while Hooker's engine was sitting on a workbench back in Connecticut. Things worsened when the engine builder's tenant began litigation about missing rent payments. Hooker had to fly to Connecticut and have an attorney intercede in order to legally enter the garage and remove his engine. He boxed the components and shipped it back to himself in Nashville.

Hooker had the rest of the Black Shadow restored by a specialist in Canada. He actually owned an N.O.S. rear frame that he used in the restoration.

"This guy came up to a friend of mine at a bike show and told him that he and his brother had collected motorcycles and parts for years but were now in a family feud and selling everything," said Hooker, who admitted that most barn-find stories never pan out, but he also knows that all must be followed up. "He said he had some Vincent parts in the barn, including a bent-up front fork from a Black Shadow he had wrecked years earlier."

Hooker's friend bought the bent front forks and an upper frame and realized they also came from the very first Black Shadow.

"On the early bikes, you have to add the engine [number 696] with 1899 to determine if it is a matching-numbers bike," said Hooker. "The upper frame was number 2595, and he called me and said we must reunite the engine with the upper frame."

Hooker traded parts for the upper frame. They were pretty mangled, but he wanted to keep them.

"I've never seen anything quite that bad," he said.

He also had hoped to purchase the front forks, but his friend wouldn't part with those.

The upper frame was straightened and installed on the already restored motorcycle, which is now acknowledged as the very first production Black Shadow as documented in every owner's manual. The irony is that Vincent exported it to North America. There was a prototype that stayed in England. It was found by a lucky man there who recognized it when it was sitting in the back row at a dealership.

Vincent expert Somer Hooker of Tennessee purchased a basket case of Vincent parts that included engine number 696—the very first Black Shadow engine. Hunting for as many of that first bike's original components, including the very twisted upper frame, he reassembled the first example. *Somer Hooker*

The Hyperterrestrial Hopper

Dale Walksler has an unprecedented advantage when it comes to hearing about hidden old bikes. He owns the Wheels Through Time Museum, where nearly every visitor has an interest in motorcycles and many have stories to tell. Walksler believes that during the seven years the museum has been in existence, between 350,000 and 400,000 people have been through the doors.

One museum visitor, Earl, had been there three or four times. He was obviously an enthusiast, but during the last trip, he developed even more of an interest. Upon returning to his home in South Bend, Indiana, Earl spent some time on his computer, specifically on Craigslist.

"Earl hits the 'enter' button on his computer and low-and-behold, right in his neighborhood is a listing for four old Indian motorcycles that had been posted there for less than a week," said Walksler of the October 2008 episode.

"He called the woman who had placed the ad, the granddaughter of Harry R. Paul, and [she] described the bikes to him. Earl went over to the lady's house and identified the bikes, checked out the serial numbers, and took photos. Then he emailed all the information to me."

Walksler was interested in the four bikes, but over the next 10 days, two of them were sold to other purchasers.

"These bikes had sat in one place for 46 or 47 years, and all of a sudden we were in this speedy negotiation to try and secure the remaining two," said Walksler. The two bikes included a mid-1930s Indian Scout race bike and a 1946 Indian Chief.

Earl met with the woman and told her he was negotiating on behalf of a museum. She was apparently impressed, because when an Ohio friend of Walksler independently heard about the bikes and contacted the woman, she told him the two remaining bikes were already sold, even though the deal hadn't been closed.

"Mentally this gal had prepared herself that if the dollars were right, the two bikes were going to wind up in a museum and not to somebody who would re-sell them at a profit," said Walksler. "I find this is the responsible method for a family member in a custodial position to valuate old bikes."

Finally, a deal was done. Even though Walksler had never actually seen these bikes, he committed to purchasing the two Indians plus a mysterious sidecar that nobody had seen. The final negotiations were made while Walksler was on the road for two weeks, so a museum volunteer, Jack, took the truck up to South Bend to pick them up.

"We arranged for several cashier's checks to be cut in case we had to break it down in some way," said Walksler. "Jack drove up to South Bend, met with

Earl, and the two went over to the woman's house to do a final evaluation of the motorcycles.

"When they pulled the sidecar out of the garage, they discovered it was just a body with no chassis. So after some phone conversations with me, we determined a fair and equitable value for the two bikes plus the sidecar body to be $20,000.

"Plus I gave Earl a finder's fee for securing the deal."

Walksler believes he paid what the bikes were worth, nothing more, nothing less.

"They were two dirty, old machines, so I don't think I paid a bargain-basement price," he said. "On the plus side, what came with the bikes was probably as interesting as the bikes themselves: an interesting history of Harry Paul himself, his racing photographs, a collection of Indian memorabilia, and interesting information on a strange club he apparently belonged to called the Hyperterrestrial Hoppers.

"It is my belief that Harry Paul was the guy in the community who worked on bikes for himself and other people—often the guys who performed period modifications on their bikes, which can be seen on the two motorcycles at hand."

Dale Walksler found four Indians listed for sale in late 2008. By the time he was able to respond, two had been sold. The bikes had been sitting for more than 50 years and were listed for sale by the granddaughter of Harry R. Paul. *Dale Walksler collection*

Here is a vintage photo of Paul, likely taken about 1940, on the racing Scout. The installation of the Chief motor probably added 15 to 20 horsepower, according to Walksler. *Dale Walksler collection*

Obviously Paul was no slouch when it came to mechanics. What he built was the two-wheeled equivalent of stuffing a Chrysler Hemi into a 1932 Ford. He installed a 1,200cc Indian Chief motor into the lightweight frame that was built to hold a 750cc motor.

"The legendary Max Bubeck went 138 miles per hour on a similar bike in about 1940," said Walksler. "He called it a 'Chout' because it was half Chief and half Scout: small frame, big motor. The difference is probably a 15- to 20-horsepower increase, but the real difference is the Chief motor, which has tremendous torque. It would have been a kind of torque monster of a bike."

Bikes that were modified in this way were typically used for scrambles or flat-track racing, depending on the type of tires that were installed. When the bike was delivered to Walksler, it had knobby tires installed, which probably means it was used for enduro events.

"It's likely that they changed wheels and tires, so there may have very well been a set of road-racing tires or a set of flat-track tires installed at some time," said Walksler. "Unfortunately, all the spare parts went with the other two bikes that were listed on Craigslist and sold before we could commit to them."

In deference to Bubeck, who is 92 and healthy, Walksler decided to rename the bike a "Scief."

"We haven't started the Scief yet, but we feel it will start without too much effort, probably in less than one hour," he said. "It's a totally intact machine.

"An interesting note is that this bike has brand-new tires mounted on it, with the 'nubs' still on them. It says to me that Harry Paul, even in his later years, decided that his motorcycles would always be ready to run, so he installed new tires on it."

1946 Harley Dreamcycle

Paul also built another custom bike. Originally the Indian Chief was designed for touring. The big, heavy bike was full-fendered, full-sized, full-weight, but Paul had other ideas for the frame.

"I think while dreaming up his dream cycle, Paul was knowledgeable enough to know that a mid-1930s Scout motor would fit into a Chief frame," said Walksler. "Back then they were called Standard Scouts by the factory and were manufactured by the factory for a couple of reasons: one, to use up parts, and two, it was a way to offer customers a lower-priced, full-sized machine because the Scout motor was less expensive to produce than the Chief motor."

Harry R. Paul was quite a mechanic: He installed a large Indian Chief engine inside the smaller Indian Scout frame. Switching only tires, the bike was used for both scrambles and flat-track racing. *Tom Cotter*

The other bike on the Craigslist discovery was this Indian Chief, which has the smaller Scout motor installed in its frame. Walksler calls it a "dreamcycle" because it was a full-size bike with a lightweight and maneuverable motor installed. *Tom Cotter*

Here is a photo of the same bike taken in 1954, prior to the installation of the smaller motor. The granddaughter was not sure if the two bikes simply had their engines swapped or not. *Dale Walksler collection*

236

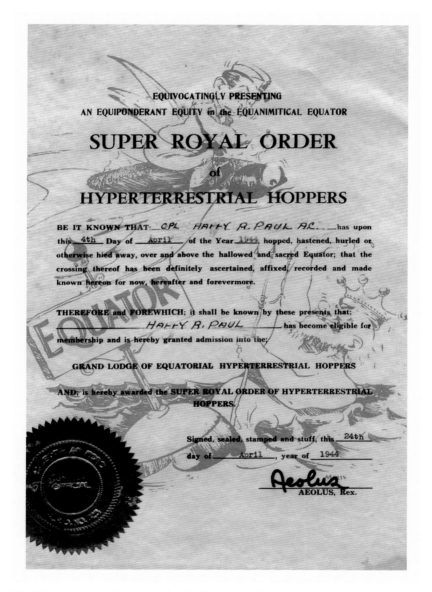

Nobody is quite sure what the Super Royal Order of Hyperterrestrial Hoppers means, but apparently Paul thought enough of it to have joined on April 4, 1944. Perhaps an exclusive motorcycle group?
Dale Walksler collection

Part of the stash of memorabilia Walksler received with this bike included a 1954 photo of the bike when it was a bone-stock Indian Chief.

"It was the same bike, but it was entirely different," he said.

The bike still has a 1953 skirted front fender and a 1946 rear fender.

Walksler compares the bike he purchased from Paul's granddaughter to that of Burt Monroe's 183-mile-per-hour Scout featured in the movie, *The World's Fastest Indian*.

"It was a conglomeration of parts," he said. "Obviously Paul knew a thing or two about interchangeability and ingenuity, because he came up with a magical combination," he said.

"He took a Scout lower end and put the latest hot rod, big-base Indian Scout cylinders on it. It actually has 750cc racing cylinders on it."

Paul also ran a magneto ignition instead of a battery ignition.

So Paul built himself a bike that was a lightweight, full-sized touring bike with a souped-up 750 motor.

"I call this concept a Dreamcycle, because it's a full-sized bike that's lighter than a full-sized bike, probably more maneuverable and easier handling because it's lighter," said Walksler.

"Interestingly, this bike is a Chief with a Scout motor and the racing Indian is a Scout with a Chief motor.

"His ability to mix and match parts and make them mechanically functional was a tribute not only to Indian's ingenuity but to Harry Paul's ingenuity. He was indeed a Hyperterrestrial Hopper Supreme."

CHAPTER SEVEN

Star Power

Winnie's James

James motorcycle number 3689214 just might have the most colorful history of any motorcycle on earth. As part of the Imperial Register Motorcycle Squadron, the James saw action in Great Britain in 1943, France in 1944, and later at the D-Day invasion in Normandy.

After its war duties were over, the bike was given to Winston Churchill by the squadron for his "supreme efforts in ending World War II."

It is said that Churchill rode James number 3689214 until late in his life and once proclaimed: "This was a true gift in every sense, a truly historic example of England's finest motorcycles. I am proud to ride this motorcycle as the brave and noble men before me did."

After Churchill's death in 1965, the James motorcycle was sold to a renowned British newspaperman, Ian Potsworthy of Surrey, England. Potsworthy kept the James until 1972 when he donated it to a fledgling military museum in Suffolk. The under-financed museum went out of business in late 1973 and the James was sold at auction to New Zealand land baron Kenneth Magorey. Magorey took the

Winston Churchill (third from right) inspects the Imperial Motorcycle Registry Squadron in Bicester, England, in 1944. The bikes are all James motorcycles. As the story goes, Churchill received James number 3689214 as a gift for his efforts in ending the war. *Tim Fortner collection*

motorcycle to New Zealand and rode it for several years on his many square kilometers of property.

After Magorey's death in 1986, the James was unceremoniously dumped in a sheep barn, in total disrepair, until found by its next owner in 1999.

The James motorcycle number 3689214 was painstakingly and authentically restored to the condition it was in when Sir Winston Churchill received it at the end of World War II.

This fine example of British history has been displayed at such prestigious events as the British War Museum opening, the Society for the Preservation of Churchill's Heritage, Churchill University in Oxford, British Veterans of World War II Reunion in 2001, and the 2003 Military Motorcycles Convention in Montreal, Canada.

While on display at the 2003 Military Motorcycles Convention, James motorcycle number 3689214 was awarded the coveted "Judges Award for History and Authenticity."

Truly, this is an incredible story, almost too good to be true. That's because it is. The real story of the James motorcycle is quite different but equally entertaining.

The present owner of James number 3689214 is Tim Fortner of Brookings,

Oregon. Fortner restores vintage racing cars out of a shop in Sonoma, California. Mike, a friend of Fortner's from San Luis Obispo, California, was once racing a Formula Atlantic in New Zealand when he struck up a conversation at a bar one night.

A New Zealander friend of his had this James motorcycle for sale and asked if Mike would consider buying it for $800 NZ. Mike wound up buying the bike and stowed it in the container with all his racing equipment and shipped it back to the States. When it arrived, he tried to get the James started, but it wouldn't.

British Office of the Defense Ministry
Archives Department, Mood Hall, Floor 3
Suxtent, Middlebury, Oxton Road
Cameron Place, London Y43 4SD

British Defense Ministry Certificate of Authenticity

September 8, 2001

Reference: *Research finalisation for James Motorcycle Serial Number 3689214*

To Whom It May Concern,

In reference to research and studies completed, and in reference to authenticated documents submitted to this office, and pursuant to British Defense Ministry authentication form (s) #CY112, and CY897, and CY932, the following results are hereby issued:

1. *That James Motorcycle #3689214 was utilised in the service of Her Majesty's Imperial Register Guard Motorcycle Squadron from 1941 until the end of hostilities in 1945,*

- and -

2. *That James Motorcycle #3689214 did participate actively in military actions while in service in Britain in 1941 and 1942,*

- and -

3. *That James Motorcycle #3689214 did participate in military operations in France in 1944,*

- and -

4. *That James Motorcycle #3689214 did participate in military actions during D-Day Operations in 1945,*

-and -

5. *That James Motorcycle was deeded to and did belong to Sir Winston Churchill from 1946 until his death in 1965.*

It is hereby ordered that James Military Lightweight Motorcycle #3689214 be entered into the British National Military Register, the Imperial War Museum Records, and the Sir Winston Churchill Heritage Foundation Archives, as a record of fact to these documents and declarations, and that the authenticity of the above detailed item has been deemed to be accurate beyond a doubt.

Submitted this 8th day of September in the year 2001.

By my hand and forwarded with pleasure,

Montogomery Lewellen Hathersby

Lord Montgomery Lewellen Hathersby
For Her Majesty the Queen

This authentic-looking document states that James number 3689214 was certified by the British Defense Ministry as the motorcycle Churchill had owned. *Tim Fortner collection*

"He took it to the go-to motorcycle guys in San Luis Obispo who worked on Yamahas, Suzukis, Kawasakis, and Harleys, and they had a great reputation," said Fortner. "And even those guys couldn't get it started."

So Mike brought the James back to his shop, where it sat.

"I went down there to do some work on his race car, and he asked if I'd like to have his bike," he said. "I told him I was not a motorcycle guy and didn't want his bike. But I told him I'd make an exception and take the BSA Lightning that he also shipped back from New Zealand. He laughed and told me that wasn't part of the deal."

Mike asked Fortner again if he'd like to have the bike and was again told he didn't want a motorcycle. So when Fortner finished working on the Formula race car, he returned to his shop in Sonoma without the James.

A week or two later, Fortner was again down at Mike's San Luis Obispo house servicing the race car, and again Mike pressed, "Take the motorcycle. I don't want it," he said. "If you don't take it, I'm just going to give it away or throw it out.

"It won't start, but maybe your guys back at the shop can get it running."

Again Fortner said he didn't want the James, but after looking at its flat green paint with the James logo, he gave in.

"I said, 'OK, throw it in the back of my truck,'" said Fortner. "So I brought it back to the shop when I was finished on his car. I unloaded it, and another guy and I tinkered around with it, changed the spark plug, put some gas in it, and kicked it. It started on the second kick."

So Fortner rode it around the race shop for six or eight months.

"It ran pretty well, so another guy in the shop and I decided to fix it up," said Fortner. "But nothing happened for at least a year because we didn't know anything about two-stroke engines. It had a pretty bad piston knock, so I called a parts house in England and got all the parts we needed."

Fortner disassembled the James and began discovering various serial numbers. He sent those serial numbers to England to see if he could trace any of the motorcycle's history.

"They made so many James motorcycles," said Fortner. "But I got a couple of responses from the British Defense Ministry, and they said that many were used in military service, but they didn't have any individual records.

"So that planted a seed of an idea for me. Military service . . . hmmmmm."

The James was painted green when he received it, so it did look like a military bike. Fortner decided to have a little bit of fun.

He went down to the sign shop that made the decals for their race cars and had stencils made and some roundels.

"We took some flat white paint and sprayed the stencils. We waited a day or two and then took steel wool and Scotch-Brite pads to scratch them up."

Based on the response he had received from England, Fortner decided to make up a story, initially just for the guys in the race shop. As he was researching on the Internet, he communicated with other James enthusiasts. One of them sent an image of some military guys standing next to some motorcycles.

"So I Photoshopped Winston Churchill into the photo and wrote up that little story," said Fortner. "And with the publisher programs available now, you can counterfeit anything. So I made up these little flyers and handed them out when people asked me about my motorcycle. They'd read it, and then I'd tell them the truth.

"That's how the story evolved; it just kind of happened when we were kind of bored."

Months later, perhaps a year, Fortner was again working on his friend Mike's race car at Thunder Hill racetrack in California. One night during that weekend, the two were sitting in a bar trying to solve the world's problems when Fortner got serious and looked straight into his friend's eyes.

"Michael, I've got something to tell you," said Fortner. "I really appreciate you giving me that motorcycle, and after what I'm going to tell you in a minute, I would understand if you'll want it back. I have no problem with that."

Playing the patina theme to the hilt, Fortner has weathered the James decals and serial number markings using steel wool and Scotch-Brite pads. *Tom Cotter*

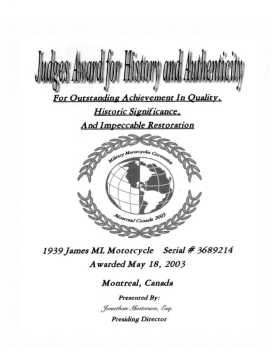

Judges Award for History and Authenticity

For Outstanding Achievement In Quality,
Historic Significance,
And Impeccable Restoration

1939 James ML Motorcycle   Serial # 3689214
Awarded May 18, 2003

Montreal, Canada

Presented By:
Jonathan Masterson, Esq.
Presiding Director

Another document made by Fortner states that the James won an award for military motorcycles in Canada in 2003. *Tim Fortner collection*

Fortner presented the "doctored" photograph and a certificate from the British Defense Ministry to Mike.

"I've traced the serial numbers and I must clear my conscience. Please read this," said Fortner. "Now understand that this is after four or five glasses of Scotch. I told him to carefully read the paperwork.

"Mike is usually quite animated, but as he started reading the history, then the Montreal certificate, and the Defense Certificate, which I had a watermark on, his animation quickly disappeared.

"'You're kidding me,' he said. "I told him, 'No, this is what I've found out.' And I again told him that I understood if he wanted it back and that I'd be happy to put it into the back of his truck.

"He said, 'Well, this thing is probably worth some money,' and I said, 'I reckon it's worth a half-million the way it sits.'

"Finally he said, 'Well, it's OK, I gave it to you. It's yours.'"

Then after one or two more drinks, Fortner turned to him and said, "Michael, it's 100 percent bullshit," he said. "He punched me in the shoulder and we both had a good laugh. 'You SOB, it was a great story,'" he said.

Believe it or not, the story does not end there.

Mike asked Fortner, "Can I take this to the guys in San Luis Obispo who worked on the James?" Fortner said, "Sure, they'll get a kick out of it."

Fortner only found out later that the two partners in the motorcycle shop were British. Very British.

"You know, God Save the Queen and all that stuff," said Fortner.

Fortner hadn't heard from Mike for a while, but at another Formula Atlantic race they were at together, he asked, "So, whatever happened with your motorcycle shop guys?"

"Well, I took the paperwork to them and had them read it," said Mike. "One of the guys sat down, put his head on his knees, and shook his head back and forth and said something to the effect, 'This was bloody Winnie's bike.'"

The other guy put his palm on his chin and his eyes started to tear up.

"We actually had Winnie's bike in our shop."

The partners asked if perhaps they could get the bike back in their shop so they could photograph the motorcycle they thought was Churchill's.

"So I asked Mike, 'So, everything is OK, right?'" said Fortner, as he looked Mike right in the eye. There was a long pause. "You did tell them, didn't you? You told them it was a joke, right?"

Fortner has the last laugh as he displays the fictional James motorcycle that he claims had belonged to Winston Churchill. *Tom Cotter*

Mike admitted, "The one guy was almost in tears and the other guy just sat with his head in his hands; I couldn't tell them I had just played a joke on them."

"Well, it's been a while; you've told them since?" asked Fortner.

"No, I can never tell them," said Mike.

So, to this day, the mechanics believe they had Winston Churchill's motorcycle in their shop.

Fortner admits he's a practical joker.

"I would never injure or hurt someone's feelings or cause retaliation," said Fortner. "But I am a bit of a jokester.

"I can just see those British guys in my mind, saying, 'Oh, mate, that was Winston Churchill's bike,' as they wipe their eyes.

"But I have a lot of fun with the bike at the racetrack. It's fun to see people read the sign next to the bike and watch their reaction as they say, 'Wow, this was Winston Churchill's bike.'

"The problem is that one day what's going to happen is that a gray-haired woman is going to be standing there, and her name is going to be Elizabeth Smyth Churchill, and she's going to be crying. And I'm going to go up to her and ask what's the matter, and she's going to say, 'That's my grandfather's motorcycle.'

"Then I'm going to be shot!"

Fortner points out that even though James motorcycle number 3689214 has been featured on ESPN's coverage of the Monterey Historic races, it probably has a resale value of about $1,200.

But the reaction Fortner has gotten from the ownership of the James has been priceless.

The Lawrence of Arabia Death Brough

By Paul Duchene

Perhaps the most famous barn find of all was performed on one of the best known motorcycles ever built—Lawrence of Arabia's 1932 Brough Superior SS-100, registration GW 2275, the bike on which he died in 1935.

Lawrence's 980cc V-Twin disappeared at the start of World War II, was found and refurbished in the late 1950s, then was bought by reclusive collector John Weekly in 1977. The motorcycle has reappeared recently at exhibitions at England's National Motor Museum and Imperial War Museum.

"Because of T. E. Lawrence I think this is the most famous road-going vehicle in existence, along with the car J.F.K. was killed in and James Dean's Porsche—if it still exists," said Weekly.

T. E. Lawrence is perhaps the twentieth century's most romantic hero, a diminutive, multilingual British scholar who led a successful Arab revolt against the Turks in Palestine in World War I in full tribal regalia.

At his death, no less than Winston Churchill said, "We shall never see his like again. His name will live in history. It will live in the annals of war. . . . It will live in the legends of Arabia."

After World War I, peace eluded Lawrence, who felt he had betrayed Arab dreams of independence. He sought anonymity in the Royal Air Force, first as John Hume Ross, then as Thomas Edward Shaw. The sole outlet for his passions seems to have been a succession of seven 100-mile-per-hour Brough Superior motorcycles, on which he rode more than 300,000 miles.

George Brough built 3,048 motorcycles between 1920 and 1940, all to customer specifications. Broughs ranged from a modest 500cc single to a bizarre 1932 four-cylinder powered by an Austin 7 engine and with twin rear wheels, and a big 1,150cc side-valve twin, often used with sidecars. His pinnacle was the Golden Dream of 1938, a four-cylinder boxer engine with geared cranks turning in opposite directions and shaft drive. Only two were built.

But the Brough to have is clearly the SS-100. In 1939, it was advertised as the fastest British bike, after recording 169 miles per hour in the hands of Eric Fernihough, who would die at 180 miles per hour trying to break his record.

The SS-100 used a J.A.P. overhead-valve 980cc V-Twin making up to 74 horsepower from 1924 to 1936, but such power reduced reliability and Brough switched to a 45-horsepower 990cc Matchless twin in 1936. In all, there were 281 SS-100s with the J.A.P. motor and 102 with the Matchless unit.

The ultimate version was the Alpine Grand Sport, six of which were sold in 1934 and two in 1935. These were "two of everything" bikes—two carburetors,

One of the twentieth century's most romantic heroes was T. E. Lawrence, better known as Lawrence of Arabia. He's shown here sitting on Brough GW 2275. He was a motorcycle enthusiast and favored the Brough brand, of which he owned six prior to this 1932 model SS-100. *Roger Hopkins collection*

two oil pumps, and two magnetos—and reputedly were tested at 120 miles per hour before delivery. This is the bike Lawrence had on order when he died.

Lawrence called his SS-100s *Boanerges* (a biblical name that means "sons of thunder") and reportedly once outran a Bristol Fighter (which has a top speed of 125 miles per hour) across Salisbury Plain. He often wrote about motorcycling in letters to people like George Bernard Shaw and Lady Astor and regularly corresponded with George Brough about his bike's performance.

"Your present machines are as fast and reliable as express trains and the greatest fun in the world to drive—and I say this after 20 years experience of cycles and cars," he wrote to Brough in 1926.

At the time, there was no more daring and dynamic image than Lawrence grinning behind the signature Brough fly screen, astride the nickel-plated gas tank in gauntlets and military cap. The timeless glamour of this man and his machine was captured by Peter O'Toole in director David Lean's 1962 Oscar-winning film, *Lawrence of Arabia*. The bike in the film is not correct, as GW 2275 was lost at the time.

Lawrence was awaiting delivery of his eighth Brough when he was killed on May 13, 1935, avoiding two boys on bicycles. The accident still has conspiracy theorists hinting at government plots and looking for a missing black sedan.

He wasn't wearing a helmet and died of head injuries six days later. The doctor who treated him later campaigned for compulsory helmet use.

"Lawrence's bike wasn't badly damaged, the accident was quite a slow-speed affair," said Mike Leatherdale, who's been the secretary of the Brough Superior club for 25 years.

"There's a photo of it on a lorry under a sheet before it was sent back to the works. The headlight and front fender were grazed, footrest bent, pannier box damaged, and gearshift bent back."

Weekly is intimately familiar with the details of Lawrence's crash and subsequent events. Lawrence cracked his skull and never recovered from his coma, dying six days later of congestion in his lungs and heart failure. GW 2275 was taken back to the Red Garage in Bovington and sat there for three months, except for May 21, when it was carried in a truck to the inquest so that the coroner could examine it.

"It was a hurried affair," said Weekly. "They held the inquest in the morning and the funeral in the afternoon, as if they couldn't get him in the ground quickly enough."

Three months later, Lawrence's younger brother Arnold (two other brothers died in World War I) sold the bike back to George Brough.

"George said he was going to keep it in memory of a great man—then turned around and sold it to Cambridge dealers King and Harper, who put it for sale in their window as belonging to Colonel Lawrence," said Weekly, sadly.

King and Harper sold GW 2275 to an ophthalmic surgeon named Munro who didn't get on with it.

"He said it was too ferocious and prone to oiling the back plug at low revs when he was going through town. Lawrence complained about the same thing. Munro took the bike back after about a year and traded it on a BMW twin. Can you imagine? What a comedown after a Brough," said Weekly.

The next owner of GW 2275 was a South African by the name of Pretorius, who was high up in the British Army. Weekly said Pretorius told the road tax authority he'd lost the logbook and got a replacement.

"Then he sold the original, but I've managed to get it back."

Weekly has managed to assemble all the related paperwork that still exists, including all the tax discs, the original logbook signed by Lawrence, and two Victorian half-crown coins that Lawrence kept in the mesh screen inside the gas tank filler.

"He'd be dressed in oilskins like a sailor when it rained, and it was hard to get to money, so he carried it in the tank."

Pretorius sold GW 2275 to Ronald Merriman Barry, who kept it for 10 years, finally selling the bike to an artist who was a member of the Royal

It was on GW 2275 that Lawrence would travel on deserted country lanes across England at speeds of up to 100 miles per hour to visit friends like Winston Churchill and Lady Astor. He also crashed this bike in May 1935, trying to avoid two boys on bicycles. He died six days later of head injuries. *Roger Hopkins collection*

Academy. It next surfaced in the hands of South Coast collector Les Perrin in the late 1950s.

"I knew it existed in 1962, I knew it was in Portsmouth, but I didn't get it until January 1977," said Weekly. "And don't ask me what I paid for it; it was a lot. I bought it from Les Perrin, who got it from a chap at work. The fellow said he had it in his garden and didn't want it and told Les, 'I'll give it to you for nothing.'

"It had a dilapidated sidecar, and the two towed it from Southampton to Portsmouth, and Les gave him a pound to cover petrol—about 20 pounds today. I was putting the bike's history together and I wrote to George Brough."

"'That's it, that's Lawrence's bike,' he said."

Weekly said that the bike had been rebuilt by Perrin, but he didn't have a lot of money and kept all the original parts.

"If that machine had been restored to a stunning bike just out of the factory, it would have demeaned it. As it is, it's just a nice oily old bike."

GW 2275 is definitely the genuine article, said Leatherdale. It has a borrowed gas tank, since Lawrence's stainless steel one was at the works awaiting his new bike, and a smaller back wheel than stock because of Lawrence's 5-foot, 6-inch height. GW 2275 still has scrapes on the handlebars and front fenders from the accident.

There are a number of period pictures of Lawrence on Broughs but only one of him on GW 2275, said Leatherdale. That was taken at Lawrence's Dorset county cottage at Clouds Hill.

Coincidentally, while the most famous Brough is seldom seen, the 1,000 Broughs known to survive are more visible than ever. An amazing 219 showed up at the annual gathering at Nottingham in August, their black paint offset by gray-haired riders.

The lineup included a 1924 SS-80, newly discovered in Edinburgh, Scotland. It's a one-family bike that's been off the road since 1930, when the owner hit a bus and promised his wife he wouldn't ride anymore.

"He passed it on to his son and he didn't ride it either," said Leatherdale.

The "barn find" phenomenon is coming full circle, said Leatherdale, with Brough Superiors heading into a different kind of anonymity, as prices for the best bikes cross the $250,000 mark (a 1938 SS-100 sold for $271,980 at Bonhams in London September 1, 2008).

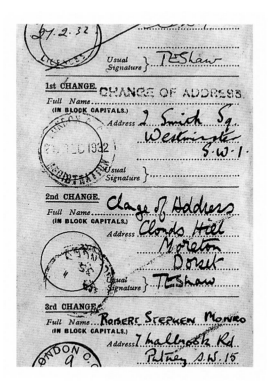

This is a copy of Lawrence's original owner's document where he entered his pseudonym, T. E. Shaw. After the crash, the bike was sent back to the Brough factory where it was repaired by company founder George Brough. *Roger Hopkins collection*

"They're getting so valuable, people are selling them at auction," said Leatherdale. "After sales like this, bikes just disappear, going into secretive private collections. Our problem now is trying to keep track of bikes we know. They're being shipped all over the world."

The recent exhibitions of GW 2275 have brought it back into public view, as the values of its brothers and sisters climb. It was rumored to be for sale a few years back, but Weekly, who is 66, is very clear on what he wants to happen to GW 2275 when he dies.

"I think it should go to a prominent museum that would make sure it's protected for the future," he said. "I think you can have an affinity with mechanical things. This motorcycle is the last thing that Lawrence touched, the last thing he thought about. There's still something about it. It's not really mine, it will always be his. He had a lot of motorcycles, but he kept this one far longer than any other, and it was his favorite."

Leno's Black Shadow

By Ken Gross

Built in Stevenage, England, in the 1950s, the 1,000cc Vincent V-Twin was billed as "The World's Fastest Standard Motorcycle." Expensive, exotic, loud, and very fast, with a shiny black stove-enameled engine, two-into-one faired exhausts, dual Amal carburetors, four sets of finned brake drums, knock-off wheels, and a 150-mile-per-hour Smiths speedometer, the Black Shadow was, and still is, the stuff of legends. Singer-songwriter Richard Thompson sang about a Vincent in his song "1952 Vincent Black Lightning," and a contemporary rock band goes by the name "The Vincent Black Shadow."

An American racer named Rollie Free took a stripped version of a stock Shadow, called a Black Lightning, and topped 150 miles per hour at Bonneville in 1950, wearing only a bathing suit and sneakers to cut wind resistance.

These fabulous bikes still appeal to people who've never even seen one in the metal. Roll up at a Harley gathering on a Vincent and you get instant respect. Today, they command six-figure prices, and as luck would have it, they're still turning up.

Tonight Show host Jay Leno loves Vincent motorcycles. At last count, he owned more than a dozen.

Here's the story of one of them:

"One day, I was going down the road on my Vincent Black Shadow motorcycle, and I see a guy stopped by the side of the road on some kind of Kawasaki. So I stop and ask him if he needs any help and baaaaammmmm!!!!, I get nailed from behind by another guy on a bike. So I dented up the gas tank on my Vincent. I came out on my crutches on the *Tonight Show,* and I say, 'a guy hit me on my bike. If anyone out there's got a gas tank for a Vincent Black Shadow, gimme a call.'

"Sure enough, I get a call from an old guy in Florida who says, 'I won't sell you a tank, but maybe you'd like to buy a whole Vincent? I have a very early 1947 Vincent Series B Black Shadow that I bought as a G.I. in England at the end of the war, and then I shipped it back here. It was one of the first ones sold. The bronze idler gear stripped a few years afterward, and I never got around to repairing it. It's still in my garage. And I'm really too old to ride it.'"

"I say, hmmm, a B Shadow, huh? They only made a few of those.

"It wasn't a bad price. So I ask him to tell me the serial number, and he does, and it's the correct F10AB/1B prefix with a really low chassis number, like 003. But I gotta double check, so I call the Vincent Club Registrar in England—this club knows where almost every Vincent ever made is, and they even have a 'spares scheme' that ensures that many critical replacement parts are still available, even cylinder heads. The Vincent Club guy says, 'Oh yes, that's the correct number, but that machine has disappeared. We think it left England in the hands of an American G.I. in 1947, but no one's heard of it since.'

"When he told me his name, I said, 'That's the guy who called me. I think I know where it is.'

"I quickly call the guy back and tell him I want the bike, and we work out a pretty fair deal over the phone. It's been languishing in his garage for decades, but it's all there. I tell him I'll send someone to pick it up and I'll call in the next day or two with the arrangements. There's a pause and he says, 'What will you have to pay to ship the bike to California?' I say, oh, probably about 800 bucks. So he says, 'Would you pay me 800 bucks if I deliver the bike in my truck?'

Jay Leno bought this 1947 Series B Black Shadow, serial number 003—one of the first built—from the original owner who called the *Tonight Show* after Leno made a plea for Vincent parts during the broadcast. Leno owns several of the iconic bikes. *John Lamm*

Vincent's sales strategy hinged on its status as the World's Fastest Standard Motorcycle, and ads like this featured the bike's speed and record-breaking potential. *Ken Gross archives*

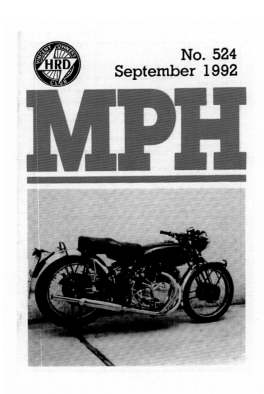

No. 524
September 1992
MPH

The Vincent Club is dedicated to the enjoyment and restoration of and acquisition of parts for all Vincent models. The bike on the cover of this newsletter is a 1947 Series B, similar to Leno's. *Ken Gross archives*

"So I say, sure, what the heck. Three days later, this battered pickup shows up in my driveway; he's got the Vincent and it's an early B Shadow, all right, and there's this bleary-eyed old guy, with his dog, who's practically driven straight through from Florida. I gave him $1,100 bucks and considered myself lucky. I had the gear repaired, cleaned it up, and the bike is a real beauty.

"I have a lot of Vincents, but this one's a favorite, as much for how I found it as for what it is."